FRONTIER COMRADES

FROM *THE* FUR TRADE *TO THE* FORD CAR

Jim Wilke

University of Nebraska Press
Lincoln

© 2025 by the Board of Regents of the University of Nebraska

All rights reserved

The University of Nebraska Press is part of a land-grant institution with campuses and programs on the past, present, and future homelands of the Pawnee, Ponca, Otoe-Missouria, Omaha, Dakota, Lakota, Kaw, Cheyenne, and Arapaho Peoples, as well as those of the relocated Ho-Chunk, Sac and Fox, and Iowa Peoples.

For customers in the EU with safety/GPSR concerns, contact:
gpsr@mare-nostrum.co.uk
Mare Nostrum Group BV
Mauritskade 21D
1091 GC Amsterdam
The Netherlands

Library of Congress Control Number: 2024047414

Designed and set in Whitman by Lacey Losh.

For James and Mary Ellen, who saw it start,
and Anson, who saw it through

Contents

LIST OF ILLUSTRATIONS ix

ACKNOWLEDGMENTS xi

Introduction 1

1. William Stewart and the Great West 15
2. Charley Parkhurst and the Gold Rush Scene 43
3. Mrs. Noonan and the Seventh Cavalry 73
4. William Breakenridge and the Human Borderlands 143
5. The "Lady Lovers" of Victorian Aspen 173
6. An Anonymous Logger in the Industrial Frontier 193

Afterword 207

NOTES 213

BIBLIOGRAPHY 259

INDEX 267

Illustrations

Following page 142

1. Oso House, Bear Valley, Mariposa County
2. Bloody Knife, General George Armstrong Custer, Private John Noonan and Colonel William Ludlow, with a Bear
3. Group on the Front Steps of the Custer Home, Fort Abraham Lincoln, Dakota Territory
4. Street in Tombstone, Arizona
5. Arizona Pioneers (Six men, two of whom are identified as Marcus Smith and William Breakenridge, early settlers of Arizona)
6. Ora Chatfield and Family
7. Logging Camp, Pacific Lumber Company, Scotia, California

Acknowledgments

This project has offered the opportunity to meet many wonderful people, whose support and interest has been crucial to its formation. First and foremost, I'd like to thank former curator James Nottage and senior curator Carolyn Brucken of the Autry Museum of the American West, where this project first got under way, together with Clark Whitehorn and Bridget Barry of the University of Nebraska Press, without whom this work would not exist. In addition, I'd like to thank the indomitable Carolyn Swift and the Soquel Historical Society, together with the late Lou Arbanas and the Pajaro Valley Historical Association, along with Charles and Tom Parkhurst; the late Doug McChristian, chief historian, Little Bighorn Battlefield National Monument, and military historian John Langellier for his invaluable input and support regarding primary documents; Ann Sneesby-Koch, assistant curator of serials at the Stephen H. Hart Research Center at History Colorado; Lisa Caprino, Reader Services, Huntington Library; Chatfield family descendant Catherine Severeau for her kindness in lending photographs; the Aspen Historical Society; Donna with the Pitkin County Sheriff's Office; Michael Oliveira, reference archivist at the ONE Archives, University of Southern California Libraries; Elisha Neely, Division of Rare and Manuscript Collections at the Carl A. Kroch Library at Cornell University; and the late Keith Rutledge, for relating his experience meeting Texas cowboys in an Oklahoma City gay bar back in 1957. Special thanks to Peter Boag as the guru afar; Patty Limerick for her encouragement; and Johanna Blume, Greg Hinton, and the late Bruce Elliot for their input and ideas. More than anything, a huge thanks to Anson, for his patience and steady encouragement.

FRONTIER COMRADES

Introduction

> These are men who have faced the rigors of nature in the wild.
> They live on realities with a minimum of theory.
>
> Alfred Kinsey

On a fine San Francisco day sometime in the early 1870s, two remarkably dressed men walked down Kearny Street into the photographic rooms of Wing & Allen to have their portrait taken. We don't know who they were, at least as of yet; they are among the countless people whose lives, remarkable or plain, survive by the most remote and ephemeral of artifacts—in this case, a tiny tintype portrait, framed in paper. Its image is impressive. The two men stand together, comfortably and intimately, smoking their pipes, looking off into a shared distance. Their working clothes were common to men in the outdoor wilderness: corduroy trousers with a checked shirt on one man, a woolen double-breasted shirt on his companion, one of its buttons hanging loose from wear. This was completely unlike the street suits worn by nearly everyone else in the city. Their very short hair, nearly like a modern butch cut, was a unique but practical style among frontiersmen and mountaineers who expected to be in the wilderness for some time or farther afield, in areas where they feared scalping. Again, this was completely unlike the longer, oiled hair that marked the fashionable men of 1874, thus serving notice to all of their wilderness alliance. Beyond all this was their pose, one man's arms reaching around his comrade's, grasping the material of his shirt, while the second man in turn lays his arm on his comrade's leg. Their alliance was as rooted in each other and a shared internal sense of self as it was in the larger landscape that fostered it, a frontier comradeship as at home in the City by the Bay as it was among the scoured granite of the Yosemite Valley, principles reflected in their appearance for the world to see. Both men have long since turned to dust, but their photograph survives as a record of a way of life, both inherently western and inherently singular, that lay far beyond the drawing rooms and parlors of mid-nineteenth-century America.

For most of the nineteenth century, traveling into the frontier West gave the sensation of passing some kind of indelible gulf and into a vast and undefined land where the old familiar rules of life did not apply. Ordinary Americans found themselves in an extraordinary place where the landscape revealed frontiers of human existence at a time when the lives of lesbian, gay, bisexual, and transgender people were not yet defined and as yet open to exploration. On the surface at least, this frontier seemed like paradise. In its early days this frontier had little room for arbitrary conventions, and modern definitions of sexuality did not yet exist in any clear form. This vacuum fostered degrees of pragmatism and social latitude in every aspect of western life, especially in isolated regions and industries, which simultaneously allowed lesbian, gay, bisexual, and transgender westerners the potential to engage life with something approaching equal footing.

In looking further, though, we find that a far more complex picture emerges. The West could feel like a paradise away from the trammels of East Coast civilization, but moving into it inevitably brought the very civilization that many sought to avoid, thereby building and reproducing nets of entanglements that would tamp down these new freedoms and make way for the rules and shush of civilized life. Over time the standards of civilization, arbitrary or not, became increasingly dominant in the West. At the same time, new developments in medical science were diminishing old latitudes by framing and marginalizing unconventional lives through pathological models. Because of this, the maelstrom of opportunities and conflicts that made up the West affected lesbian, gay, bisexual, and transgender westerners in intrinsically personal ways that became uniquely critical to their success or survival.

What then, was their life like in the Old West—was it a paradise as some imagine, a land of freedom far from rules and traps of civilization, a land of frontier romance? Or was it something else, something difficult or hard?

Frontier Comrades: From the Fur Trade to the Ford Car examines this experience through six accounts of lesbian, gay, bisexual, and transgender life in the nineteenth-century American frontier. It is the true story of people who ventured forth into the West, often finding themselves among its vast and unforgiving lands in a place where, if they were plucky, they might enjoy a life unimaginable in the eastern states. Each account interprets this history in different parts of the West at different periods of time, moving chronologically from the fur trade era to the dawn of the automobile age. These narratives show very generally that people farther out in the frontier wilderness could live lives on their own terms, while those closer to the demands and requirements of civilization were obliged to jump through more hoops. This is admittedly a simplistic and antiquated perspective within western studies, yet it nonetheless broadly prevails in the chapters presented here. We'll see the former at work in the first and last chapters, while the latter is emphatically clear in the third and fifth chapters. In addition, many people lived somewhere in the middle, between the bores of the wilderness and the developing West, a life represented in chapter 4. Still others glided past it all, living their lives uninterrupted and often with full knowledge of their associates, as in chapter 2.

This is not a typical work from the field of gender studies and is probably not a work of gender studies at all. Instead, it's a portrait of the American West and the frontier experience through the lens of six lesbian, gay, bisexual, and transgender lives, examining how their self-perception was shaped and defined by their occupations and relationship to the lands that surrounded them. This is in part because several comprehensive works have already focused on social and theoretical perceptions of sexuality and gender itself and in part because basic and reliable background data on these people has long been missing from even relatively familiar western accounts, such as the circumstances of military culture that contributed to and propelled the emotional immolation of a Seventh Cavalry soldier following the death of his transgender wife. It's important to note that this book addresses only a small part of a much larger subject and as such leaves many aspects of gay, lesbian, bisexual, and transgender life among westerners to future researchers. Furthermore, this book does not formally address Native and First Nations traditions of North America, of which the most familiar are the Two-Spirit and *bote* traditions of the Plains and southwestern cultures. These traditions form an important and ancient role in the spiritual life of the Native world; they deserve their own work and authorship that will do them justice.[1] Fortunately, new work is beginning to progressively uncover these and many other similar accounts, and it is hoped that authors in these fields will bring greater attention to them over the coming years.[2]

Because this book covers the nineteenth and early twentieth centuries, a period of tremendous change both in the West and for gay, lesbian, bisexual, and transgender people, it is both useful and necessary to address the choice of terms used throughout the text. To begin with, this book employs plain and simple terms for gay people wherever possible, even when anachronistic, largely for reasons of practicality. Any number of terms and phrases have been promoted over the past two centuries, often by gay people themselves, each with their advocates and detractors. While the terms used here may be somewhat arbitrary, this approach is nonetheless efficient and avoids the cumbersome and confusing complexity of specialized literature or the drudgery of phrases such as "people who in later eras would be considered gay."

Likewise, in this book "the West" generally refers to that part of North America that lies west of the lower Missouri River. This is also somewhat arbitrary, but it describes what most Americans considered the West in the mid-nineteenth century and covers the accounts contained within this book. These accounts begin in the second quarter of the nineteenth century, when Americans began to look toward the West with an eye to territorial expansion. Those goals were not unique in this regard: contests for territory and hunting grounds had occurred in this region for many thousands of years, and the Europeans were only the latest entries in a long business. There was little doubt that the nineteenth-century United States would take this direction, and there was absolutely no doubt that it would achieve its goals. Its growing population, proximity to western lands, and its technological capacity were reinforced by a spiritual justification, a "manifest destiny," as they said, "to overspread the continent allotted by Providence for the free development of our yearly developing millions."[3] For the Americans, a policy of expansion would bring a Pacific foothold, massive amounts of potential farmland, and a colossal gold rush in California, the first of many to come in these western territories. For the First Nations and Native American societies, this process was, and remains, especially and unimaginably hard. Tribes had warred among themselves since antiquity, but the relentless capacity of this new opponent, together with the unprecedented scale of its goals, was unstoppable and ultimately overwhelming. It was also shockingly fast: the series of treaties, force, and attrition that the Americans called the Indian Wars progressively overturned eighteen thousand years of Native society within the space of one or possibly two lifetimes.[4] "Manifest destiny is no longer a subject of abstract speculation," the New York Times reported in 1853. "It has a consistency, concreteness, and certainty of fact."[5]

A contest between the ideas of *frontier* and *civilization* became an ongoing theme among nineteenth-century Americans. They shared a general understanding about what the two meant, at least to them, both individually and in contest, and this book accordingly uses both terms in this nineteenth-century way. The word *frontier* generally means a border between one territory and another, or the outer limits of a given territory, and accordingly people of that era talked of crossing the "frontier line" or the "frontier of civilization" on their way *into* the West, meaning that they were crossing the farthest boundaries of the civilized world, such as what the Missouri River represented in the 1840s and 1850s, to pass into the western lands beyond.[6] However, the term is also fluid and could (and often does) describe wild or unexplored and uncivilized regions, which to nineteenth-century Americans, as well as their modern counterparts, lay both physically and mentally beyond the lines of a given place or civilization—something to be experienced or conquered and tamed, like the northern plains, or the deepest oceans, or space. Likewise, while the word *civilization* generally refers to any type of advanced cultural life or society found around the globe, in the nineteenth century it nearly always referred to an idealized and morally progressive Euro-American culture, one that its possessors and advocates considered superior to all other societies and the pinnacle of human development. When applied to the American West, the term "civilization" was also considered an action, the act of taming, or *civilizing*, an open and wild land to make it a cultivated, constructed, and constrained one. In the popular press there arose a narrative that described the ongoing war or crusade of civilization upon the frontier, where the onrush of American civilization into the West was nothing less than a preordained and inevitable triumph of a moral and muscular society. Although a few contemporary writers suggested that what they called the frontier period had been useful for the American character, far more saw the state of the frontier as a threat to the social order.[7] For them, the frontier period was a necessary but momentary stage in civilizing and taming the West, with the goal of transforming it into something on par with the rest of the civilized world, making it safe for social engagement and productive for global investment. "We don't want to cultivate in Europe," remarked a Sacramento man as late as 1888, "the idea that this is a rude, rough section with civilization in the shell and savagery as yet but partly eliminated."[8] Buffalo Bill, he added, had done enough damage as it was.

This book also uses "the West" and, by extension, "the frontier" as terms to reference and encompass a pragmatic, no-nonsense way of life that arose from the necessity for survival in the frontier wilderness. This again is somewhat arbitrary, but it allows a reasonably practical means of describing a functional consensus of plains manners that became a necessary, everyday way of life. No one was exempt from this reality, even Oregon- and California-bound emigrants, forced to throw aside their cargoes of civilization in desperate attempts to lighten their wagons in the face of alkali dust and no water.[9] For those who lived in the West itself, the temporary expedients of the trail became an everyday way of life, adopted through practical use by group consensus and relayed from one generation to another within a given trade or region. This in turn fostered perspectives on life that left behind arbitrary or unrealistic traditions of civilization, reflecting the requirements of their conditions and their work within them, a unique and often shocking perspective to civilized observers. "Ninety percent of them was infidels," remarked Edward Abbott, a straight Montana cowboy who worked the northern ranges in the 1880s. "After you come into contact with nature," he explained, "you get all that stuff knocked out of you—praying to God for aid, divine Providence, and so on—because it don't work. You could pray all you damn pleased, but it wouldn't get you water where there wasn't water. Talk about trusting in Providence, hell, if I'd trusted in Providence I'd have starved to death."[10]

For gay and bisexual people, this way of life also meant that arbitrary values and prejudices could potentially be set aside, blunted by the realities of survival in unforgiving territory. "These are men who have faced the rigors of nature in the wild," remarked sociologist Alfred Kinsey. They had been rained on, stampeded upon, and otherwise forced to endure whatever nature brought. "They live on realities," he added, "with a minimum of theory." From his research in the early twentieth century, Kinsey discovered that "there is a fair amount of sexual contact among older males in Western rural areas. It is the type of homosexuality which was probably common among pioneers and outdoorsmen in general. Today it is found among ranchmen, cattle men, prospectors, lumbermen, and farming groups in general—among groups that are virile, physically active." They were conscious of their attitude in life, their masculinity as a reflection of the same, and of being westerners rather than having an identity as gay people, a term then largely associated with urban men. "Such a group of hard-riding, hard-hitting, assertive males," he added, "would not tolerate the affectations of some city groups that are involved in the homosexual; but this, as far as they can see, has little to do with the question of having sexual relations with other men."[11]

Just what homosexuality *is* was a debate that dates back, in protomodern form, to the mid-nineteenth century. At that time the concept of inherently lesbian, gay, bisexual, or transgender people was not yet fully understood. Society instead generally imagined that being gay was not something one *was* but something one *did*, a kind of bizarre choice on the part of otherwise ordinary people, who might be misled, or wicked, or merely confused.[12] Some of these attempts were rather dramatic: in 1874 social reformer Victoria Woodhull blamed restrictive marriage rules, amounting to what she considered social slavery, for the spread of homosexuality among people seeking less entangled venues for relief. "The repression of law ... and the resulting enforced and unwilling relations in marriage," she stated, "are already yielding their natural fruit—a growing disgust, sexually, between the sexes [and the growth of] Sodomy in man and its antitype in woman."[13] Others were simple and direct: in 1903 the Pinkerton National Detective Agency simply called train robber William Miner a "sodomist" and left it at that. Miner engaged both men and women when useful or convenient, so this term, describing an action, habit, or indulgence on Miner's part, indicated that Miner was a "sodomist" in the same way one is a "bicyclist" and not a bicycle.[14] While developments in medical science would eventually fit people like the bisexual Miner into specific and scientifically determined categories, they were as yet on the far horizons of public perception.

Only recently has scientific study revealed the internal and inheritable genetic portraits driving the lives of LGBTQ people, revealing a powerful, ongoing, and extraordinary picture of human life. This is because human characteristics are the result of complex arrangements of multiple genes, some strongly associated with a given trait, others less so, that shape and guide the human life and determine receptiveness to forms and identities within that life.[15] Few single genes control any one element of human behavior, and most traits rely instead on various combinations of genes for their development and internal cognition, the same hereditary combinations of genes that govern eye color, height, or even the shape of earlobes. The effect is similar to scattering bits of multicolored corn upon a floor and observing the various patterns: one combination of colors might result in one set of traits, while another combination might provide a person with another, very different set of traits. These internal genetic portraits are inevitably shaped further by outside experiences such as the conventions of one's place and era, similar to how a plant may grow, depending on the strength of the wind, the composition of the soil, or the angle or amount of sunlight.

The first steps toward a scientific recognition and understanding of the biological origins of gay, lesbian, bisexual, and transgender people would occur only near the end of the nineteenth century, as part of a larger coalescence of scientific thought and study regarding the natural world. In the course of this development, scientists and doctors began to recognize the inherent genetic and hereditary origins of homosexuality and other human characteristics, even if the exact means of heritability were not yet fully understood. It was a necessary and important step toward the development of modern science and medicine but one that was initially prone to classifying misunderstood elements of human life as pathologies or diseased traits.[16] One influential perspective came in the late 1880s from a German writer, Richard von Krafft-Ebing, who described gay people as inheriting a degenerative vice, one by which they would sink below the standards of social normalcy.[17] This basic concept of an inherited but defective condition began to shape and influence scientific and social thought well into the twentieth century. "We are just beginning to realize the prevalence of abnormal psychology," remarked an observer in 1925, "and we are discovering deviates from the normal in the most unexpected places."[18]

These two developments—the rise of medical science and the associative crusade against people now defined by it—were joined by a third: the association of gay people with weak and unmanly stereotypes. The most significant of these were drawn from the exaggerated character of London playwright Oscar Wilde, who didn't invent the stereotype but became internationally famous as its representation. Wilde's global fame came while touring the United States in 1882 and giving lectures to promote Gilbert and Sullivan's new comic opera *Patience*, a lampoon of Britain's aesthetic movement in the arts. *Patience* was not as miserable as it might have been, but the subject of its lampoon was so regional and ephemeral that its promoters hired Wilde, outlandishly dressed to represent the opera's fictional comic protagonist, to warm up American audiences before the opera went on its American tour. Westerners were not impressed: he was unoriginal, they said, and seemed to be possessed by "an insane desire to exhibit himself." In Colorado the "verdict of Leadville," remarked observers, "is that Mr. Wilde is a conspicuous failure."[19] The appalling sensation of his performances, and accordingly the impression of the character stereotype upon the public, was so strong that when Wilde was placed on trial in London for homosexuality over a decade later, the publicity that followed this "nasty mess" not only cemented the fictional lampoon character upon him but eventually upon all gay people, giving a heavily publicized face to the idea of a monstrous weakness that threatened a national crisis. The lampoon character of the opera *Patience*, along with Wilde's untethered embrace of it, unwittingly brought in its wake untold decades of prejudice, fear, and repression.[20]

If society at large did not have a conception of an actual gay identity prior to its formal recognition or description by medical science, this did not mean that gay people had not already done so themselves, and according to their own ideas. In fact, they were quite capable and actively working toward a nascent sense of self-recognition, motivated in part by contemporary movements in the sciences and humanities. At different points in the nineteenth century, gay individuals in Europe began to recognize themselves as distinct individuals, develop terminology, and even take tentative steps toward what would later be called gay civil rights movements. This movement was not restricted to Europeans: in 1889 an ordinary Colorado postmistress recognized this identity independently, calling her passion for women her "being's destiny," for want of more cohesive words.[21] That she lived effectively isolated from others like herself, in a community incapable of recognizing her reality and subsequently hostile to it, makes her determination all the more remarkable. It is likely that people like her were independently reaching similar conclusions, whether or not they had the ability to communicate with others like them and whether or not they had a forum in which to advance their recognition.

Just what homosexuality *was*, as well as how to measure or define it, was perplexing to some, and assessments of its nature varied. This work uses the "Kinsey scale" as a useful reference for gradients of human orientation, developed by Dr. Alfred Kinsey in the first half of the twentieth century. It describes a continuum, from fully heterosexual people on one side, fully homosexual people on the other, and bisexual people in between, with the spectrum usually drawn as a chart with a sliding scale, for example, from black to gray to white. Some of the people in this book might best be described as entirely homosexual while others are best considered bisexual to various degrees, and people like them make up a moderately significant part of the population. While not perfect, the Kinsey scale offers a reasonably robust and practical approach to understanding the complexity of human life for many of the people described within this book, especially those who are just outside of familiar or more formalized categories, similar to the interludes between night and day that reflect the genetic and chromosomal scatterings building the working foundation of human life.

Over the course of these developments, gay people sought to define themselves through language, thereby seeking a place in the world on their own terms. The scientifically framed words *heterosexual* and *homosexual*, invented by a gay man in the 1860s, follow the rules of classically derived nomenclature and have been adopted by the field of medical science, along with the more recent and equally straightforward words *bisexual* and *transgender*. Other gay-coined nineteenth-century words, such as *uranian*, *dioning*, or *invert*, rose and fell from use, while *lesbian*, another nineteenth-century introduction, and *gay* have endured into the present.[22] The 1990s saw the politically framed term *queer* become popular among the activist and social academic set, while younger people have more recently adopted it for its feeling of generalized otherness. The initialism LGBT and its variants have also come into common use, largely through their simplicity.

While no practical, rational, or functional reason for antigay prejudice exists, prejudice against gay people has nonetheless been historically widespread. Its existence, and the potential lack of it in the wilds of the West, underlies the bulk of the accounts within this book. Broadly, antigay prejudice draws from a variety of external and unrelated sociocultural elements, such as unfamiliarity, fear or hostility, or as motivation for political or strategic advantage, or from combinations of these and similar elements, often aimed at minority population groups, often for the advantage of power. To represent and enact this hostility toward gay people, many states and territories employed variations of biblically named "sodomy" laws. While sodomy convictions represented the social indignation of civilization's arbiters in material form, they could also be somewhat ambiguous and were generally used to describe a variety of actions, typically involving nonprocreative intercourse, between any number of parties, heterosexual or not, willing or not, human or not. In the nineteenth century, accounts of "sodomy" included a self-proclaimed Presbyterian preacher whose attempts on the ladies of his congregation were "too grossly vile for publication," along with another attempted heterosexual assault upon a woman in Kentucky. At least one cowboy song described sodomy with women in brothels, presumably as a form of birth control.[23] Sodomy cases could also be somewhat rare: of some sixteen hundred court cases tried in Sacramento between 1853 and 1854, only one was for sodomy, and this, given the looseness of the term, does not necessarily involve a gay person.[24]

In the nineteenth century, prison terms for gay people so convicted appear to have averaged from three to ten years, often with the terms intended to impoverish and ruin the convicted. An 1858 Nebraska law, for example, specified that the "infamous crime against nature . . . shall subject the offender to be punished for a term of not less than one year, and may extend to life." The law also specified that Nebraskans convicted of "sodomy, or the crime against nature," would be "deemed infamous" and permanently denied the right to vote, hold office, or serve on juries, effectively removing those so convicted from public or civic life, a kind of de-citizenship.[25] Bail amounts ranging from $20,000 to $70,000 were upheld for a group of San Francisco men arrested in 1918, intended to prevent the men from meeting bail and thus force them into prosecution.[26] At San Quentin, prison life tended to "harden their [prisoners'] conscience beyond redemption," remarked observers in 1874. "Ribaldry characterizes their speech," they added, "and sodomy their actions."[27] Yet while sodomy laws could be harsh, there were occasional moments of mercy, as with a San Francisco teenager pardoned from a sodomy conviction in 1873. His youth made him "ignorant rather than criminal," according to the court, "and [he was] probably not aware of the nature of his offense." Even so, he was ordered to leave the state for several years.[28] Sodomy laws also required evidential proof, which meant that on occasion some people charged with sodomy went free "for want of evidence," as with two San Francisco men arrested in early 1873.[29] To eliminate potential loopholes and aid in prosecution, some states and territories began to tighten restrictions, as with an 1876 Texas measure that would "define and punish sodomy," along with adultery and sex outside of marriage.[30]

The shape of antigay prejudice motivating these laws has evolved over time, usually as a mirror of other contemporary concerns, whether real or imagined. In the nineteenth century, antigay prejudice focused on the idea of repudiating a loathsome vice, one akin to gambling or consorting with prostitutes, that is, a wicked form of antisocial conduct. In the early twentieth century, the rise of medical science formalized antigay prejudice as a kind of scientifically backed civic duty against deleterious forms of humanity, with "purity crusades" targeting gay people as a set group, even in private homes, and using the same methods used to target brothels, speakeasies, and opium dens. During the Cold War, antigay prejudice was politicized into a "war on homosexuals" waged by public figures against a perceived national security threat, with mass firings, imprisonment, and blacklisting. More recently, antigay prejudice has been revived and has taken on a mix of religious, conspiratorial, and "culture war" narratives, aimed at setting back the success of gay civil rights, particularly marriage rights, along with those of transgender people, with a goal of marginalization and eventual recriminalization.

Despite these challenges, a steady and impressive rise of gay civil liberties in the United States and across the world has taken place since the late twentieth century. Gay people have recognized a change in society, public opinion, and law, culminating in the public rise of gay civil rights movements in the late 1960s and a steady increase in civil rights recognition, including the elimination of sodomy laws and upholding of the right to marry. A critically important step in this process was the American Psychiatric Association's 1967 affirmation of gay people as normal and healthy Americans. Another was the push for gay rights, especially after the Stonewall Uprising of 1969, when gay people grew tired of police raids upon their bars and began to fight back as people worthy of rights and respect. Since then, and despite adversity, gay people have enjoyed a tremendous rise in public support and civil rights up to the present time. Whether this lasts, however, is uncertain.

The people discussed in this work are not distant abstractions. They were real and often unremarkable people who found themselves negotiating the boundaries of frontier and civilization in a remarkable place at a momentous time. Their lives were integrated with the West itself; they hunted its buffalo, met the great chiefs and mountain men, knew survivors of the Donner Party, served with the Seventh Cavalry, romanced Curly Bill Brocius, and worked the region's mining claims. They saw the arrival of the railroads and the overnight transformation of half a continent. Their experience in turn is intertwined with our own, whether we know it or not: today people drive along the old roads where Charley Parkhurst drove his stage, or past the old general store where Clara Dietrich kept the books and dared plan her elopement. Their frontier is our frontier; their lives, like our own, were and are interwoven with the Great West and that great cacophony called the American world.

1

William Stewart and the Great West

For tens of thousands of years, herds of bison dominated the North American plains. They are among the largest animals on the continent and once numbered in the tens of millions, roaming the landscape in gigantic herds up to several miles wide, a constant parade of rutting, mating, and searching for fresh grass. Migrating herds moved along familiar paths worn into the ground by generations of animals that preceded them, and this in turn dictated the movements of people who hunted them. At that time, all hunters pursued the bison on foot, and skilled hunters earned respect among their peers while ensuring the spiritual balance of life through the act of the hunt. The calendar of their lives and the lives of their families followed these seasonal transformations of meat, sinew, bones, and hide into food, shelter, tools, and clothing, in a pattern as regular as the movements of sun and moon. This ancient pace of life had quickened dramatically by the eighteenth century, when horses brought into North America by the Spanish and French offered a new, fast, and nimble platform for tribes and hunters, enabling them to hunt more efficiently. Mastery of the horse meant mastery of the plains, thereby increasing the scale of the hunt along with the wealth and status of tribes, as well as the measure of a hunter's personal capacity, and all of this within the predetermined spiritual path of their world.

For sporting Europeans such as William Stewart, the North American buffalo hunt was at once a primal and compelling spectacle. It possessed a sphere of influence, he thought, akin to a ritual or spiritual presence, distinct from the rest of the world, especially from his native Scotland.

"There is a religion in hunting," he later wrote, "and like the fire worshippers, or any other culte [sic], it should form its own government and its own laws; nothing gives cause to strife like disputes in hunting grounds, death ensues, and the race of man having fought for their prey, rendering their chase, that of the hunter being hunted."[1] This sense of intense power appears to have appealed to him immensely. He portrayed it in his later semiautobiographical novels as a rite of passage within a kind of mysterious and powerful drama, in effect a late Romantic-era measure of capacity and strength, established and enacted upon a distant and heroic stage, unsullied by the mundane rituals and restraints of daily life. "The dust was now suffocating," he wrote of hunting while trapped on his horse within a stampeding herd, and "to choose a mark would be impossible, or to distinguish sufficiently to follow up the choice—the thunder of so many thousand feet over the hollow sounding prairie—the ominous look, and threatening approach of those on whom I pressed, the bewilderment of being carried along on the cloud of monsters and a whirlwind of dust, on an animal, though of whatever merit of speed and endurance, was of a height which added dread of being overwhelmed to the other perils of this extraordinary chase."[2] He pursued this experience for several years in the 1830s, annually traveling into the western North American plains and mountains to seek out and deliberately engage its contest of endurance, testing and proving himself in the process.

The hunt brought something else as well—a pragmatic way of wilderness life that allowed him to foster relationships with men, the most important of these forged in hunting. Doing so was possible on the frontier of the American West but dangerously illegal in Stewart's Scotland and Great Britain overall. The American West brought Stewart some of the best years of his life, and it also brought a challenge in his ultimately unsuccessful attempt to interweave the freedoms of the West with the responsibilities of Great Britain, a challenge he was never able to fully reconcile.

In the early nineteenth century, Europeans such as Stewart looked to buffalo hunting in North America as a distant, dangerous, and visceral sport whose vitality had not yet been diluted through the management of gamekeepers and private preserves. Hunting in Europe had evolved into a formalized activity, in effect a ritual demonstration of the hunting and martial prowess that once made up the nascent aristocracies of ancient Europe; now relegated to demonstrations of tradition and taste, the hunt on European soil was almost completely free of danger. For a Great Britain exhausted from the decadence of George IV and wary of the Industrial Revolution, stories of buffalo and the American Indians who hunted them paralleled and sometimes merged with romantic tales of ancient European chivalry, pretending to the ideal of an age when aristocracy was earned and men were men, not voluptuaries propped up in the saddle while someone else shot their trophy for them. Stewart transferred this impression of vitality to the American plains, creating in effect a vast stage setting for an imaginary drama that resurrected the origins of prowess, manhood, and strength, enacted in blood on a vast and completely real scale.

Stewart's own path to the West drew as much from his willful personality as from his self-perception, one that was founded and shaped in accordance with and defiance of the aristocratic social norms of Great Britain. He was born in 1795 to a member of the minor nobility, Sir George Stewart, fifth Baronet of Murthly and seventeenth Lord of Grandtully, and was the second son of six children. The Stewarts had occupied Murthly since 1615, gradually building it up into the comfortable and unassuming estate that Stewart had grown into, but by virtue of an ancient tradition of primogeniture, the estate's lands would automatically pass to the oldest son, John, while the heir's younger brothers were expected to take up positions in the clergy or, in Stewart's case, the military. In 1813 Stewart's father purchased an entry rank for him within the Sixth Dragoon Guards and then, at Stewart's request, a transfer to the Fifteenth King's Hussars as a lieutenant, which required further expenditure and sent him to Spain, where he fought Napoleon's army during the Peninsular Campaign. A year later he was back in action, as a lieutenant during Napoleon's defeat by the Duke of Wellington during the Battle of Waterloo in June 1815. He prospered within the military structure and considered its training in duty, endurance, persistence, and obedience to be essential for the qualities of manhood, and he employed its training in marksmanship and horsemanship throughout his hunting trips.

The majority of Stewart's early life was spent away from the estates and among men. A military career combined with hunting trips, travel, and the London club life placed him within congenial male environments where he seems to have felt most content. In fact, life among gentlemen, military officers, and sporting men of all kinds appears to have been Stewart's favorite environment, one where women were largely and conspicuously absent. He seems to have dallied with women from time to time, but his emotional relationships appear to have been, as much as possible for him, among men. The only exception was marginal: Christine (or Christian) Stewart, a maid or servant on a neighboring farm, with whom he dallied and subsequently married in 1830 after she bore him a son, William George Stewart, legitimizing a potential heir. The marriage made her an "honest woman" in the eyes of her contemporaries, but she saw very little of her husband and never lived in the main house or enjoyed the deference of her eventual rank, a transgression of class that was socially impossible. He provided her instead with the means to live respectably in distant Edinburgh and to educate their son, who went into military training.[3] Marriage outside of his social station shocked Stewart's counterparts and enraged his older brother, yet it also allowed an heir with minimal responsibility on Stewart's part, along with unlimited opportunity to travel and live as he pleased. Just as significantly, it effectively blocked social pressure to marry within his own social rank, eliminating the demands and requirements of a wife of his own social standing.

His long-standing animosity toward his older brother increased after their father died in 1827, leaving John Stewart with control of the estate and the monies set aside for William. John immediately began plans to replace the old Murthly manor house with a monumental new structure, significantly larger and correspondingly expensive. In the realm of his older brother, William Stewart perhaps found himself a bit like a minor character in the first of his semiautobiographical novels, as someone who had "a will of his own, and that it had been in some degree thwarted."[4]

In 1832 a significant argument between the two siblings sent William storming off to North America for an extended hunting trip of several years, leaving his family and his dismissive brother so that he might partake of the pleasures of life amid the fraternal camaraderie of the North American plains.

The American West had its own challenges, very different from British ones, but of a type possibly more to Stewart's liking. Success and survival in the frontier required vigor and skill, making it a place where men such as Stewart could establish and demonstrate their own sense of worth, perhaps in Stewart's case as much to those he came to meet and travel with as to himself. He had not been long in New York when he met another former military man, J. Watson Webb, who provided a few valuable contacts in St. Louis, among them Thomas Benton and particularly William Clark, whose travels through and passion for the Rocky Mountain frontier whetted his appetite to go there and see it for himself. His most important meeting was with twenty-nine-year-old Robert Campbell, the experienced head of the packing division of the Rocky Mountain Fur Company. Campbell was preparing for the spring departure to the 1833 rendezvous, scheduled to be held along the Green River of present-day Wyoming, and Stewart asked to go along. Campbell had been in the Rocky Mountain fur business for over eight years, starting out with a party of men led by Jedediah Smith in the fall of 1825.[5] He proved his mettle in the field and over time and worked his way up to company clerk. He saw the work as useful but difficult, with little of the romance implied by people like Stewart. Only the year before, Campbell wrote to his brother Hugh in Philadelphia about that "mode of life that *necessity* and *choice* have caused me to adopt" during a return from the rendezvous. "To confess the truth," he wrote, "I am sick of it."[6]

Anyone traveling west of the Missouri River in the 1830s found it necessary for the sake of safety to travel in large parties. For small parties and individuals, the most desirable (and often only) option was to accompany the annual trade caravans operated by companies active in the Rocky Mountain fur trade. Traveling with a caravan was in effect following a commercial supply chain to a source of furs at trading events held every year at prearranged locations, known by the French term *rendezvous*. At the rendezvous, furs that had been trapped over the previous fall and spring were exchanged for trade goods and supplies brought out by the company caravans. A timely or early arrival to annual rendezvous was essential to gain access to the finest, choicest, and most profitable furs, and while Campbell could expect that his own company's trappers would save their furs for their employers, free trappers and Indians looked to the most advantageous trade in all circumstances. Stewart rapidly found that his British rank of captain and aristocratic birthright had no more sway along the upper Missouri River than his advanced age of thirty-eight. Campbell refused to take him, sizing him up as bored greenhorn and thus a liability in the practical environments of the West.

Campbell's refusal to take Stewart was simply business. Greenhorns, no matter how grand, brought the risks of delay in reaching the rendezvous and a resulting material loss of economic profit, and Campbell's train was already burdened by supercargo, including the alcoholic son of General William Harrison, seeking a cure in the western air. Campbell was persuaded only after Stewart agreed to pay his way as a passenger, essentially providing liability insurance covering any potential losses as a result of his presence. Stewart would take his place in the train and be treated as any other man, complete with assigned duties he was expected to fulfill.

Caravans were traditionally organized along lines broadly resembling that of a ship or a military hierarchy. Up to sixty men were governed by captains, officers, and others assigned specific duties appropriate to their role within the group. Every one of the forty-five men in Campbell's caravan was expected to know and do his share of the work, as well as to contribute to the success of the trip and the safety of everyone in the caravan. Stewart, a man accustomed to his social lessers doffing their hats, now found himself unexpectedly outranked by what his society considered common men, all by virtue of their earned experience, and these men refused to accept Stewart's direction, even when Campbell had assigned Stewart to a given duty. As head of night guard on one occasion, Stewart was required by Campbell's rules to punish a man who had neglected his post. But in that social context, greenhorns had no place telling experienced men how to behave, and the packers complied only after Campbell demanded their respect for the authority he had vested in Stewart, rather than Stewart himself. Over time, Stewart was able to establish himself on his own merit, gradually rising within the ranks on the basis of his military training, his endurance, and especially his marksmanship among people who came to genuinely regard him with, if not admiration, at least earned respect. He would never be one of the boys, but in another sense he came to be entirely one *with* the boys, or at least a sport, on recognition of these facts. For Stewart, the caravans were just a necessary and convenient means to travel in an open country. And apart from the nuisance, the men who led the caravans probably had little interest in Stewart either. For them, this grandiose Scotsman was only the latest of curiosities in a very old business.

The North American fur trade was already two centuries old when Stewart arrived. The primary object of trade was the North American beaver, *Castor canadensis*, whose fur provided exceptionally fine felts used in hat making, and the North American river otter, *Lontra canadensis*. The most fundamental form of trading, an exchange of furs hunted by Indians for trade goods offered by Europeans, was far older: the Native peoples of Newfoundland and Labrador briefly traded furs with Norse Greenlanders as early as the eleventh century.[7] Some six hundred years later, new generations of French, Spanish, and English traders were establishing alliances among the Indians, generating geopolitical spheres of influence that breathed with war, treaties, and trade.[8] The Spanish moved northward from present-day Mexico into much of the Southwest, while the British moved westward across Canada from Hudson's Bay into the Pacific Northwest. The French had progressively moved from Quebec and Montreal south and westward into the Mississippi region, an area they named La Louisiane after their king and that remained deeply French in manners, habits, and jurisdiction even after it temporarily passed into the hands of Spain following the Seven Years' War in the mid-eighteenth century. By the time Napoleon had reacquired and subsequently resold Louisiana Territory to the Americans in 1803, it extended to the Continental Divide and perhaps beyond; no one was really certain, and the far western border remained undefined for several decades. The farthest border possible was the Pacific coastline, which the Lewis and Clark Expedition was assigned to explore by President Thomas Jefferson, even if it meant crossing contested territory to get there. Meriwether Lewis duly reported back what everyone else already knew—that the country was "richer in beaver and otter than any country on earth," but apart from a sliver of the Northern California coast claimed by the Russians, or an 1817 treaty allowing joint occupation with Britain, the Pacific Northwest was effectively British, discouraging American trappers from establishing any meaningful presence or trade.[9]

The Americans turned instead to the upper reaches of the Missouri River and the Rocky Mountains, where claims of possession were reasonably secure. Every spring, when the water was high and the grass green, a small host of American companies, some well organized, some barely so, swarmed along the banks of the Missouri before heading west to tap the riches beyond, with varying degrees of success. Between 1815 and 1830, American agents reported total profits at just over $1.6 million, for some 390,000 buffalo hides and 375,000 beaver pelts.[10] The largest and by far most formidable of these firms was John Astor's American Fur Company, which achieved near total control of the fur trade at the Great Lakes before expanding westward in the early 1820s and setting up a system of trading forts like those employed by Britain's Hudson's Bay Company. Between 1829 and 1831, the American Fur Company was reported to have processed over 17,000 beaver skins, 386,000 muskrat skins, and 112,000 raccoon skins, followed in proportions by rabbit, buffalo, deer, elk, fox, bear, bear cub, otter, fisher, mink, marten, lynx, wildcat, wolf, wolverine, panther, badger, polecat, squirrel, and opossum.[11] Stewart associated with Astor's principal American rival, the Rocky Mountain Fur Company, a nimble affair led by William Ashley, who field-tested a variety of business models before settling on a free trapper and rendezvous system in the mid-1820s. Effective organization was one of Ashley's strong points; seeking to eliminate as many cost risks as possible, he eliminated the trading posts and restricted field operations largely to the carriage of trade goods to the rendezvous and the hauling of furs on the return trip, and he "drew up, and published among his men, a code of rules for the better maintenance of order," which "by their general adoption, the dangers and difficulties of the mountain trade have been more than half removed."[12] But by the time Stewart traveled with the caravans, the fur trade was already past its prime. The math was simple: years of intensive trapping had severely reduced the populations of beaver, making it difficult to support trade economics as before. Even Stewart was able to sense that his first trip out in 1833 was the last of the really good ones. With the American market in shambles, the Hudson's Bay Company effectively wiped up what remained.

The brigades of trappers that Stewart met at the annual rendezvous, as well as the men with whom he traveled on the trade caravans to get there, made up a distinct culture unlike anything he had known in Britain. Practicality trumped tradition in the West, and the restrictions of formal conduct demanded in the society drawing room were relaxed and scattered among the companies assembled for rendezvous; these men took on their own sense of conduct, defined among unspoken rules drawn from common agreement regarding respect and dignity. This contributed to a certain latitude in terms of socialization, which reflected the different cultures and individuals who convened to trade, as well as an easing of restrictions upon conduct that could be considered taboo in other worlds. The men who went west were largely young, with the physical stamina necessary to withstand the rigors of the wilderness; they were adaptable and amenable to the practical aspects of mountain life. Trappers lived in the mountains year round, usually working together in brigades of up to sixty men at a given base camp where they wintered between the fall and spring trapping seasons, when beaver were active and furs thick. Their society, like their buckskin and trade clothes, was a mix of what could be made locally or obtained in trade, an adaptation of social and material culture to the ways and needs of mountain life.

Some of the men courted and married Native women they met over the course of time, forming alliances with nearby tribal groups and adapting Indian ways. Just how many men married is hard to say, although at the 1826 rendezvous some fifty Indian wives and children accompanied the hundred or so trappers assembled there.¹³ For them, assimilation into Indian society offered not only a wife and children but also a sense of family, place, and home, along with a stability that was valued as much by the fur companies that bartered with them as by the trappers themselves. The Indians in turn saw marriage as way of tapping into the political power of the Americans, much as they had with the French and Spanish before them and as they continued to do with the British. But these alliances were often conditional: trappers who returned to East Coast cities with their Native wives would find cold receptions. "Among civilized people," wrote a Hudson's Bay trader of a man who moved to Montreal with his Indian wife, "neither himself nor her can be happy[;] to join in anything like civilized society with her is out of the question."¹⁴ Of the men who did not marry, security within their group and occasional relationships among them provided similar senses of stability and family.¹⁵ Ultimately, all of these men, whether married or not, recognized each other as members of a small but distinctive society existing beyond the frontier of the civilized world. It created a sense of separatism and identity that spoke of having one's own standards of conduct and habit and of making one's own choices.

Stewart conducted his hunting trips as a gentleman, with the capacity of adopting regional habits when comfortable or necessary, in effect paralleling the adaptability of mountain men to the requirements of wilderness and its society. This duality of order and versatility was shared by other gentlemen traveling abroad, a habit that demonstrated not only taste but the ability to retain one's own sense of self while adapting to the fecundity of nature. "Going native" did not necessarily mean adopting the style of the locals—although some did—or becoming one of them—which some did too—but it did mean that gentlemen could adopt such habits as practical for intercourse and good relations, along with a few momentary and situational freedoms socially impossible in Great Britain. Along the way, Stewart gained a reputation for marksmanship in hunting buffalo and fame for staving off a grizzly, and over time he became a familiar, even remarkable fixture among the Indians and trappers. The process inevitably brought new ideas about what defined a gentleman, and such ideas seem to have been central to Stewart's rediscovery of self during his years in America and the West. During his visit to Fort Vancouver, Stewart probably saw the British post as an ideal in its practical and nearly elegant mix between Native and European ways, a world of Indian marriage and black broadcloth that demonstrated an ordered, stable, idealized adaptation on an institutional scale. The model existed from the top down, for the head of the post, its chief factor, John McLoughlin, had himself married a Métis woman.[16] Fort Vancouver was their own branch of Britain in the world, remade to suit their own requirements through measures that encouraged stability and good relations with local Indians. This collision of manners represented an approach to life that infused Stewart's concepts of a gentleman with the plasticity of the wilderness.

This plasticity offered Stewart the opportunity to enjoy a series of male relationships, including one with a Métis man who became the love of his life. Stewart's associations began on his first trip out West, with a handsome young packer named George Holmes. Holmes was experienced on the trail and exceptional in having a formal education, making his working life among men in the open plains an unusual and apparently deliberate choice. He was also exceptional for his bright personality, which differed substantially from the quieter masculinity of the other men, who knowingly called him "Beauty."[17] He appears to have been enraptured by the tall Scottish captain, but Stewart seems instead to have seen Holmes as a momentary convenience, freighted by the encumbering nuisance of affection and demonstrable clinginess. They paired up on the trail and even built and shared a bower at the rendezvous on the upper reaches of the Green River, but their inherent disparity became evident when Stewart ejected Holmes from their bower one evening to spend time alone with someone else. Holmes eventually departed but "left his saddle, the usual pillow of the wanderer," inside their bower as an implied statement of possession. To seek another tent would admit defeat, and Holmes slept instead just outside the bower, closest to his imagined right of place but nonetheless exposed in the open air.[18] During the night, he was attacked by a rabid wolf that raced violently through the scattered camps. "All hands got up with their guns in pursuit of the animal," recalled Charles Larpenteur, a clerk for the company, "but he made his escape." Holmes was "badly bitten on the right ear and face," and his wounds would prove fatal.[19] Symptoms of the rabies virus that promote transmission through abnormal aggression in animals create similar disturbances in humans, who descend into an agitated and dangerously delirious state. This tortured state of mind ultimately led Holmes to suffer an unyielding series of increasingly intense fits. By that time, the rendezvous was over, and the caravan was back on the trail. "For some days," Larpenteur wrote, Holmes "could not bear to cross the small streams which they struck from time to time, so that they would cover him over with a blanket to get him across; and at last they had to leave him with two men until his fit should be over. But the men soon left him and returned to camp. Mr. Fontenelle immediately sent back after him; but when they arrived at the place, they found only his clothes, which he had torn off his back. He had run away quite naked, and was never found."[20] Many years later, Stewart offered some suitably pious and public regret over the incident, claiming impressively that "his bones were left, we could never learn exactly where, on the branch of some stream, and the bough of some tree, where I would have willingly made a pilgrimage to render the last tribute of regret, and contrast the living memory with the dead remains." With the windup came the pitch: "There has never quitted in my breast a reproachful remorse," he wrote, "for the part I played him on that sad night."[21] Whether Stewart was simply posturing or had to some degree grown genuinely remorseful in his later, lonely years is hard to say. But in reality, by the time Holmes lay dying, Stewart had abandoned him to his fate and already ridden far away.

The leveling effect of plains life that obliged Stewart to rise by his own efforts in the esteem of the men with whom he traveled fostered a newly recognized sense of self within their forthright society, while at the same time investments in the New Orleans cotton trade allowed him enough independent income to travel in style. With each season his trips out West increased in scope along with the trappings of his retinue; he visited William Clark at St. Louis in 1837, became known for a perfectly tailored white buckskin hunting coat, and once famously presented mountain man Jim Bridger with a cuirass and helmet sent from Britain—an elaborate, completely useless gift that took months of preparation.[22]

Over time, Stewart's annual travels became less of an extended hunting trip and more of a way of life. His western sense of self was probably at full flower in 1837, when he invited a Baltimore artist named Alfred Miller to accompany him and record his trip to the Rocky Mountains and the rendezvous on the Green River for posterity. Miller had just moved his studio to New Orleans and unexpectedly found in Stewart a client and engagement that would ultimately define his career. Miller's drawings, rendered in quick, light strokes reflecting a kind of ease and grace inherent to mountain society in the midst of summer, present Stewart as a great sportsman, a magnificent grandee in white buckskin with a fine London rifle—a picture of splendor and determination, leading his party of men. Privately, Miller later wrote that Stewart could be imperious and hard to deal with, that he was a "military martinet" in terms of discipline and a man who wore grandiosity somewhat thinly on his sleeve. There was something else as well, something impulsive and disconcerting, that Miller encountered one day on the grasslands. While Miller was carelessly absorbed in sketching the scene, Stewart silently crept up from behind and grabbed him, physically pinning him down on the grass for a full five minutes—a lesson, he claimed afterward, intended to teach him to never be caught unawares in the West, where enemies of any kind would take advantage. Miller recalled how "suddenly I found my head violently forced down & held in such a manner that it was impossible to turn right or left." At some point, Stewart appears to have satiated his impulse and released Miller, admonishing him in tones that concealed and recast his intensity as dominant and justified principle.[23] Any genuine lesson would have been learned in the first minute; anything longer edged toward a sense of impulsive near ravishment, explaining itself away, once the impulse had passed, as instruction.

It's not that Stewart had anything for Miller: by the time Miller joined the party, Stewart was traveling extensively with Antoine Clement, a young, handsome, and expert hunter he first met at the 1833 rendezvous. Clement was in his early twenties, one of nine children raised and baptized in St. Louis and its surrounding communities by his father and namesake, who died in the same year that Clement met Stewart. Clement was twenty-one then, with a respected reputation as a hunter on the plains, along with a famous temper. When they first met, Stewart was so taken by the sight of Clement, so simultaneously challenged and enraptured, that his later description of the event, in his semiautobiographical novels, reads with an immediacy and in words that anticipate Whitman's "secret and divine signs," what Stewart described as "those mysterious sympathies which are conveyed by the touch as well as by sight."[24] Over the next several years Stewart and Clement continually engaged, disengaged, and reengaged. There was a tension and challenge between the two from the beginning. "Here you might suppose," wrote Stewart many years later, "the two classes were represented; and the bearing of both was such as if neither would yield to the other, even in a glance."[25] Clement had the ability at times to bring Stewart into a fascinatingly unfamiliar position of supplication. Stewart described Clement at length as a man of "faultless beauty" and wrote how he felt hopelessly inadequate to embrace Clement's "grand simplicity of bearing" on anything like even terms. When they first encountered each other, he set aside his formal British manners on a hunch and spoke to Clement in French, and in Clement's style, thereby meeting Clement on his own ground or at least in imitation or tribute of the same. Clement had just brought down a buffalo and deliberately offered Stewart the opportunity of making the first cut, perhaps knowing Stewart had no idea what to do next. This opened a comedic tango of manners as Clement taught the flummoxed, embarrassed Stewart how to cut and pack the fresh meat, essentially teaching Stewart as Stewart's superior. As they left the site and headed toward their respective camps, Stewart was "anxious to have made some propositions about meeting again, but there was something about my Indian friend that checked any advance; and I was both attracted by a hidden spell, and repelled by a half haughty smile."[26]

When Stewart encountered Clement three years later, Stewart was traveling for pleasure with Adolf Sillem, a young German man he had met in St. Louis.[27] Sillem was experienced, willing, and reasonably interesting, to the extent that Stewart invited him along to the 1836 rendezvous, where he was mistaken for a "young English blood" by one member of a passing missionary group.[28] For the first time, Stewart had chosen to travel with a tent, a rare item on the plains, where men normally slept on blankets in the open air. It was also a complicated device, which had to be set up each evening and taken down again the following morning, an effort intended above all to provide private space as the two men slept together, away from the rest of the caravan. Sillem was game, but after eight months of each other's continuous company, Stewart appears to have reconsidered. Toward the end of the rendezvous, Stewart took Sillem and several other men, including Clement, on a side trip for hunting, offering Stewart the critical opportunity to gauge Clement the hunter against Sillem the blood. It's not known what transpired, but when they returned to St. Louis, Sillem was gone and Clement remained.

"Antoine, by which name Mr. Clement is almost exclusively known," remarked a man who met him a decade later, "was born in the mountains, his mother being an Indian woman, his father a Frenchman. He was reared in the wilderness, and though an intelligent man, seems reconciled to no other life."[29] Miller found Clement's personality to be easy, comfortable, and genuine. Even before the trip, Miller recalled their spending time together casually playing card games in New Orleans, waiting for the spring so their trip out West could begin. His drawings and sketches, made once the trip was underway, show Stewart and Clement constantly side-by-side, with Stewart in the foreground enjoying the center of attention, as appropriate to the patron of Miller's artwork, while Clement sits, stands, or rides quietly and assuredly alongside. Yet where Stewart appears to have been constructed and self-conscious, continually attempting to project, establish, and justify some sense of self, Clement appears to have been at one with the world and genuine in his engagement within it, a disparity that marks one of the elements that make Stewart's trip so remarkable. Western life, and what Clement specifically represented, appears to have challenged Stewart into rising to the occasion, something he seems to have relished as much as resented.

Yet, though Stewart was drawn to and enraptured by Clement's presence, old habits persisted, and he appears to have objectified Clement on several levels, as if the younger man were a specimen. Most broadly, Stewart's attraction to Clement follows a pattern typical of British gentlemen traveling abroad, later described by Christopher Isherwood as a desire for men who were "younger, and preferably foreign."[30] In other words, British gentlemen desired relationships with men who were twice removed (by distance and lack of seniority) from challenging the dominant social position of a British gentleman, who could therefore set aside rules of engagement that would have been at play in encounters with another Britisher and essentially adopt the freedoms of someone who, in a sense, didn't count. It was extremely Roman, and for all of Clement's innate qualities, nonetheless placed him in the same basket as Holmes and Sillem. But Clement had something that neither Holmes nor Sillem could touch, at least in Stewart's eyes, something equally attractive and equally objectified: a dual French and Cree ancestry. Of Clement, Stewart later wrote "there was something to be liked about this half-breed, and I had kept by his side all morning; there was not much to be got by direct questioning, but occasionally he put forth some symptoms of the most extraordinary sagacity, as well as in respect to hunting as to the ways of man and the brute with whom he was in the habit of coming in contact."[31] Stewart was drawn to and fascinated by Clement in part for this reason and regularly defined Clement in his later works as a "half-breed," "a young *Metis*," or "Indian," emphasizing and objectifying their differences to increase the symbolic significance of their engagement and the imagined magnificence of his experience.[32] In one of his later semiautobiographical novels, Stewart wrote of entering through Clement a state of personal wilderness, a longing to run about naked with Clement in the sun while their clothes, wet from crossing a stream, dried. When Clement moved to leave for his camp, Stewart lamented that there was "some further intimacy to be longed for; I knew not very well what, but there was an enchantment over me, one of those mysterious sympathies of romantic affection, as well as of the most rational and practical intercourse."[33]

In his mind, Stewart was "going native" in the most interior sense possible, imagining their relationship as a kind of manifest force drawn from a physical blending of the Old and New Worlds, much like Clement himself, the most intimate possible merging of societies and traditions, a tempting incandescence where all thought of time is lost. But unlike the trappers he met at the rendezvous, or McLoughlin at Fort Vancouver, Stewart's motivation for a Métis partner drew not so much from practicality or alliance as it appears to have been from fascination, opportunity, curiosity, vanity, and idealism. Enchantment and "mysterious sympathies" did not prevent Stewart from lumping Clement into a trophy cabinet or treating him like a prized horse or hunting dog. This mix of passion and carelessness appears to be typical of Stewart, something he employed in one way or another throughout his life toward all ends, but it also shows how he may have for a moment nearly risen out of it, or at least perused its edges.

What Clement saw in Stewart is unclear. Stewart was approaching forty when they began to engage each other, and if he was carefully constructed, he was still a man demonstrably commanding in both presence and bearing and palpably interested in Clement beyond ordinary measure. Their strengths and character most closely worked in harmony while hunting, where marksmanship and persistence established a functional measure of mutual respect where all focus was upon their prey, the two men acting as one in concert. It is possible, too, that through their consuming engagement in the hunt Stewart may have momentarily forgotten himself in the ecstasy of the moment, something British gentlemen would not otherwise allow in public view, or even privately, thereby providing Clement with a glimpse of something genuine, compelling, or appealing beneath his usual countenance. Clement also seems to have been among the very few men who could face up to Stewart, ride off his temper, and get away with it, and the hunt plays a role in its most memorable demonstration. On the plains, Miller recalled a terrible fight between the two men after Stewart berated Clement for not fastening something properly. Just as Miller thought they would come to blows, they were distracted by buffalo calves in the distance, immediately riding out together on the hunt and later returning, laughing, the argument forgotten.

Gentlemen who travel abroad to experience life on native terms generally do so with the understanding that it is a temporary state of existence, a momentary and presumably beneficial indulgence with an implicit purpose of improving their own state, along with that of their country, upon their return. Stewart was no exception, and his western life officially remained an extended hunting trip, albeit one that had been transformed into a form of exile in a sportsman's paradise. Yet, for some time, letters from Murthly had been advising Stewart of his older brother's illness along with the expectation that he would be inheriting the estates as well as the title and responsibilities and that he should thus return immediately to Scotland. John died while in Paris in May 1838, was "brought by steam to Scotland," and buried the following month at Murthly. "As the late Baronet left no issue," reported the *Caledonian Mercury*, "he is succeeded by his next brother, Captain William Stewart, now Sir William Drummond Stewart, who is at present and has been for some years in North America."[34] Letters were immediately sent to Stewart's address at St. Louis, but they sat unopened until the fall, when Stewart returned from the season's rendezvous. Although the contents were clear, Stewart seems to have been ambivalent about returning. He lingered further, writing to inquire whether John had left a son and heir, even as he prepared for the trip back. The answer arrived in December that there was no heir and the estates were his; even then he did not depart for Murthly for another four months. The delay avoided wintertime travel in the rough seas of the North Atlantic, but Stewart's real motivation seems to have been a desire to remain in America as long as possible, even as he started preparations for his return. He began the collective program that would result in a forced remaking of Murthly as a westernized home away from home, employing the pretext of collecting specimens and trophies to both prolong his experience in America and re-create it once again after arriving in Scotland. Writing to thirty-nine-year-old fur trader William Sublette shortly after hearing the news of John's death, Stewart dealt in household matters of a sort, as if he were still at work preparing for the next season in the field: news about a cask of wine, that he trusts Sublette is "getting on better with your other boy than Silas who is not a fairy," some financial matters, and a request for some errands, and that Sublette would "be good enough to send for Antoine and tell him I wish him to get some gourds of the best form for dippers, also some red birds and keep them in cages as I wish to take them to England. I expect him to be ready by March. I trust you can procure me some tame deer."[35] He invited Clement to come along with him to Scotland for the winter, with a pleasure trip through Turkey and Constantinople on the side and a return to North America in time for the 1840 rendezvous.

Stewart and Clement arrived in Glasgow in mid-1839 before moving overland to Murthly. The old house remained much the same as when Stewart last saw it, an understated ramble of stone and oak that his late brother intended to demolish once the new house was completed. This was countered to some degree by the empty shell of the new house, long left unattended, along with John's astounding debt of a quarter million pounds. Stewart refused to complete his late brother's house, and its gigantic unfinished shell loomed over the estate for another century, torn down only after World War II.[36] After settling immediate affairs in the castle, he took Clement on a several months' trip to Egypt, Turkey, and the Middle East, departing in November 1839. It was a type of Grand Tour, and Stewart guided Clement through a world he had traveled in his twenties, a sort of revisiting of his life as impressed upon Clement's person, through a part of the world and culture that momentarily released them from the strictures of Britain. But Murthly's unattended estate matters overwhelmed any idea of returning to America for the 1840 rendezvous, and Clement was forced to hunker down while Stewart looked after matters. Worse, the old societal patterns were again dominant, and to some degree there was boredom in store for Clement as he faced the rules and manners considered appropriate for his lesser status in life on the soil of Great Britain. Murthly was Stewart's, but the mores and manners of Great Britain ultimately governed the estate and, by extension, Stewart himself.

Stewart was understandably, if fatally, determined to bring the West back to Scotland with him. It was necessary that Murthly reflect his experience and his derived philosophy as much as possible, and he began to reconfigure the ancient estate almost immediately. The grounds were planted with native American flora, including a particularly impressive set of Douglas firs, named for the Scottish botanist David Douglas, combined with medieval oaks and specimens of European foliage. This merger of two continents, expressed through a botanical synthesis of old and new natural worlds, prepared visitors for what they would encounter within Murthly's ancient walls. Stewart's redesign of the estate first provided visitors with the emblematic environment of the hunt and the West, and then, within the manor house, visitors would see rooms hung with ancient battle flags, antlers, and horns, as provocative and battle weary as the lances and armor cuirasses that surrounded them. Room after room displayed exotic objects from North America and the Middle East, intermixed to create a striking display. This effect reveals itself through letters Alfred Miller wrote home during a two-year stay at Murthly and its outer lodges while working on new paintings commissioned especially for Stewart. "The floor is overspread with Persian prayer carpets fringed with silk," he wrote, "and the walls covered with cloth (crimson) hangings. A glittering tomahawk, the one worn by him in the mountains, is placed on a small table near the divan. . . . In one corner are numerous Indian pipes, Turkish chibouks, Meerschaums, etc., with long cherry stems."[37] Even more impressive was the small herd of genuine buffalo, captured on the plains as calves and exported to Britain by sea at Stewart's direction; they grazed on imported buffalo grass in a sort of miniature prairie Stewart had arranged for a neighboring estate.

On the surface, it was a traditional and fairly common, if carefully staged, presentation of worldly experience, a kind of *Heldenleben* for the knickknack shelf, typical of well-traveled gentlemen and sporting bachelors, using exotic objects to impress visitors through irrefutable statements of some inherent and manifest value cherished by the owner. Stewart's relics hinted at a kind of heroic journey into a creation myth for any number of imagined truths and principles, the engagement of a wilderness long lost to a Britain that had grown soft with the complacency of civilization and under threat from the disruption of steam power and industrialism. None of this was new, and careful displays of exotica had been the standard trope of gentlemen of leisure for several centuries. Even so, Stewart's firsthand experience in the West placed him in a unique position to explore them. They were personal fragments of his attempt to express and justify his own ideas about what mattered in life and, at Murthly, his ultimately unsuccessful attempt to find and establish common ground between the compelling pragmatism of the West and the compulsory responsibilities of civilized Great Britain. During his stay at Murthly, Miller furthered this effect by transforming his light mountain sketches into finished paintings—an illustrated narrative of Stewart's travels—guiding and reinforcing his thematic concepts through scenes of hunting, men gathered round their campfires, or Stewart on horseback, effectively transforming the house into a gallery demonstration of who Stewart thought he was, or how he wanted to be seen, and resurrecting a life he had been obliged to leave behind. "These recollections," Miller wrote somewhat saliently, "must be to him grateful and pleasant for our remembrance of pleasure is always more vivid than the reality."[38]

Two of Miller's works stand out especially. One is a small and deeply intimate watercolor study of Stewart and Clement, a double portrait with their profiles placed against each other, looking resolutely into the distance.[39] The other is the large oil painting it appears to have been a study for, *An Attack by Crows on the Whites on the Big Horn River East of the Rocky Mountains [Crows Trying to Provoke the Whites to an Act of Hostility]*, placing Stewart and Clement within an incident that occurred on the trail, when a large number of Native men raided Stewart's camp, making off with livestock and provisions. In Stewart's telling, Clement, who spoke the Crows' language, cautiously advised Stewart to remain absolutely calm no matter what, for the Crow men would not strike unless their outnumbered opponents did so first. This not only placed the two men together but gave them purpose as they converged into a unified whole, merging Clement's knowledge of the country with Stewart's self-possession, thus saving their lives in the combination. It was

Stewart's way of inserting himself into a heroic marriage of nature and civilization, where Stewart stands center stage and, as a contemporary observer remarked, remained "calm and composed . . . knowing that the safety not only of himself, but of all who trust in him depends entirely upon his complete command of self . . . a position worthy of a hero."[40] Beyond the painting's safe and authoritative demonstrations of outward capacity that impressed contemporary visitors to Murthly lay a more subliminal portrait, suggesting a specific set of strengths and attractions possessed by and between Stewart and Clement that coalesce into an early and nascent statement of personal identity, justified and idealized through noble purpose for a greater good. The portrait of Stewart and Clement on its own, and within the context of the painting, is among the earliest representations of what would eventually evolve into something akin to modern concepts of identity, a demonstration of self-worth aligned with higher principle (or at least a noble bearing) that has a place and function within the world, adding deep purpose, value, and importance to the commissioning of the painting. As with all things Stewart, it is mixed and combined with several other ideals to create a variety of deft and sophisticated statements about the power of earthly strength and human bonds.

Despite these noble and determined statements, Clement was a sort of desperate human souvenir, ultimately little different from the buffalo and tomahawks that littered the grounds, introduced and practically demonstrated to Stewart's Scottish friends as a romantic reminder of his old hunting trips. This casual indifference to Clement's dignity is an element that appears to be consistently innate to Stewart, but it may also suggest that Stewart was slowly resuming the manners and authority expected of and consistent with the British gentleman, at the price of the mutual respect the two men had formerly shared on the plains and through the imposed and inescapable hierarchies of a manor house. Yet even if Stewart had attempted to bring Clement up into full rank, there was only so far Stewart could go, in fact hardly far at all, before reaching impenetrable barriers: reconciling Clement within Stewart's Scotland posed a challenge he was never fully able to resolve, undoubtedly because it was impossible but perhaps also because he seemed to have stopped trying. Stewart's own society would never accept a "half breed" as a gentleman, much less anything like an equal, and any idea of intimate companionship was absolutely illegal. Only five years earlier, two London men named Henry Pratt and John Smith were actually sentenced to death for "a nameless offence [sic], committed in the borough of Southwark," and subsequently "hanged at the front of Newgate" prison for what British law considered an "unnatural crime."[41] The laws that put them to death and that by extension threatened Stewart, had been in place since the 1530s and had only recently (1826) been revised to no less lethal effect, at least for Pratt and Smith. That they were the last men sentenced to death in Great Britain for having a sexual relationship was little comfort, at least for them, and offered little assurance to anyone, including Stewart, that they might not be the last.

Because of this, Stewart deliberately disguised and justified Clement's presence by employing him as a valet, or "his man," an arrangement a later British author would call "the classic British ruse," in that it offered male couples the appearances of social propriety and conformity combined with the ability to live and travel together without suspicion but at the price or requirement of appearing and outwardly functioning as master and servant.[42] It was an efficient, neat, and minimally dangerous tactic, but it also worked best with men accustomed to and accepting of the hierarchical societies of Great Britain or Europe and therefore fit within and accommodated its perimeters, even while secretly expanding them. This sort of faux servitude was probably strange, discomfiting, and insulting for someone like Clement, but the absolute requirements of life within the hierarchical social context of Great Britain in 1841 held firm and fast; anyone who disputed it faced the full force of that society at their peril.

It was not until the late summer of 1842 that Stewart and Clement returned to America for his final, long-promised trip to the West. Clement could only have been too glad to go back. They boarded the steamship *Great Western* for a transatlantic crossing and arrived at New York that September. Stewart, reported one newspaper that fall, "is one of the most eccentric and remarkable personages of the age. It is only a few years since he terminated a sojourn of seven years on both sides of the Rocky Mountains, where he employed himself in hunting the buffalo, wild boar, and other denizens of the American Forest." It continued, noting that Stewart was "a man of very unassuming manners, remarkable taste, and considerable talent. We understand that Sir William now intends proceeding to his old haunts, and resuming his forest life."[43]

The trip Stewart planned was entirely unlike anything he had gone on before, not only for the party itself but the world around it as well. The landscape remained much as it had for centuries, but the conditions and people traveling into it had dramatically changed. When he set forth in the spring of 1843, the old fur trade economy had grown dim; no rendezvous lay ahead, and the caravans had vanished, replaced by parties of nervous emigrants bound for the Oregon country. Five thousand people would flood into Oregon's Willamette Valley by the mid-1840s, enough to overwhelm the local populations and decisively shift the balance of power.[44] Already they were mustering along jumping-off points for the West, stocking up on last-minute supplies, while an expedition under John Frémont was already out in the field, mapping the best routes for them to take. Some of these emigrant parties could be colossal. In the spring of 1843, one of these parties, called the Oregon Company, was nothing short of a gigantic moving city, with 1,000 men, women, and children; 121 wagons; nearly 700 oxen; nearly 300 horses; and nearly 1,000 head of cattle, all bound for Oregon and the "new country."[45] Despite its size and difficulties crossing a river, the Oregon Company by late June was already 250 miles out, "getting along smoothly," and its 2,000 animals, a group larger than most buffalo herds, were grazing a conspicuous path westward.[46]

In contrast, Stewart's excursion was nothing more than a well-prepared pleasure trip, one where Stewart placed himself as host and star. The old familiar figure of fur trader William Sublette was there, along with a few other seasoned men to provide familiar and welcome faces while dressing the trip in the trappings of the old fur trade. Clement brought along his younger brother François. A few scientists were invited to cast the outing in an enlightened glow, while some Jesuit priests tagged along with the party as far as the Rockies before continuing on to the Northwest. To set up the tents and make meals, there were some servants, including two from Murthly, among them Stewart's actual valet, a Scottish man named Corbie. Bizarrely, the remainder of the party was made up of inexperienced greenhorns. This decision was both impractical and imprudent, but Stewart appears to have deliberately if somewhat randomly selected these men, apparently as an audience for his lessons about survival in the West, which he imagined would be taught in the field from the position of his authority. As it was, it went smoothly enough. The younger, inexperienced men chafed a bit at the strict order of things but learned to pack and prepare themselves for the day and gradually fell into the rhythm of the trip. One man was lost for a few days, another was dragged by his horse, but both survived. Things grew friskier when three Pawnee men sought protection among Stewart's party from a group of Osage warriors, who rode up and tried to pull the Pawnee men away from them. They shadowed Stewart's party through the afternoon but eventually lost interest and rode off.[47] By midsummer, though, reports began to trickle back about Stewart's "overbearing rudeness" combined with desertions, some men even having "threatened to shoot him if he continued in his tyrannical course."[48] Stewart's associates denied the story, which appears instead to have been the inevitable result of attempting to impose forcible enlightenment upon a captive and inexperienced audience.[49] Troubles or not, they had made it to the Rockies by August, where they held a semirendezvous of their own, relaxing among the trees and mountains, gambling skins for trade goods, and in general having a great time.[50]

During the trip an unexpected tragedy affected Clement in a personal and deeply saddening way. While heading west on the North Platte River, his younger brother shot himself by accident when pulling a firearm by its barrel from under a tent. François Clement was hit in the chest, just below his lung, an impossible wound for the medical science of the 1840s, especially in the open wilderness. He lived for a few hours, cried out that he was dying—"Mon Dieu! Je suis mort!"—and died as the evening's light faded into dark. One description of his death put him in the arms of Stewart. "He was but fifteen years old," wrote Matthew Field, a New Orleans reporter going along with the trip, "the pet of his mother at home, and a forward, smart boy at everything that pertained to hunting or forest life." He was buried the following day with services and poems, in a grave that was deliberately hidden to protect it from wolves.[51] The party returned to camp in otherwise good condition, set up its farewell dinner, clinked glasses, and moved on. Stewart wintered in New Orleans as usual before his planned return to Murthly in the spring of 1845. Clement chose to remain in America rather than return to Scotland for a tangential life with the increasingly grandiose and aging Stewart. He was reported to have married not long after and, at thirty-one years old, set about re-establishing both his status as a skilled hunter and respect as his own man before heading off to fight in the Mexican-American War, seeing firsthand some of the military life Stewart had known in Spain and Belgium.[52] Having won praise for his actions in battle, Clement had just returned from duty in the field when, in the summer of 1847, a correspondent from St. Louis described him as one of the social lions of the city. Clement had been part of a small American force that outmaneuvered their opponents at the Sacramento River near Chihuahua, Mexico, thereby gaining the field. "At Sacramento," according to a report, Clement "volunteered as cannoneer" in Captain Richard Weightman's artillery, "and it was by his advice that the artillery was planted within fifty yards of one of the redoubts[.] 'Fight close—fight close!' said Antoine, 'dat is de vay ve vip de Spanish and Indian!' and sure enough, it was the way that Sacramento was won. Every man went into the engagement on his 'own hook,' and was a host in himself."[53]

At Murthly, Stewart turned his attention to the estate, rebuilding a dining room damaged by fire and remodeling a chapel on the estate grounds (to the frustration of his Protestant family), occasionally visited his wife, now living in one of the estate houses a few miles away, and heard from their son William George, whose own military career was on the rise. The first of Stewart's semiautobiographical novels, *Altowan*, was written in the mid-1840s; the next, *Edward Warren*, was finished a decade later. Each offered him opportunities to revisit the West, where imaginary protagonists replayed his western adventures in a manner that allowed him to publicly memorialize his experience while explaining as much as possible his view of the world and opinions of life, a sort of justification for himself. Over the ensuing years the estate's trees matured, the animals survived or not, and the collection at Murthly took on an inevitable patina. He lived the remainder of his life surrounded by his art, his tomahawks, and his memories, turning to the comfort of sentimental representations where he stood center stage with Clement by his side. Before his death in 1871, he commissioned *The Red Book of Grandtully*, a chronicle of the Stewart family that depicted several of the ancient trees of the ancestral estate along with many of the new growths, and he arranged for an engraved portrait of himself with Clement to be featured in its pages, symbolically placing Clement within the Stewart legacy.

Stewart looked to the past and the future. He hunted buffalo in the ancient fashion and saw the hunt as a test of character requiring physical stamina that belied the prerogatives of birthright. Hunting with Clement forged a bond possible on the frontier but that crossed boundaries of custom and manner in a way that is both traditional yet startlingly modern. The display of a heroic narrative of his western travels, told in part by his collections and commissioned works, reflects an impossible longing, his concurrent attempts to reconcile the West he loved with his native Scotland: loved, but also obligatory. Stewart sought to align elements of these two worlds into a singular whole and, in doing so, define himself by commenting on the power and ideal of romantic and masculine nobility. But the rules of the natural world could not be followed easily or without cost in Great Britain, and Stewart found that it was far easier to introduce a few civilized comforts into the wilderness than attempt to reinvigorate the clipped lawns of the Old World with the brutal vitality of the North American frontier. The compelling story is perhaps not so much what Stewart brought to the world—he saw no evidence of natural selection nor did he actively document Indian life through a coolly forensic lens—but rather, how a man stumbled into himself, in a sense, by traveling into the West and, when compelled to return home, tried to find himself again by attempting to knit it all together.

Stewart was grandiose and careless, but the opportunities he longed for, along with the happiness he found possible in the West, would be readily understood and appreciated. Over time, the West would change, and it was already showing signs of a dramatic change that would occur over the next century. The contrast between frontier and civilization that Stewart found at work between the North American West and Great Britain now began to play itself out in the West itself, cutting out the transatlantic middleman and compelling westerners to reckon with newly imposed ways of life, whether wanted or not. Over the years to come, what people like Stewart would find in the West depended in part on how they engaged the West and how the West in turn engaged them. This evolution would provide as many opportunities as it would eventually provide dangers.

2

Charley Parkhurst and the Gold Rush Scene

At the same time William Stewart was traveling through the West, a young hostler named Charles Parkhurst was beginning to make his way through life among the stables of Providence, Rhode Island. He could not have known it at the time that a tough but splendid life awaited him in the far and distant West, where his sheer existence eventually led him to permanent fame, all for his simple yet determined path in following his nature and prudently refusing to bend to others.

Parkhurst left no written record of his world and seems to have made no effort to perpetuate his memory. Few people in his working field did. These men could enjoy respect within a circle of close associates in their line of work, but they were otherwise subsumed within the cultural and social boundaries of life and largely unknown beyond fragmentary glimpses. Parkhurst seems to have especially shied away from publicity. His most reliable image is drawn from within the peripheral shadows of mundane miscellanea—city directories, county registers, a lawsuit, and an occasional notice. An equal amount draws on anecdote and recollection, the flood of memories that poured out on both sides of the nation after news of his death revealed and confirmed what many had long imagined—that his body was that of a woman. Most of these early and contemporary memories related mundane details of his life, yet they often included the impressive idea that many people had already long perceived him as something distinct from ordinary men and then simply let it be.

According to the *Providence Directory* of 1836, the earliest direct reference to his life and career, Charles D. Parkhurst was a hostler, working among the horses of a livery stable in central Providence.[1] Twelve years later, Parkhurst had risen up the ladder to the position of coachman, and by that time, in 1848, he had met a young man named Bartholomew Moore. Moore later recalled that Parkhurst "used to drive a hack for Charles H Childs" in Providence and "was quite a favorite among the boys and, indeed, his employer had the greatest confidence in him."[2] His stablemates agreed. He was "exceedingly popular with his associates and with the people for whom he worked," the *Providence Journal* later reported. His "judgement as to what could and could not be done with a wagon was always sound, and his pleasant manners won him friends everywhere." The origins of Parkhurst's success and earned respect were summed up by another of his old Providence associates, an old-timer who remarked that "there wan't [sic] no reason why Charlie should not get on well. He understood his business; he was pleasant and stiddy [sic] and sober, and with them any feller can do well."[3]

Parkhurst's stablemates also knew he was someone special, and they appear to have simply accepted him as such. "Now that it is known that Charlie was a woman," the *Providence Journal* reported in 1880, after his death and the discovery of his female body, "there are plenty of people to say they always thought he was. No doubt they thought he was not like other men, indeed, it was generally said among his acquaintances that he was a hermaphrodite." This acceptance wasn't from the idea that nineteenth-century Americans necessarily had a place for transgender people in their society but perhaps rather from the reason that when they encountered people like Parkhurst at least, they had no model to necessarily cast them negatively and looked to his actions, person, and circumstances for a guide in this absence. The *Journal* added that while Parkhurst's shape was "more womanly than manly [it was] accounted for by the mysterious word generally pronounced 'mophodite.'"[4]

At that time, the word *hermaphrodite* was popularly used in a matter-of-fact way, referring to any variety of things that combined features of two separate things, from botanical experiments to aphids, politics, the sailing rigs of vessels, shellfish, or even railroad cars. A hermaphrodite brig combined two styles of sailing rig on as many masts, while hermaphrodite politics combined separate political planks or described political duplicity. Hermaphroditic strawberries were frequently discussed. The term was not entirely neutral and sometimes referred to something that was either inert, useless, or monstrous as a result of its combination, but this characterization does not appear to have been applied to, or associated with, Parkhurst by his associates.[5] If anything, they appear to have respected and enjoyed him. In the nascent science of the mid-nineteenth century, Parkhurst was just another interesting marvel or curiosity of nature, as much a part of the world as Darwin's barnacles, reflecting a pragmatic acceptance that seems to have occurred throughout his life.

Despite this, Parkhurst appears to have continuously guarded his inner world against discovery or interruption. This cautiousness was both lifelong and occasionally necessary. "His mates used to try to get him drunk once in a while in order to see if he would not betray himself in some way," continued the *Providence Journal*, "but Charley kept his wits about him, and after one or two glasses would begin to 'pass.' In vain did his comrades urge a few more drinks. Charley was not dry, and when he was not he would not drink."[6] Parkhurst's caution protected his associates as much as him, by deflecting material knowledge that might have obliged them to act, whether they wanted to or not, and in so doing he avoided attempts by others to stuff him into a skirt or otherwise oblige him to live an unfamiliar or unwelcome life. He navigated a knife's edge between a society that was relatively bemused at the thought of someone like Parkhurst and one that would nonetheless be obliged to social convention, separate and apart from personal feeling. If his associates in the stable did not care, its owner, Charles Childs, might, and if Childs did not care, his clients might, and if they did not care, word would inevitably reach some official or body in Providence or elsewhere that would involve itself in Parkhurst's affairs out of, if not claims to decency, then from decorum. By maintaining his guard up to the end, Parkhurst was effectively able to live life on his own terms and as he wanted, not even as a natural curiosity but as Charley Parkhurst, and in doing so he likewise allowed his friends and associates opportunities to enjoy him as he was, without interference or bother.

His origins are uncertain. "He is the Enigma of the stage-coach business," remarked stage superintendent William Buckley, who later met Parkhurst in California. "I do not even know where he was born or when he came to California."[7] Parkhurst seems to have been deliberately vague, although he could apparently open up somewhat on occasion when it suited him. "He told one of his associates that he came from New Hampshire," reported the *Providence Journal*, "but did not tell the name of the town. He told others that he had came from the poor-house in Worcester, from which he had run away."[8] Whether he knew of others like him is also uncertain, although he was not alone. In the winter of 1835 he might have read about the death of one Captain Wright in Britain, a social yet eccentric gentleman with a "grotesque and unique appearance" whose death revealed the body of a woman.[9] More ominously, in the spring of 1838 he might also have read about a divorce case between a transgender bricklayer and his wife, where the aggrieved wife threatened her husband with betrayal and interruption in order to obtain better terms in the divorce settlement. They had been married for over twenty years when the wife took her case against her husband, a clear and unavoidable warning that time, trust, or affection alone offered no promise of security and that even the most intimate of partners could prove dangerous. The bricklayer had pursued his "trade of a more ordinarily masculine and hazardous description, with a degree of skill and ability" that paralleled Parkhurst's own career in the stable and stagecoach world, framing this distant misfortune in very immediate and personal terms. Parkhurst's deep and careful reticence, as well as his lifelong bachelorhood, may have been informed by the dangers demonstrated through examples such as this, pointing to the wisdom and security of a life entirely on his own terms, even if at the cost of a social life.[10]

Parkhurst seems to have moved through life at a consistently slow and steady pace. If he wasn't methodical, then there is at least no evidence of rash ideas or sudden, impulsive decisions. He spent about ten years in Providence as a hostler, grooming and feeding horses and setting harness and rigs. Livery stables maintained their own horses for hire by customers, either in harness or saddled, and stabled other privately owned horses whose owners had ridden into town, in a business model akin to the services offered by a full-service parking garage.[11] It was sometimes dangerous work; all animals could have a temper, and more than a few hostlers were kicked by impatient, anxious, or unfamiliar horses while grooming them. Most were fortunate to escape with a broken leg or bad gash, and Parkhurst himself was later recalled to have lost an eye at some point from a kicking horse, which led to nicknames like "one-eyed" and "cockeyed," used among those who remembered him years later.[12] Despite the dangers, the stables offered invaluable instruction on the carriage-driving world through firsthand experience, something he put to good use. He transitioned to a coachman sometime between 1844 and 1847, successfully navigating the rungs of the hostler's ladder from the stall and pitchfork to the driving seat and reins. His new rank was accompanied by an increased status: a prominent position within the livery world, one that represented a mark of earned ability.

Driving was a skill in life, something simultaneously respected yet expected, a basic hallmark of ability. To be able to drive meant that one had capacity, whether in the means to afford the trappings of driving or, for men like Parkhurst, the means to earn a living by driving—in other words, wealth or the ability to gain wealth. Drivers who knew their horses displayed an ease in driving that other sound drivers recognized in their passing, which engendered respect and reinforced their status as gentlemen. Parkhurst was "considered one of the best drivers in the city," his associates recalled, "and his services were sought for by the best people. Quite a number of wealthy families always depended upon having him for a driver if they ordered a stable team."[13] At the stable of Charles Childs, Parkhurst was among the cream of the Providence stable trade, catering to "some of the richest families in the United States," many of whom relied on hired livery rather than undertake the expense of keeping horse and stable themselves. He "drove the best team in the stable," the reporter continued. "The horses were gray, exactly matched, and it was quite a sight to see Charley guide them through a crowd. He always took care of this team himself. He was fond of six in hand, and called it nothing but fun to handle four spirited horses."[14] Parkhurst's associates later remembered that he dressed fashionably when he was in his thirties, almost a bit ahead of his fellows. They felt that he seemed to enjoy it. He always wore gloves, which they considered unusual but easily explained. "He was thought to be putting on style," they said, "but as he always dressed well, the gloves were looked upon only as a part of his high toned ideas."[15]

A material measure of the respect held for Parkhurst survives in a story that lingered in old-timers' memory, a story originally told among stablemen as a way of saying Parkhurst had the requisite know-how. "He never was known to have more than he could do with his team, but once," they recalled. While working for Charles Childs in the late 1840s or early 1850s, Parkhurst drove twenty-five couples to a dance in Pawtucket, a few miles outside of Providence, using a six-horse rig and with Liberty Childs keeping him company on the driver's seat. It was a "dreadfully cold night," and on the drive back "the air was so cold and the horses were so frantic, that Charley's hands became numb, and he got Liberty Childs to drive the leaders, while he took charge of the other four horses."[16] That is, when Parkhurst's freezing hands became too numb to safely manage all six horses, he turned the reins of the most critical pair over to Childs, whose hands had been kept warm inside coat pockets and were able to safely handle the task, while Parkhurst's numbed hands retained the reins for the next four horses, whose jobs pulling the weight of the vehicle required less care. The story was remembered for a reason, clear to anyone in the stable trade: Parkhurst neither gave up on his commitment to the rig and his employer, nor did he endanger his rig by stubbornly refusing help out of false pride. Instead, he asked for just as much help as necessary while holding his own—a work ethic that demonstrated both dignity and prudence, an anecdote told and retold among stablemen everywhere as measure of his earned respect for decades to come.

Parkhurst left for California in 1853. People in Providence recalled that he went west at the request of James Birch, a fellow Providence coachman who had jumped into the gold rush frenzy four years earlier to start a California stage line, aware that a staging business would thrive in a new country where no rails yet existed. "About 1849," the Providence residents were reported as saying, "James Birch and [his business partner] Frank Stevens went to California and started a stage line. After a year or two they sent for Charley to come and drive for them."[17] James Birch had worked as a driver at the O. H. Kelton & Company stables in Providence during the 1840s, a few blocks from the stables where Parkhurst worked.[18] The field of livery coachman in a small city is accordingly small, and Parkhurst and Birch likely knew each other by profession. And while Parkhurst was thirty-six years old in 1848, old enough to be settled into his career and have a long-established reputation, Birch was twenty-one and full of energy. The gold rush was mostly a young man's game, and Birch dashed off to try his luck in the melee.

Birch and Stevens were making a sound decision. In gold rush California, the staging market was both obvious and lucrative, a "rush and scramble of needy adventurers" arriving on ships daily, those vessels loaded to the bulwarks with tools and men who barely knew where to go and even less how to get there.[19] Birch soon made a name for himself, and by April 1851 his "Telegraph Line of Coaches" between Sacramento and Nevada City was one of the most profitable routes in California, a direct line to the goldfields with fares alternating between fifteen and twenty dollars each way.[20] Within a few months Birch had made his fortune. Accordingly, it was now time to return to civilization and take on a sensible married life. But while he sold the Nevada line to Hayward & Swift and returned to the States a wealthy man, quiet domesticity made him restless, and he felt compelled to reenter the fray—the perpetual urge of all energetic people.[21]

Birch returned to California in March 1853, apparently bringing Parkhurst with him to help with the new business.[22] He immediately bought back his old Telegraph Line of Coaches for $40,000 and got back into business, using seventy-five horses and eleven coaches "well crowded with passengers" in continual rotation.[23] Bartholomew Moore, who first saw Parkhurst in Providence in 1848, was selling furniture in

Sacramento with his brother Daniel when he saw Parkhurst again "in Sacramento in 1853, where he was driving stage for Jim Burch [sic], who was at that time the great stage man of California." Moore recalled the wonderful experience of sitting beside Parkhurst as he told stories during the drive, thus offering the only reliable first-person account of Parkhurst's personality and style as a stage driver. "Charley drove both to the northern and southern mines," Moore recalled, "and had many interesting adventures and some hair-breadth escapes, and it was as good as going to a circus to get a seat beside him and hear him talk."[24]

While Parkhurst was driving stages over the interesting new roads of California during the fall of 1853, Birch was at work establishing a new stage company, one that would unite all the scattered independent lines into a single, unified whole. The result was the California Stage Company, which opened on the first day of 1854.[25] At its height, it was praised as the "most useful, necessary and popular" of California institutions, with Birch as president, operating capital of a million dollars, a majority of California mail contracts, and stage connections throughout the state.[26] The logistics were impressive: to keep it all running, the California Stage Company required chains of stage stations, ticket agents in all the principal cities and towns, mail contracts, stage drivers, hostlers, blacksmiths, carriage repairmen, veterinarians, stables, and suppliers for the all-important hay, feed, and water.[27] Over a hundred of the famous red-painted Concord coaches were built to order by Lewis Downing & Sons at Concord, New Hampshire, crated up, and shipped by sea around Cape Horn to San Francisco, while hundreds of stage horses were purchased in the East and driven directly overland in herds to California at a cost of $250 each.[28] The California Stage Company's road department looked over hundreds of miles of improved roads, bridges, and ferries in all kinds of weather, whether hot or cold, wet or dry. Traffic was heavy and business was brisk, "beyond the conception of those not familiar with it," remarked an observer in August 1855. At Marysville, for example, up to a dozen fully loaded "splendid four and six horse Concord Coaches" left each morning for points across the state.[29] Its initial portfolio of routes expanded southward in late 1854 when it acquired two lines

Parkhurst would later drive: Adams & Company's staging to Stockton and the southern mines, and Dillon, Hedge & Company's staging from Oakland and San Jose westward to Monterey Bay.[30] By the spring of 1861, Birch's operations had even reached Portland, Oregon, making the 750-mile run from Sacramento in seven days.[31]

In the midst of all this, Moore ran into Parkhurst yet again, this time, surprisingly, at sea in February 1854. Parkhurst was traveling in company with James Birch from San Francisco to New York on board the Vanderbilt steamers *Cortes* and *Northern Light*, via a land crossing at Nicaragua. The California Stage Company was in business now, and Birch was heading back East to secure mail contracts in Washington, to purchase supplies from eastern manufacturers, and to see his wife, while Moore was looking forward to marrying his fiancée in New York before meeting with furniture manufacturers for stock he and his brother would require for the new showroom they would open in Sacramento that summer. What Parkhurst was doing on the ship is not known. He may have been homesick or have chosen the safety of returning to Providence and familiar friends over the risks of a transgender life alone in California, without Birch's protection.[32] The *Cortes* departed San Francisco on February 1 at noon, taking on posted mail up to fifteen minutes before the lines were cast off and the ship headed out to sea. As Parkhurst negotiated the decks of the *Cortes* when it steamed forth, he would have seen its paired rocking beam engines towering over the deck, endlessly scissoring in time with the side wheels. On the first day out, he would also have seen the steamer *Brother Jonathan* pass by inbound for San Francisco, followed by the steamer *Sierra Nevada* a few days later off Baja California.[33] The *Cortes* was a two-class ship, with its passengers ticketed for, and divided between, first cabin and steerage. For this leg of the trip at least, Parkhurst appears to have traveled in first cabin. Shortly before the *Cortes* discharged its passengers in Nicaragua, Moore recalled seeing Parkhurst in the ship's main saloon, sitting beside James Birch as the cabin stewards placed dishes along the cabin table for tips. "On the opposite side of the table to where we sat," Moore recalled, "was Jim Burch [sic], who planked down a [ten dollar] gold eagle [and] Charley Parkhurst, who sat beside him followed with $5"—generous but not lavish and thus suitable and respectable for a man in his position and in a room where "very few in the cabin gave less than $2 50."[34] Nicaragua marked the halfway point of the trip, which required a land crossing to the Atlantic side (in actuality the Caribbean Sea), where the passengers then boarded the Vanderbilt steamer *Northern Light* for the final leg of the journey, steaming across the Caribbean and up the Atlantic coast.[35] The *Northern Light* was a three-class ship, with a moderately priced second cabin offered between first and steerage. While Birch and Moore both traveled in first cabin and accordingly had their names published in the *Northern Light*'s passenger list, Parkhurst appears to have chosen the moderately priced second cabin, where names were not prominent enough to warrant publication.[36] It was a fast trip, with the *Northern Light* romping into New York with four hundred passengers and $800,000 in California gold only twenty-two days after the passengers had left San Francisco, and all this despite a delay while rescuing the crew of a foundering coal schooner, the *Teren*, not far from New York.[37]

Parkhurst's choice to return to the East underscores moments of caution that periodically appear to have pervaded his life. As long as Birch was in California, the security of his presence offered Parkhurst protection, by association as much as employment. But this security might evaporate while Birch was in New York for business, even if only temporarily. Parkhurst chose not to risk staying alone in California but to return to the security and comfort of old friends in Providence.[38] Even so, his time on the East Coast was brief; he appears to have returned to California by mid-1855 if not earlier. Just what propelled him to head west again is unknown—perhaps a California job offer from Birch or an associate, or perhaps just the shock of a New England winter compared to the mild Sacramento version.

The California that Parkhurst encountered on his return was undergoing tremendous change. The great gold rush six or seven years earlier had transformed the region overnight, from what the Americans considered to be a useful but distant newly acquired territory to, as far as the Atlantic coasters were concerned, a kind of bachelor paradise where men could take off their coats, get rich, and live free and easy, far from the shushing fingers of home. It moved from a sea of tents to a kind of wooden Boston followed by instant statehood and the Bella Union.[39] The last of the old gold rush fleet that once crowded San Francisco Bay had been towed off. A new generation of California clippers appeared with snowy white sails, and auction houses jostled with bidding for the contents of their holds: flannel shirts and cider vinegar in kegs and barrels.[40] Inland, the city of Sacramento had been built up in brick and cast iron and by 1856 was already running a railroad over twenty miles into the interior, with locomotives built in Boston and Jersey City. On the Sacramento River, the whistles of side-wheel steamers with names like *New World* and *Antelope* sounded over the waterways, while the canvas sails of an endless fleet of cargo schooners plied back and forth along the delta.[41] Already, some of the free and easy that characterized the early gold rush years was beginning to wear off, and as early as 1850 the inhabitants of Hangtown pretended to social respectability by renaming the place "Placerville."[42] These attempts toward civilization were nonetheless frisky, and for a few moments vigilance groups in San Francisco acquired buildings, put up sandbag forts, and published greatly ornamented and elegant lithographs of themselves to commemorate their work, along with a few hangings outside of buildings neatly decorated with cannons and bunting.[43] But beyond California's rivers, its urban squabbles, and its tiny railroad lay seemingly endless stretches of land, covered by plains, mountains, forests, and ranchos, all primed for staging.

The great California stage routes of the 1850s focused on three areas of travel. The first and most profitable of these routes, and the all-important backbone of California's mining economy, served the lucrative mining districts that lay along the Sierra Nevada foothills. Nearly every letter written to or received from distant families in the East was carried at some point on stagecoaches between the California steamers and the writer's desk. Every day dozens of stagecoaches rolled in and out of the California Stage Company's depots, brimming with passengers, express cargo, and mail, bound to and from the great mining centers of the mountains that lay in the distance. "In traveling over the solitary and voiceless plains of California," a traveler remarked in 1859, "the stage coach may be christened with the borrowed name of ship of the desert, with the chief part of its lading in rigging. A fully equipped ship of the line [will] carry nine inside and sixteen outside passengers, with the baggage not only complete for this compliment [sic] above and aloft, but with as many supplementary trunks and boxes as may be entered upon the way-bill and paid for."[44] The second, and equally important, route connected the urban world of the Bay Area with the city of San Jose, just south of the lower reaches of San Francisco Bay. Here the San Jose stages ran on impressively tight three-hour schedules, timed to meet the Oakland ferryboats, along elegant roads scattered with farms and oak groves—a nascent form of commuting in the immediate post–gold rush landscape. The third great route, one that Parkhurst did not drive, had emerged in 1858 over the Sierra Nevada and beyond, as part of an audacious, miserable, and dangerous transcontinental stage system called the Overland Mail, which ran across the continent from California to the Missouri River and beyond. It was splendid and frisky, especially as the coaches crossed the Great Plains. "The coaches used for this route," remarked observers, "are the celebrated Concord coaches, and each coach is provided with five Sharp's [sic] rifles, so prepared that passengers can readily use them, in case of attack."[45] In the Sierra Nevada range, reports of road conditions were regularly posted in 1858 and 1859 by a stage driver named Henry Monk, who soon became a national hero for humble-shaming the influential New York editor Horace Greeley on a drive over the Sierra in July 1859.[46]

Editors of California newspapers later thought that Parkhurst had driven the first two of these great routes, first from Stockton to Mariposa and the southern mining districts, and then from Oakland to San Jose. He drove a third route as well—not one of the great ones but instead one of the countless unassuming local lines that threaded together everything else, in this case a simple local jaunt between Santa Cruz and San Juan by way of Watsonville on the Monterey Bay, where he was "the boss of the road."[47]

Taken together, these three routes provided him with a well-rounded experience of California staging. Parkhurst's run from Stockton to

Mariposa was one of the longest in the state, around one hundred miles across the great Central Valley of California to the farthest of the southern Sierra mines, and all for a ten-dollar fare. A passenger on the Mariposa stage in the summer of 1860 described a departure from Stockton at five in the morning and a stop for breakfast three hours later. He recalled the "level and uninteresting" country and slow driving, frequent stops to water or change horses during the hot summers, an impressive suspension bridge over the Stanislaus River, and a more conventional cable ferry over the Tuolumne River by Osborn's Ranch.[48] It was as splendid as it was strenuous, and the view from the top of the stage was magnificent. In the 1850s the San Joaquin Valley positively shimmered with green grass and pronghorn antelope, while enormous condors wheeled overhead and the Merced ran cold, clear, and speckled with fish. There was little doubt that one was in a wilder country. From deep within Sierra canyons came stories of grizzly bears, "more numerous than agreeable," and rumors of colossal trees, the biggest in the world.[49] In Mariposa, a man who shot his wife's lover appeared "cheerful, as he ought to, for he has done his duty."[50] At Snelling's, a stage stop that Parkhurst would have passed on the Merced River, William Snelling was shot to death in his own tavern during supper by a man in a buckskin coat. Snelling's murderer, a man named Edwards, was eventually caught in the Carson Valley, but the people there, loath to extradite, hanged him themselves.[51]

Mariposa was the center of the southern mine region, with a landscape and geology that required a style of mining infrastructure unlike that of its northern counterparts. It had "suffered more, perhaps," remarked *Hutching's California Magazine* in 1859, "than almost any other mining district for the want of water for mining purposes, [yet] owing to its quartz leads and rich, flat gulch, and hill diggings, it has generally been very prosperous. . . . Its streets at certain times of the year present a very lively appearance."[52] At that time, the ranch and mines known as Las Mariposas were owned by John Frémont, who had adventured into California in the 1840s to claim control of the state in the name of manifest destiny.[53] With the gold rush in full swing and hungry miners everywhere,

Frémont found his own Mariposa-area properties besieged in turn, and his wife Jessie complained about the "Indians, bears & miners" that ruined things. It's not known whether Parkhurst ever saw the Frémonts. They traveled between Mariposa and Stockton by private carriage, and at the time Parkhurst most likely drove the route to Mariposa, Frémont was in New York, a reluctant presidential nominee for the newly formed Republican Party.[54]

The California Stage Company's interest in the southern mining regions was short-lived. It had overextended itself in terms of practical stage management, and in 1856 it chose to sell off its southern routes to one of its own officers, Charles McLaughlin, general superintendent at Marysville. McLaughlin added it to a portfolio that also included the San Jose and the Santa Cruz lines that Parkhurst would later drive.[55] It's uncertain whether Parkhurst may have known McLaughlin, but it's likely he knew his superintendents and to some extent appears to have chosen or have been offered routes within McLaughlin's business. Parkhurst was "the best all-round driver in California," according to stage superintendent William Buckley, and "as brave as Julius Caesar."[56] This respect and affiliation offered the same associations of safety and security that he had known while working for Birch, especially after Birch moved on to new projects in the mid-1850s. McLaughlin himself lived a vigorous life. He pursued mail contracts throughout the state, at one point looked into a mule line, and was once attacked by a three-hundred-pound woman in a carriage, who "fired the whole six barrels of an Allen's revolver at him and then drove off."[57] He survived the shooting and by 1860 was actively involved in building the San Francisco and San Jose Railroad, whose steam trains reached San Jose in 1864.[58]

At some point Parkhurst landed a seat on McLaughlin's Oakland-to–San Jose run, trading the dusty San Joaquin Valley for the cool breezes of San Francisco Bay. The route from Oakland to San Jose was a pleasant, thirty-mile trip by way of San Leandro, Hayward's, and the relatively ancient Mission San José. It was also a suburban whirl, a three-hour drive timed to depart Oakland after the arrival of the morning ferryboat from San Francisco. Northbound stages were likewise scheduled to depart from San Jose in time to reach Oakland for the afternoon boats. This made for snappy driving that allowed coachmen abundant opportunity to show their stuff.

Driving was everything. "With the horses trotting loosely in their harness," one passenger recalled, "and the driver on the brake, we streamed around the curves. . . . They were dainty, elegant little animals, those leaders; at one moment, with their reluctant heads reined towards their flanks, they danced like wild deer along the verge of the precipice, and the next, the inexorable driver was grinding them against the bank—but never a sign did they give of leaving the road, so thoroughbred were they. The swing horses, a trifle larger, followed the movements of the leaders, but more sedately. The wheelers [were] big steady fellows."[59] Every horse had a role when in harness, each having a specific and interrelated function, somewhat similar to instruments in an orchestra. A first-class rig employed six horses, enough to do serious work with minimal trouble. The lead pair of horses, at the front of the harness, were called the leaders, used to steer and lead the team into a curve or turn, pulling the tongue of the vehicle into a desired direction and creating a cascading effect as the other horses followed. Leaders required more tact than power and were generally the smallest horses in a team. Next in line were the swing horses, whose role combined and transmitted the directional value of the leaders with the pulling force of the wheelers behind them. The heaviest horses, harnessed closest to the vehicle, were called the wheelers, powerful animals who bore the brunt of the pulling work of a coach or wagon. They required brawn over brain and generally followed wherever the leaders went. All of this was controlled by a sturdy set of harnesses, controlled by a leather-ribbon network of reins and tensions that conveyed commands from the driver to the horses, allowing for slight tugs and pressures that would steer the animal into a desired direction.

Much of the horses' work was helped by the design of the Concord coach itself. Concord coaches employed a unique system of leather strap suspension that allowed the coach body to sway independently of the chassis, or "gears," checked in its side-to-side motion by buckled leather straps on each side. "By allowing the heavy body to rock fore and aft," remarked William Banning, the son of an early California stager, "they enable the force of inertia to supply a timely boost to relieve the team of strain due to obstacles of the road. The horse was the vital consideration. The less taxed, the more he could pull and the faster he could go. The coach that could run the easiest with the greatest load was the best for the horse. And the Concord was that coach."[60]

Parkhurst probably enjoyed staging on a well-graded road, particularly when it made driving a pleasure, but coaching on the Oakland-to–San Jose run required careful driving. The San Jose roads were crowded with vehicles—private carriages, business wagons, gentlemen on horseback, teamsters in freight wagons, buggies darting in and out like frightened rabbits. Any upset would make the news. Sometimes this was impossible to avoid, as with a stage that was upset during the summer of 1857, when trying to drive past a drunken teamster whose slow, weaving lumber wagon blocked a clear path.[61] The San Jose roads were also a prime spot for opposition stage lines, the local start-ups that inevitably appeared to compete with whichever large stage company was dominating the field at any given time. This competitive spirit bred racing, as rival coaches dashed down the road for advantage and glory in a sport as popular as it was condemned, often by the same people and in the same breath. Parkhurst left no record of such recklessness and appears instead to have driven prudently at a smart yet approved pace.[62] But the San Jose run is also where Parkhurst was recalled to have had his first known incident since that bitterly cold night outside of Pawtucket many years earlier. "It is told that once," an account later remarked, "while driving a fractious four-in-hand from Oakland to San Jose, the team ran away so suddenly as to throw Parkhurst from the box. Still retaining his grasp on the lines, he was dragged along until he succeeded in turning the runaways into the chaparral, where they caught among the bushes and stopped. To show their admiration of the driver's pluck the passengers made up and presented him with a purse of $20."[63] Runaway teams were a serious and all too common problem: an anxious team or even a single frightened or unbroken horse made a stage difficult to manage and could result in disaster. If the horses knew the road and carried on with minimal fuss, its passengers were fortunate, but more often they spooked and bolted for some cause fathomable only to the equine mentality, and a subsequent upset that wrecked the stage was all too common.[64] Common or not, it was a driver's duty to always maintain control of the team, and a driver who lost his team cast doubt on his abilities and blemished a proud career. And while Parkhurst displayed mettle in holding onto the reins as he was dragged off the coach, the prize offered by his grateful passengers for saving their lives would have only made it worse: in effect, they were rewarding him for saving them from a problem of his own making.

By this time, Parkhurst was approaching his mid-forties. Whether related to this incident or not, Parkhurst moved on to another McLaughlin route sometime prior to the summer of 1859. The new run was a relaxed, local jaunt with two-horse coaches, neither long nor fast, a good match for an older driver. It ran along the coast range of mountains from San Juan (now known as San Juan Bautista) westward along the Monterey Bay toward Santa Cruz.[65] The road through this generous land was pleasant and leisurely. There was the familiar, if extended, presence of McLaughlin; an annual sea of mustard flowers that rose en masse across the southern range of the Pajaro Valley; crops of wheat, potatoes, and strawberries; and the occasional sight of gulls and pelicans over Monterey Bay, hovering and wheeling over shoals of mackerel a mile wide.[66]

On the southernmost end of this route, San Juan was marked by the presence of Mission San Juan Bautista, an adobe brick structure Spanish missionaries began building in 1797.[67] Across from the mission was a grassy plaza and the Plaza House, a large adobe hotel with a ground floor built in the 1810s and nearly as old as Parkhurst, topped by a newly built second floor. Stage offices and dining rooms for travelers were located here, and Parkhurst would likely have taken his meals there. Directly next door to the Plaza House was a two-story adobe house, originally owned by General José Castro, a Californio who served as interim governor of Alta California in 1835 and military commander a decade later while defending California against Frémont and other invading Americans who had "daringly introduced themselves into the country" with an eye toward acquisition.[68] Disheartened by the loss of his beautiful

Alta California to the subsequent American conquest, Castro left the region and eventually sold the San Juan house to the Breen family, who had survived the disaster of the Donner Party to get there. The Breens were among the thousands of people who headed west during the 1840s amid the manifest destiny push and with Frémont's maps highlighting bright green farmlands in the "new country" of Oregon and California. Wise travelers, new to the country and unfamiliar with its face or ways, followed the established trails, especially the Frémont-surveyed Oregon Trail, that ensured hardships but also the greatest chance of success. Others risked taking alternate or newly discovered routes in hopes of saving time or wear. The Donner Party, with the Breens among them, were among the latter and took the Hastings Cutoff, which split off from the main trail to run south of the Great Salt Lake before rejoining the California Trail. Late starts and ill considerations led to the party's late arrival at the foot of the Sierra Nevada just at the onset of winter.[69] They were trapped by snow while crossing, famously driven to cannibalism to survive, and instantly notorious by the time the survivors had finally made it down the other side. Despite this trauma, the Breens did as best they could, and one of the Breen children who survived the Sierra ordeal and lived at the San Juan house for much of her life became the last surviving member of the Donner Party when she died in 1935, after decades as a living witness to the tragedy.[70]

By 1860 San Juan had become a relic of the Spanish colonial past or at least an island of provincialism before the new Coast Line of stages for Santa Barbara and Los Angeles revived the action. Its importance to northern stage traffic was waning, and as early as 1858 a new road had been cut over the Santa Cruz Mountains, from Santa Clara straight through to Santa Cruz, providing a direct if rudimentary line between the Bay Area and Monterey Bay. In late 1860 a second turnpike road opened, this time between Gilroy and Watsonville, now known as the Mount Madonna Road.[71] A third turnpike had replaced the original one over the Santa Cruz Mountains by 1862. It ran more efficiently, connecting with McLaughlin's stages and, by 1864, McLaughlin's new San Francisco and San Jose Railroad. This connection shifted everything: one could go from "the cars" directly to Santa Cruz by stage and turnpike, cutting out Watsonville and San Juan entirely. The local staging was also changing. McLaughlin turned his focus to the Bay Area and railroad building, while new stage companies took up his old routes. Dillon & Company ran to Mariposa now, and Adams was running through the Pajaro Valley.

Stage driving was hard work; its drivers took a battering in the open air, and few stagers drove into old age or lived long enough to do so. Parkhurst retired from staging around this time, perhaps when he turned fifty in 1862, or perhaps a few years earlier, in 1859. It was also around this time that Parkhurst reentered the primary record for the first time after leaving Providence, in an account book for a Watsonville dry goods store: on Saturday, August 6, 1859, Parkhurst purchased two pairs of overalls at $1.50 and tobacco at $1.00.[72] He was known to have been farming by 1865, having leased approximately five hundred acres of farmland on the Soquel Augmentation Rancho, located roughly halfway between Watsonville and Santa Cruz. The lot that Parkhurst had leased, lot 5, was part of a Mexican land grant to María Luisa Cota Hodges in 1844, as an augmentation to her existing rancho, one of some five hundred or so ranchos that existed along the coast up to 1848.[73] It had been deeded in rapid succession, mostly among French investors, during the early 1860s and eventually landed in the hands of Felix Gambert, a thirty-year-old San Jose businessman who in turn leased the land to Parkhurst for thirty dollars a year, with the stipulation that Parkhurst not cut wood apart from that for personal use, such as firewood or fencing, nor attempt to work the coal mine that had been dug into a hillside.[74]

Parkhurst's Soquel Augmentation lease was ideal for a retirement farmer but was burdened by a significant problem. A competing claim to the land had been filed by Frederick Hihn, a Santa Cruz businessman who was determined to acquire and control the Soquel Augmentation tract for himself and was capable of, and inclined toward, prolonging fights and relentlessly draining others through litigation to achieve his goals. The thirty-six-year-old Hihn had studied business in Germany before immigrating to California during the gold rush, and once there he found that securing Spanish and Mexican land grants could provide a substantial profit and that Santa Cruz offered good opportunities. His focus on the wooded Augmentation lands stemmed in particular from their potential value as fuel and lumber sources, but they also offered the reward of easy pickings among landowners ill prepared to defend themselves. Offers for the land were plentiful enough, but partitioning cost money that families rich in land and hides did not have.

Hihn claimed ownership of tract number 5 through an April 29, 1859, agreement with María Louisa Cota Juan and her then-husband, Ricardo Fourcade Juan, to purchase "an undivided one-third of one-ninth of the said several tracts of land" for $375.[75] Somehow complications showed up to Hihn's advantage (as they frequently did in Hihn's transactions), and the costs of partition were levied against the Juans, leading to a sheriff's sale, one of many Hihn regularly employed against property owners of all kinds and that could be found posted on the county courthouse door, always using Hihn's own language. Mariano Vallejo, who managed to keep his estates intact, saw men like Hihn at work throughout the state and recalled how "these legal thieves, clothed in the robes of the law, took from us our lands and our houses and without the least scruple enthroned themselves in our homes like so many powerful kings. . . . The number of California families despoiled of their lands under one pretext or another by means of arbitrary actions of the courts ran into the hundreds."[76]

Things came to a head on July 9, 1866, when Hihn attempted to claim physical possession of Gambert's land, with an attempt to evict Parkhurst from his lease in the process. He underestimated his target: Parkhurst absolutely refused to be evicted and instead "ousted" Hihn from the property. The following day, Hihn wrote a legal complaint against Parkhurst on pale blue paper and in his characteristically clear, well-practiced handwriting, arguing that Parkhurst had "unlawfully and without right or title trespassed and entered upon said premises, and took unlawful possession of same and ousted Plaintiff [Hihn] therefrom and has since retained and does now retain possession of said premises," and Hihn wanted "restitution of said premises, for the sum of one hundred dollars as damages, and for the sum of ten dollars for each and every month the said premises have been and still may be detained from him [Hihn] and for costs of rent."[77] A summons followed, and battle began; it led to suit after suit, filed in the Santa Cruz courts like the heavy and unyielding broadsides fired from a Nelson three-decker.

Hihn's tactics were relentless and persistent but also very much reminiscent of a hawk that springs from its perch to surprise and quickly overwhelm its prey. Gambert's and Parkhurst's tactics were in turn slow and absorbent, removing the element of surprise while slowly wearing Hihn out. Year after year, the case went back and forth as one judgment or another was overturned or was otherwise set back into motion—a long, slow process that effectively denied Hihn any claim to the land during Parkhurst's lifetime, as well as for some time afterward. All of this was long after Parkhurst's original three-year lease had expired, suggesting a fight on principle together with the suggestion of something approaching contempt on his part for Hihn's actions. All of this was noticed and admired by the surrounding community. Parkhurst, a newspaper reporter pointedly remarked after his death and the discovery of his female anatomy, "was put in possession of the land at a time when the struggle over the property was such that only a brave and determined man was believed equal to the task of holding it against Mr. Hihn and his agents."[78]

Through it all, Parkhurst farmed. He listed himself as "farmer" when everyone in the county registered to vote in April 1867, and in 1871 he may have seen his first locomotive in many years, one of the big Southern Pacific machines with its splendid brass trim that ran onto a newly built Watsonville branch by way of Gilroy. At some point in his post–staging life, he lived near, and may have played a part in managing, the Seven Mile House, a stage stop and tavern located roughly halfway between Watsonville and Santa Cruz. People who knew him during these years describe him as a tempered man, good with stories and sociability. "He smoked, chewed, drank, played card[s] and was 'one of the boys,'" a newspaper later reported, "but was never addicted to loose life."[79] He was "always social, but never convivial," another associate recalled, "a pleasant but not a jovial companion."[80]

Storytelling was a sacred rite of stage drivers. At that time, the absolute undisputed champion of storytelling was stage driver Hank Monk, the "cock liar" of Carson City whose tales were best taken, observers advised in 1877, "*cum grano salis*." Monk's stories generally ranged from tall tales about frozen jackrabbits to outright pranks, such as his coolly informing a woman passenger in 1874 that her cumbersome Saratoga trunk was being sawn in half in order to get it up a mountain.[81] The stories associated with Parkhurst were of a very different type: surviving examples all tell of how Parkhurst confronted one obstacle or another, always saving the day along with his coach and passengers. In one, he makes the instant decision to race across a bridge that was crumbling during a flood, driving his horses on just as the timbers gave way behind him and fell into the swollen river. In another, he fends off the infamous bandit "Sugarfoot" with his pistol, sending the highwayman onto "his last journey" while saving the coach and passengers from robbery.[82] Neither of these stories was genuine.

The story about the flooded bridge did bear some possible elements of truth. Every year heavy rains and spring snowmelt transformed streams flowing down from the Sierra Nevada into raging torrents. In 1861 four horses attached to a stage were drowned in Auburn Ravine while "all the bridges from h-ll to breakfast were washed away."[83] Travelers forced to navigate these roads during flood season did so extremely carefully, and occasionally stagecoaches with all their passengers could be stranded between washed-out bridges for days at a time. "The Mokulumne is roaring down with great fury, and the Calaveras has overflowed its banks," reported observers during a particularly strong storm in late 1859. There was "little prospect for the arrival of either the Mariposa, Sonora or Mokulumne Hill stages," remarked observers, while another stage running between Visalia and Hornitos had "capsized at Mariposa Creek, drowning two horses" a few months earlier, in March 1859. The driver, a man named Alden, was nearly drowned himself while saving his passengers, along with the mail bags.[84] Despite this, Parkhurst's collapsing bridge sounds more at home in melodrama than reality. A similar incident did occur a few years later, and just outside of Santa Cruz, but this involved a burning bridge instead of a flooded one: in the fall of 1864 a stagecoach passing through a low-level forest fire in the mountains above Santa Cruz lost one of its wheel horses while attempting to cross a bridge that seemed solid but had actually burned out to the brink of collapse, an event that Parkhurst would have undoubtedly heard of almost immediately after it happened.[85] Parkhurst's story was either an exaggeration of a drenched but mundane event he or others encountered during floods in the Sierra foothills, or an appropriation of Alden's lost stage, or the burning bridge incident, or any combination of these, reset through the lens of drama and the distant Sierra Nevada, far enough away to escape serious scrutiny.

The same situation applies for the bandit "Sugarfoot." Highwaymen inevitably appeared along the roads of gold rush California, but at first they avoided the armed stagecoaches in favor of easier pickings such as lone travelers and teamsters. They did not attempt to rob a stage until August 1856, when the unsuccessful but infamous Camptonville stage robbery made up for lost time with a first-class shootout between both parties, driving off the bandits at great cost to each side.[86] After that, a small handful of stage robberies, both successful and attempted, began to occur with some regularity, generally favoring the northern mining districts outside of Marysville or Nevada City. There was the Rabbit Creek robbery in February 1857, another in Nevada City that spring with One Eye Jack, and an attempt to rob the Forest City stage in September 1858 by a group of robbers that included Dutch Kate, a cross-dressing stage robber.[87] Some stage drivers fought back. In October 1858 stage driver Oliver Wiswell clobbered a would-be highwayman on the road between Stockton and Sonora using a heavy iron king bolt. Wiswell's defense was so sudden, violent, and complete that the second robber was "appalled" and fled in terror despite being armed with a gun. The first robber had "not spoken since," the *Sacramento Daily Union* reported, "and probably never will."[88]

Parkhurst was involved in none of these, and there is no evidence Parkhurst was involved in a stage robbery at all, especially one that ended with the shooting of a bandit, a major incident that would have been significant news. Nor were there reports of a bandit named Sugarfoot in 1850s California.[89] It was, however, the nickname of a Stockton stage driver, Joseph Horsley, who drove the Stockton-to-Mariposa line and died of exhaustion at the age of fifty-five in October 1880.[90] While the shooting of Sugarfoot was a tall tale, two of its elements did relate to men running stages out of Stockton, people whom Parkhurst may have either known personally or have heard of: Oliver Wiswell and his defense of his coach with fatal consequences for the robber, and Joseph Horsley's nickname, Sugarfoot (or Sugar Foot) Joe. Parkhurst may have blended these or similar elements to build a story that suggests and potentially reveals a desire for personal heroism, something Parkhurst may have dreamed of but hesitated to achieve in his actual life, lest it bring attention to him along with the danger of interruption to his carefully guarded world.

Wherever these stories did come from, a combination of nerve, horsemanship, and dedication combine to offer a portrait of Parkhurst saving the day and refusing to be taken advantage of, by nature or villain. The one story Parkhurst did not appear to personally relate was the one where he saved a coach from a near-disaster of his own responsibility, by holding back his runaway horses while driving a coach on the Oakland-to–San Jose run. This context offers the possibility that this third story could be genuine and reflects actual heroism on the part of Parkhurst in refusing to lose either his grip on the reins or his ability to regain control of his startled team. Anything could have spooked his horses, but good drivers are responsible for the control of their teams at all times, and Parkhurst was accordingly dragged off the coach and onto the ground, where he managed to steer the animals into roadside chaparral, thereby stopping their runaway and reestablishing control of his team and the safety of his coach.

Parkhurst turned sixty in 1872, around the same time that his health began to break down. He began to disassemble his world in response, eliminating the burden of unmanaged assets as he prepared for later life. That spring, he put some eighty head of "young American gentle cattle" up for sale, mostly heifers that roamed Bean Ridge, the land he had more recently farmed in the shadow of Bean Hill, and he authorized

Cumming's butcher shop in Soquel as agents.[91] He was reported to have settled into a cabin on land owned by Charles Moss, a fellow Pajaronian who had known him since at least 1859. The Moss family owned a nice-sized lot that ran alongside the stage road, near the Seven Mile House north of Watsonville. Parkhurst grew increasingly frail with each season. The *San Francisco Call* reported that "he had been so severely afflicted with rheumatism as not only to be unable to do physical labor, but the malady had even resulted in partial shrivelling [sic] and distortion of some of his limbs."[92] Rheumatism is a broad term that can encompass several diseases, such as osteoarthritis, which affects cartilage and subsequent joint motion, or bursitis, which inflames points along the body related to muscle use.[93] His condition worsened with the appearance of what was thought to be cancer on his tongue, the likely outcome of his longtime tobacco habit. Doctors offered to relieve this by inserting a silver tube down his throat, but he demurred. His reasons for refusing this treatment are unknown but may suggest a last effort to avoid an examination that might have revealed a female anatomy, as well as recognition that a lifetime on his own terms did not warrant interruption at the very end. "As the combined diseases became more aggressive," reported the *San Francisco Call*, "the genial Charley became not morose, but less and less communicative, till of late he has conversed with no one except on the ordinary topics of the day."[94] As the fall of 1879 moved into winter and the weather grew cold, he took a further series of turns for the worse and, as a stager later remarked, "was driven over the Great Divide." He died on December 28, within days of the new year, and was buried on the afternoon of December 30 in a small plot just outside of Watsonville, facing the old stage road that he used to drive.[95]

With Parkhurst's death followed the inevitable discovery of a female anatomy and the irrefutable confirmation of what just about everybody had already long imagined. As the news spread, it was clear that Parkhurst really was someone special. This knowledge extended back to his associates in Providence in the 1840s, and everyone had their own take.[96] In Monterey Bay, the *Castroville Argus* reported that people "who were well acquainted with her say that the disguise was suspected and talked about years ago."⁹⁷ That is, they considered Parkhurst to be a woman living a man's life, and they also accepted him as such and took a pragmatic approach by letting things be. In doing so, they were allowing Parkhurst to live the life he pleased without interruption while saving themselves from the responsibility for, or nuisance from, such an interruption. Not all people saw him as someone in disguise, however: a Santa Cruz editor refuted the Castroville position by describing Parkhurst as something else, something in between. "We have seen several people," the editor wrote, "who assert that they always considered 'Charlie' neither man nor woman, but both."⁹⁸

All of these people were right in a way, even though they seemed to be talking about different things. Mid-nineteenth-century Americans practiced a habit of talking about specific things in a general way, characterized by the phrase "like this, but different," thereby comprehending a standard and its variations within the same sphere. This was akin to binocular vision and allowed a three-dimensional perception of ideas, variety, and patterns to be understood simultaneously and exist in harmony. Occasionally, a wet rag like the editor of the *Providence Journal* attempted to transform the account into an object lesson: that for all of Parkhurst's bravado, tongue cancer got him in the end, which the *Journal*'s editor moralized as the inevitable result of his conceit in assuming the God-given place of man.

The people in Castroville knew Parkhurst personally and therefore talked about him as a woman in disguise in a very matter-of-fact way. Other newspapers drummed up a romanticized mystery in a way that suggests their editors were more enthused at the marvel of Parkhurst than genuinely perplexed. "There may be a strange history," remarked an article that appeared in both the *Daily Alta California* and the *Sacramento Daily Record-Union* on the same day, "that to the novelist would be a source of inspiration; and, again, she may have been disgusted with the trammels surrounding her sex, and concluded to work out her fortune in her own way."⁹⁹ A Petaluma editor was equally adamant that whether Parkhurst's life was from "necessity or phantasy the certainty remains that in the latter years, there must have been many dark hours when poor Charles Parkhurst longed for a little sympathy which is accorded every woman."[100] A Santa Cruz newspaper laid it on thickest, wondering if reports of her supposed motherhood "may date back to that proud eminence by which virtuous women alone can fall, fall by the deception of some man monster, but there must have been a cause, a mighty cause."[101]

Henry Monk took Parkhurst's death as an opportunity for a joke, not on Parkhurst particularly, but on life and stage drivers in general. By the time Parkhurst died, Monk had retired from staging and was holding court around the Ormsby House bar in Carson City, where he entertained friends and flummoxed strangers. When told by a newspaper reporter about Parkhurst's death, he paused for a moment as if in reflection and, once he had thought up a joke, started up: "Je—hosiphat! I camped out with Parkie once for over a week, and we slept on the same buffalo robe right along. Wonder if Curley Bill's been playin' me the same way."[102] Monk was joking that maybe all the other stage drivers were also really women, pulling a fast one on him. It was a blend of Monk's two favorite joke styles: the tall tale and the prank. The tall tale was that maybe all the other stage drivers were really women, while the prank was that they were all in cahoots to have some fun fooling Hank Monk. Curly Bill, who drove stages out of Reno in 1860 and once shot himself in the leg by accident, had absolutely nothing to do with Monk's story except to have his name used as a prop to advance Monk's punchline. Monk's towering reputation as a jokester—he was called the champion or "cock liar" just two days after Monk's Parkhurst story was printed—together with his appreciation of this reputation as the source of his fame and its attendant benefits, along with the implicit understanding that the Carson City editors were fishing for a joke when they approached him with the news, suggests Monk's Parkhurst story was made up on the spot for fun. Monk sang for his supper.[103]

Bartholomew Moore also conceived of Parkhurst as something of a mystery but in a more spiritual way. Moore had known Parkhurst personally since 1848, had sat beside him on stages, and had once traveled with him by sea for several weeks. As far as Moore was concerned, Parkhurst's existence was from origins less of biology and science than the divine; to

Moore, Parkhurst might be conceived of as a mysterious spiritual entity, something that inhabited and fulfilled the corporeal body. Parkhurst was a kind of indefinable spiritual experience, contained within, and manifestly different from, the dull flesh. At the end of Charley Parkhurst's life, Moore later wrote, "what was called Charley Parkhurst died and an unknown woman was buried in a lone grave, where life and death will forever be a mystery."[104]

The most extraordinary comments appeared in the *Sacramento Daily Union* on January 3, 1880, only days after Parkhurst's death. The author remarked that if the reports of Parkhurst's body were true, there was "nothing intrinsically incredible about the story" and compared Parkhurst to the account of "a woman [who] spent the greater part of her life as a common soldier, and engaged in many battles, fighting as sturdily and bravely as any of her male comrades." He then proceeded to compare Parkhurst to the famous Chevalier D'Eon, whose life as interchangeably both man and woman engaged the courts of Louis XV and Louis XVI as well as Georgian England and was famously depicted as a woman in a *robe à la polonaise* while fencing in 1787 before an audience that included the future George IV. Upon D'Eon's death at the age of eighty-four in the spring of 1810, the *United States Gazette* remarked that after assuming female dress in 1777 D'Eon was "universally regarded as a woman [and that] by the reception she met at the court of Louis XVI. and by the expressions of esteem made to her by almost every person in the kingdom—she was deserving of the highest praise."[105] The *Sacramento Daily Union*'s reporter was using these comparisons to demonstrate that people like Parkhurst were not only recognized but that others like him had achieved great feats of strength, walked within the highest social strata, and earned great success and fame in life.[106] But this description and comparison constituted merely a warm-up for what the Sacramento editor had next in store. "If the story of Parkhurst is true," he continued, "it will add another and a particularly consistent and well rounded instance to the catalogue of abnormally masculine women. In such a case it is evident that the masculine character is present in the fullest sense, and that the physical marks of sex are scarcely more than abortive developments. Such a woman," he concluded, "is very much more of a man than anything else, and in adopting male clothing and habits she only obeys the law of her nature, which is in such cases no doubt the safest guide."[107] The Sacramento editor, writing from his desk in the tawny cast-iron Sacramento cityscape, punctuated by steam whistles and the endless ordinary bustle of an inland California city in 1880, was pointing out that Parkhurst was a natural product of nature and that the feminine element of Parkhurst was merely incidental to the masculine sense that was nature's path for him. As for Parkhurst's following this path, the writer emphasized a perspective that parallels something of our current understanding of transgender people: that Parkhurst's nature was innate and that in living his life as he did, he was simply following nature—the best policy and the "safest guide."

3

Mrs. Noonan and the Seventh Cavalry

Over the first few days of August 1868, a line of military wagons under the command of the U.S. Army's Seventh Cavalry Regiment made their way southward across the windswept plains of central Kansas. They were in Indian country, moving slowly and cautiously over rough roads between the cavalry's summer headquarters at Fort Hays, Kansas, to temporary duty at Fort Larned, a small post some fifty miles away on the Pawnee River. The wagons were packed with supplies to support a distant army, as well as with civilian employees of that army—mostly women employed as company laundresses along with a few of their children.

Years later the Seventh Cavalry's First Lieutenant Edward Godfrey recalled a singular incident from this mundane trip that opens a window into a remarkable person. During one of the wagon train's periodic stops, and as troops and civilians set up a temporary camp while the animals were fed and watered, a laundress assigned to the Seventh Cavalry's Company A worked her way out of a wagon and walked in Godfrey's direction. Women working in the open country quickly learned from experience to wear practical clothes to protect them from the sun, but this laundress also wore a stylish green veil sheathed around her lower face. She approached Godfrey with complaints about traveling with the other women in the tightly packed wagons. She disliked the crowded conditions, he remembered her saying, and claimed the children "angered her" with their constant crying and noise. She wanted permission to ride alone in a separate wagon, away from the other women for the rest of the trip. She was "tall and angular," Godfrey later wrote, "and had a coarse voice." Yet as they spoke, "a stiff breeze wished [sic] the veil off her face and revealed a bearded chin."[1]

The issue wasn't, Godfrey realized, about children at all. What the laundress actually wanted was privacy, a place to hide a growing beard from the other, potentially suspicious laundresses, along with, as the startled Godfrey was quickly coming to understand, a male body. Her claim about the noisy children was just a ruse to protect herself, one of many she periodically employed to avoid disruption in her path of life. This was critically important to her long-term survival and was especially difficult while traveling in the field. Concealing her physical sex in the cramped confines of army wagons made her life perilous. At any moment another laundress could point her out and make a fuss. "It was a hard life for her," Elizabeth Custer, wife of the Seventh Cavalry's famous general, later remarked of this laundress specifically, "camping out with the other laundresses, as they are limited for room, and several are obliged to share a tent together. In the daytime they ride in an army wagon, huddled with children and luggage."[2] Every moment of life was a perpetual game of risk in situations where she could be discovered at any time, as Godfrey found that day on the Kansas plains in 1868, when he got the surprise of his life. Yet despite these dangers, she developed an outstanding reputation among the military command and would count Elizabeth Custer, among other wives of the Seventh Cavalry's top officers, as her longtime employers. Her last husband was likewise respected; he was a career soldier who had served as an orderly in the Custer command and had rapidly climbed the ranks of noncommissioned officers. The people such as Godfrey who knew her circumstances maintained a discreet silence that drew from an intricate web of social and military etiquette.

After arriving with the laundresses at Fort Larned on August 5, the twenty-three-year-old Lieutenant Godfrey sought out the captain of Company A, Louis Hamilton, and "rallied Hamilton of my discoveries and suspicions when he told me the story of her employment."[3] Hamilton explained that he had hired her earlier that year at Fort Leavenworth but that they had known each other a few years before that, when he was an infantry officer in Colorado. At that time the future laundress had not yet transitioned into the identity of a woman and was as yet an ordinary teamster, driving army supply wagons on the Santa Fe Trail while doing Hamilton's laundry on the side when in fort.

Hamilton's explanation to Godfrey of his relationship with the Laundress did not come from a popular acceptance of transgender laundresses, nor did it come from a familiarization with the unusual.[4] Instead, it probably reflected Hamilton's confidence in his security within the systems of decorum and military manners. Until the news became public a decade later, Godfrey never spoke of the matter, believing discretion and practicality the better part of honor. A conservative man, Godfrey respected the laws of propriety and, aware of Hamilton's stature, prudently avoided embarrassing a captain. Godfrey would soon be married as well, making it necessary to keep his career as steady as possible for his own security as much as that of his future wife. Reporting on one of his own would do little to advance his career security, especially regarding an unusual but ultimately trivial matter. Hamilton's confidence might also have arisen from his distinguished family lineage, one that drew directly and literally from the foundations of the United States. His paternal grandfather was Alexander Hamilton, a veteran of the Revolutionary War who served as the first secretary of the Treasury under President George Washington. His maternal grandfather, Senator Louis McLane, served as secretary of state in President Andrew Jackson's cabinet. His father, Philip Hamilton, had been judge advocate with the Brooklyn Navy Yard before serving as a prominent judge in Poughkeepsie, New York. Louis Hamilton found his vocation in the military, entering the army at the age of eighteen to fight in the Civil War. Family influence helped bring him a commission as a second lieutenant of the Third Infantry within two months, a commission personally endorsed by President Abraham Lincoln, who pointedly mentioned Hamilton's family background. Perks aside, Hamilton earned a reputation as an able commander and rose up the ranks to first lieutenant in under two years. He led a company of men during the Battle of Fredericksburg and won brevet honors during actions at Chancellorsville and Gettysburg.[5]

With the close of the Civil War, the U.S. government turned its military focus in part toward American expansion into the West. By 1866 Hamilton and the Third Infantry had been stationed at Fort Lyon, a small post in southeastern Colorado along the banks of the Arkansas River in Comanche territory. The fort's men protected the settlers, farms, and irrigation ditches that were just beginning to spread out from Fort Lyon northward, but the fort's original duty was much older: it was built to protect the Santa Fe Trail, the eight-hundred-mile dirt road connecting the ancient New Mexican capital at Santa Fe with the steamboat landings on the Missouri River at Independence and Leavenworth. The trail was old but not ancient: it had been blazed during the height of the fur trade in the 1820s by Missouri-based merchants who wanted to take advantage of trade with Mexico after its newly established independence from Spain.[6] The trade was poor at first, but over time it became immensely profitable and worth protecting; by 1829 military forces of the Sixth Infantry Regiment based at Leavenworth were accompanying the trade caravans as far as American territory then reached. This type of military presence along trading posts, trails, and eventually railroads formed a foundation for the American military presence in the West and shaped its engagements with tribes that encountered them.[7]

A trip to Santa Fe had once been a seasonal job, like the fur trade caravans: out in the spring, back in the fall. By the mid-1860s, however, it was a year-round affair running like loose clockwork along well-trod roads. A stage line to Santa Fe ran regularly, while long trains of freight wagons, called "Mexican trains" for their commercial link to New Mexico, were constantly passing Fort Lyon in each direction, stopping to water their mule teams while camping nearby for protection. In the summer of 1863 one train of 30 wagons carried 45,000 pounds of New Mexican wool into Leavenworth before returning with "dry goods and groceries" such as sugar, coffee, tea, rice, dried apples, and molasses for Santa Fe. A few days later an enormous Mexican train from Santa Fe arrived at Leavenworth with 150 wagons, 1,800 mules, and 150 men.[8]

The army had its own trains of freight wagons, operated by private contractors to supply military requirements. These "government trains" of freight wagons carried everything from food and everyday supplies, like thirty thousand bushels of corn due for shipment to Fort Lyon by June 1865, to materials necessary to build or repair the military's network of forts and trails; a government train of seventy wagons carrying lumber, sash, and building materials for constructing military posts traveled along the Smoky Hill route that November.[9] The government trains were organized in part by the Chief Quartermaster's Office at Fort Leavenworth, while additional quartermasters at each fort handled these shipments in the field. Captain Hamilton rose to the rank of regimental quartermaster for the Third Infantry on June 8, 1865, which placed him in charge of military supplies as well as hiring and contracting with civilians, as needed, to provide specific services for his post. Everyone from clerks and telegraph operators to wagon masters, blacksmiths, forage masters, and teamsters were hired and accounted for under his eye. One of these anonymous workers would eventually become the remarkable laundress that Godfrey encountered that day in 1868.

At that time, the future Laundress was an ordinary teamster, one among the multitude of anonymous, unsung men driving the "government trains" of wagons that supplied Fort Lyon and other military forts across the West with food and materials. He drove an impressive "six-mule team from New Mexico to Kansas" for the Fifth Infantry between 1866 and 1867, one soldier later recalled, and was well remembered at Fort Hays for years afterward.[10] Godfrey's description of the Teamster as Mexican, together with accounts of others who recalled him as being of "Mexican birth, and familiar with all the towns and cities from the Missouri River to the Rio Grande," suggests that the Teamster came from within the former Mexican territories and spent part of his early years on the Santa Fe Trail.[11] He was probably born in the 1840s, just as U.S. claims of manifest destiny, as well as a political and military willingness to press them, brought the Southwest into American control after 1848. Despite this shift, it was still "Mexico" in the persistent vernacular of many who traded in the region, following an inherited identity that survived war and territorial evolution by the stubborn force of custom. Wherever the Teamster came from, though, and whoever he was, a teamster's life with the U.S. Army offered protection and stability in an uncertain world. Life on the trail also brought unforgettable experiences with a rich array of stories carefully told over the years. It was a life on the road among men in nature, a life spent traveling between the red earth landscapes of Taos and Santa Fe and the open plains of Kansas, a life watering the stock and tending to harness, the steady creak of the wagons and splitting the blankets with fellow teamsters beneath starry nights, lending a private sense to the human realm.[12]

The Teamster's skill and versatility extended beyond wagons: when Hamilton needed laundry work done, Godfrey recalled Hamilton telling him that "a Mexican teamster [who was one of] his employees volunteered to do the work and did it to his satisfaction."[13] In other words, one of Hamilton's teamsters offered to do Hamilton's laundry on the side, when he wasn't driving wagons on the trail. The Teamster liked laundry, Hamilton, or the extra income—or any combination of the three—well enough to offer to do the work, while Hamilton either liked the laundry or the Teamster (or both) enough to employ him. Godfrey personally offered no further explanation of Hamilton's relationship to the Teamster beyond laundry, saying simply that the man "did it to his satisfaction," but then Godfrey was famously and prudently reticent to relate any account that departed from traditional narratives of military honor, and Hamilton's teamster occupied a place on the far horizon of Godfrey's perception. But regardless of whether Hamilton's relationship with the Teamster was passionate, strictly business, or simply a momentary convenience at a distant fort, it was brief.

In May 1866 Hamilton was summoned back East to Washington to prepare for service in the newly organized Seventh Cavalry. This was a significant promotion toward a glittering new career. He would also be commissioned as a captain, all shortly after his twenty-second birthday.[14] The Seventh Cavalry was one of a larger complement of newly organized army units that rose from a necessary military reorganization following the close of the Civil War. The Army Act of July 1866 pointedly included several new cavalry regiments within the larger postwar military structure, many of them to be positioned across the expanding western environment. The Seventh Cavalry was to be based at Fort Riley, Kansas, an old post near the confluence of the Kansas and Republican Rivers, directly west of Fort Leavenworth. Hamilton was confirmed by the Senate and headed westward again to Fort Riley for training and service. The Seventh itself consisted of twelve distinct companies of soldiers, designated A through L. Each company had seventy-eight enlisted men (a number later reduced to sixty men) commanded by fifteen noncommissioned officers who had risen from the ranks, as well as two commissioned officers who received appointments. Each company of the Seventh also had trumpeters to signal directions on the battlefield, blacksmiths and farriers for the cavalry horses, and five laundresses to wash the soldiers' clothes and bedding. Hamilton was appointed captain of Company A. The companies of any given cavalry regiment were dispersed and stationed where needed, giving a flexibility to the operations reflected by the companies themselves, whose men were likewise dispersed as necessary, whether for post work, scouting, escorting supplies or captives, or other duties. The Seventh's permanent fame came from its second in command, Lieutenant Colonel George Custer, who bore the honorary, or brevet, rank of general and had active day-to-day command in the field. Custer graduated from West Point at the bottom of his class, but his service and fast rise during the Civil War distinguished him, and in June 1866 the new Seventh Cavalry was his. He had not yet discovered his passion for fighting Indians, and the campaign season of 1867 began with unusually wet and dreary weather, the worst since 1844, which slowed everything down. Snow, mud, and ice created a desolate landscape where chasing Indians was largely futile, and the plans of several generals were plagued by confusion.

The American claim to the West had been purchased from France some sixty years earlier, in 1803. No one really knew what to do with the territory at first, and for years the Americans largely left it alone, a useless wasteland suited only for distant societies of Indians and fur trappers. In this land of Native societies and seasoned frontiersmen, sociability went far, and years of experience generated familiarity and respect, both necessary and genuine, for the manners and customs of Indian societies met along the way. But over time, the sheer numbers of restless Americans and drumbeat claims of manifest destiny guaranteed a steady incursion into lands the Spanish and French had scarcely touched. This new West and its swarms of settlers had little experience with plains traditions or Indian manners and didn't care to learn: their sole focus was business, and they saw the West as nothing more than open land on which to expand their model industry. "These plains are not *deserts* but *the opposite*," explained Colonel William Gilpin in 1857, "and are the cardinal basis of the future empire of commerce and industry now erecting itself upon the North American continent."[15]

The Americans approached the Indians living on these lands as unwanted tenants who had to be managed or cajoled, and they absolutely refused on the basis of social prejudice to engage them as equals. Vigorous debate focused on how to approach them from ethical and logistical standpoints, but the thrust of the arguments revolved around how to handle them as a problem and ultimately how to most efficiently acquire land. What Gilpin portrayed as an "advancing column of progress" was enforced by the American military, at first by guarding travel routes through the plains and then by maneuvering Indian nations off hunting lands claimed for use by the Americans, usually through a series of treaties.[16] The Americans themselves readily admitted that treaties were primarily tools, and a contemporary remarked that these treaties were "nothing more or less than convenient frauds for the momentary pacification of some tribe or tribes at war, made on our part with the mental reservation that they shall not be kept a day after it becomes profitable or popular to break them."[17] By that time there was no discussion of whether treaties should be made at all, and many people were already embracing a growing view of Indian society as a backward stage of human development, worthy of being wiped off the map.

In the midst of this turmoil Hamilton repeated his past military achievements, on one occasion turning back a sizable force of attacking Indians near the Republican River with only a handful of his own men. But warfare on the plains was very different from the formalized maneuvers employed during the Civil War. On the plains, raiding parties or decoys could catch troops unawares, and a small party of Native men, easily chased, would suddenly become a much larger group, just as soldiers found themselves outside of the protective range of their own men. This is where Hamilton found himself on June 24, 1867, when he chased a raiding party along the confluence of the Republican and Kansas Rivers with a small detachment of men intending to recapture some horses, only to be suddenly confronted by nearly twice as many Native riders. Hamilton's military instinct took over, and he ordered his men to crouch down into a defensive position, holding off the attackers for several hours with no casualties among his party save a horse. Custer described it as a "gallant fight" in his report to his military superiors and praised Hamilton along with two other officers for their "pluck and determination" in staving off attacks over the following days.[18]

The late summer and fall of 1867 brought the installation of a thirty-six-year-old Civil War veteran, General Philip Sheridan, to command the Department of the Missouri, as well as a treaty two months later by order of the U.S. Peace Commission to achieve a settlement with the southern Plains Indian nations. That October about five thousand Indians gathered at Medicine Lodge Creek in Kansas to negotiate the treaty. While there, representatives for the federal government promised annuities of food, supplies, and support to compensate for the loss of hunting lands and made these goods available to all those who left those hunting lands and moved to a reservation between the Platte and Arkansas Rivers, set aside for their use separate from the Americans and their travel routes. Two companies of the Seventh Cavalry under the command of Captain Albert Barnitz were present as escorts for the peace commissioners. The Cheyennes "were suspicious," wrote Barnitz in his journal, "in regards to touching the pen, or perhaps they supposed that by doing so they would be 'signing away their rights'—which is doubtless the true state of affairs, *as they have no idea that* they are giving up, or have ever given up the country which they claim as their own, the country north of the Arkansas." Although impressed by the crowd and the ceremonies leading up to the signing, Barnitz had a cynical view of the event and concluded that the Medicine Lodge Treaty "amounts to nothing, and we will certainly have another war sooner or later with the Cheyennes, at least, and probably with the other Indians, in consequence of misunderstanding the terms of present and previous treaties."[19]

By November 1867, the Seventh Cavalry had moved to winter headquarters alongside several companies of infantry at Fort Leavenworth, Kansas, on the banks of the Missouri River. Leavenworth was a venerable old relic, established during the fur trade era, and its seat on the Missouri made it a gateway to the West, a vast nerve center for all military affairs extending westward to the Rocky Mountains, and a vital hub of distribution and supply for distant forts, troops, and communication. Leavenworth was also exceedingly cosmopolitan, at least as cosmopolitan as an army post on the edge of civilization can get, and its society was imitatively formal, conscious of upholding and displaying the fullest possible standards of eastern civilization in manner, dress, and splendor. "All things taken into comparison," Jennie Barnitz wrote from Leavenworth that winter, "I think there is no life in the world quite as pleasant as Garrison life. Every morning at 9 O'C is Guard Mounting on the Parade ground in front of our houses. The band is out, & the ladies usually sit out on their porticoes & see & talk with their friends. At sunset, of pleasant days, we have Dress Parade, which is very imposing. Then evenings everybody visits. It actually spoils me for any other life."[20]

The eastern end of the Santa Fe Trail passed through Leavenworth to reach the Missouri River. In those days, rows of powerful steamboats lined the riverbanks at Leavenworth, as wagon trains fresh in from New Mexico Territory unloaded bundles of wool and raw materials onto their decks before returning to Santa Fe with crates of manufactured goods brought out from American factories. One day in the early winter months of 1868 a teamster driving one of these freight wagons on the streets of Leavenworth caught Captain Hamilton's eye. "Their recognition," Godfrey later recalled, in his simple and understated way, "was mutual."[21] He was the same man Hamilton had employed two years earlier to do his laundry at the infantry post and who had spent the past two years driving mule teams for the Fifth Infantry between New Mexico and Kansas.[22]

Just exactly what happened over the following weeks remains unknown, but it was neither random nor casual. A combination of factors—genetic predisposition, internal self-awareness, and a chance reengagement with Hamilton, intermixed with the opportunities and constraints of a major military post on the edge of the western frontier—all fell into place. A New Mexican teamster stepped off the driving box of a freight wagon, and a modestly powerful new woman emerged to take his place. The details of her origins had as yet to be understood at that time, and the first significant steps to developing a picture of this process would come much later, although scientists in Britain and Europe were beginning to formulate a sense of it. But whether recognized or not, the genetic, biological guide central to the human condition existed within the Teamster's own genetic makeup from birth. Her path resembled, in a way, that of Two-Spirit people, whose place in the plains and pueblos embodied a spiritual sense imbued with the harmonic balance of life. The Teamster may have encountered such people while growing up and might have known of these traditions, which may have informed and supported their own self-conception as a good and spiritually necessary part of the larger world. There would be no spiritual place for her in the military posts of the U.S. Army, though, and she would have to find that out on her own.[23]

Hamilton's part in this process is undefined yet evident. He appointed the former teamster to a position as laundress with his own company, Company A. This provided stability and employment and, with employment, presumably encouragement. More significantly, providing her with a position as laundress allowed them to keep in touch on a regular basis (within allowable limits) while attracting minimal attention. Hamilton was taking a bold risk and confidently betting on it, as Godfrey would later discover that summer, and he was doing so right in the heart of a major military post. For the Laundress, a completely different world was unfolding. She was stepping into a vast new world of hardworking semi-sisterhood, a largely anonymous yet simultaneously vital corps of around seventeen hundred women working as company laundresses for the U.S. Army, averaging five laundresses per company by army regulation.[24] This small army of women joined a larger civilian team of blacksmiths, cooks, carpenters, wagon masters, and storekeepers in supporting and maintaining the vast military network.

Around the time of the Laundress's transition in February 1868, General Sheridan arrived at Leavenworth to begin reviews of the troops in preparation for the coming summer campaigns. The pace of life at the fort picked up, the band played more often, and parades of soldiers and officers in full military dress upon the field were held, followed, for the officers at least, with rounds of visits and social calls. It was the last call for a winter spent in diversion and socializing. Inevitably the campaign season would return, and it would be time to move out into the field. Sheridan ordered Major Joel Elliott to lead several companies out to guard travel routes across the plains, in the familiar duty of protecting travelers, communication, roads, and construction crews on the new Kansas Pacific Railway. "On the 10th inst. at 9 am.," wrote Captain Barnitz, "the column consisting of Companies A D E G & K 7th Cav., preceded by the Regimental Band, marched around the parade ground, at Fort Leavenworth, receiving the parting salutations of the ladies and officers of the post & department who were to remain; and then, as the Post Band struck up the tune of 'The Girl I Left Behind Me' we marched off toward Fort Riley and the 'Great Plains.'"[25]

The cavalry moved into Kansas lands still thick with buffalo and the newly persistent sight of railroad trains, "passing and re-passing" on Kansas Pacific tracks two miles distant, trailing thin streaks of pale blue wood smoke into the vast prairie sky. The officers entertained themselves at each night's camp—"Hamilton has a cask of beer," Barnitz wrote—and stopped briefly at Fort Hays before setting up camp twenty miles farther west, at a site Elliott named Camp Alfred Gibbs. As spring melted into summer, the cavalry passed days of quiet, guarding the few travelers passing by. Small things took up importance again, and the officers began a competition for one enlisted man of their company to be chosen as orderly for the day, an assistant to the commanding officer, always chosen on the basis of his perfect appearance. "There is great rivalry," Barnitz wrote to his wife, "between Companies A and K in this matter, and I really believe that Col. West or Capt. Hamilton would either one rather lose fifty dollars than that a man of the other company should be selected instead of one from their own!"[26]

The U.S. Army was now protecting the construction of several railroads westward across the plains to the Rockies and beyond. It followed the old army tradition of guarding travel routes but now on a vastly enlarged and industrialized scale. The Omaha-based Union Pacific Railroad was the largest and most important of these, and by the summer of 1868 crews had graded earth and built tracks nearly seven hundred miles west from Omaha, all the way into Wyoming Territory, where the Thirtieth Infantry built a fort to protect the construction crews and railroad operations.[27] At that time, the Union Pacific had nearly one hundred locomotives either in service or on order and was approaching the Utah border at a rate of two miles of track a day. Its target was a planned connection with the Central Pacific Railroad of California, which had just built a line over the Sierra Nevada and was now racing eastward across the Nevada desert toward Utah Territory, gaining as much ground as possible before meeting the Union Pacific.

The Seventh Cavalry's forces were on another railroad line one hundred miles to the south, in Kansas, protecting the construction of the Kansas Pacific Railway as it built westward toward the Rocky Mountains.[28] By the summer of 1868 the Kansas Pacific's tracks had reached three-quarters of the way across Kansas, much of it along the Smoky Hill River, cutting across the hunting grounds of the southern Plains nations. Its trains were already spooking buffalo herds, and now commercial hunters were beginning to take advantage of the newly laid tracks to slaughter buffalo on a mass scale before loading buffalo hides onto trains for shipment east. At the same time, the first cattle drives into Kansas were using the Kansas Pacific's facilities at Abilene, at the end of the newly scouted Chisholm Trail. Thousands of head of cattle now rode out of Abilene on Kansas Pacific stock cars, drawn by handsomely polished locomotives, glibly named after different Native American nations.[29]

Godfrey's encounter with the Laundress came while the war in the southern plains was taking a significant new turn. Forebodings of war were rising, this time late in the season. A month earlier, in July 1868, Lieutenant Colonel Alfred Sully, commander of the District of Southern Arkansas, had ordered the troops of the Seventh Cavalry to Fort Larned to oversee the distribution of annuities, food, and supplies promised to the Kiowas as part of an agreement between the U.S. government and Kiowa Nations to leave their traditional hunting grounds and come onto lands set aside for them as reservations. But while the Kiowa, Comanche, Plains Apache, Cheyenne, and Arapaho Nations had gathered there for annuities, the Indian agent there refused to distribute them in reaction to a Kiowa hunting raid on traditional enemies that had transpired earlier that year. The agent and his superiors thought that the Indians had agreed to lay aside all conflict, and the officials thus took the raid as a deliberate provocation, while the Kiowas thought their agreement with the white government entities was separate from their relations with other Indians. This led to a conflict of expectations, especially after Indian men who had already agreed to live on a reservation found themselves denied the other part of the bargain. The agent's actions struck them as pushy and rude. Why, they wondered, had Washington interfered in their own affairs, and why was the punishment put on all of them and not just the specific hunting party?

Over the course of the 1860s, tensions and hostilities between Indians and settlers on the southern plains steadily grew. Indians increasingly felt there was little difference between settlers and their traditional tribal enemies, while settlers saw no difference among Indians at all: to them, all Indians were inscrutable, wary, and dangerous. One group held as much enmity as the other, and raids and retaliations peppered the increasingly violent landscape. The Americans were inclined to blunt force, which they called "admonishment." As the fall of 1868 progressed, General Sheridan and his officers drafted a new type of warfare to force the issue: a winter campaign that would launch with a surprise attack on hibernating villages deep in snow, when ponies were thin and warriors could be caught off guard, enabling the army to force weakened tribes onto reservations where they could be managed and subdued.[30] Sheridan arranged for Custer to lead the campaign, and troops headed out from Leavenworth into the field, moving westward across Kansas before crossing into present-day Oklahoma.

By the early morning of November 27, 1868, the cavalry had taken up positions on the banks of the Washita River and then lay in wait, shivering deep in the snow outside the sleeping Southern Cheyenne camp of Black Kettle, the Cheyenne chief who had tried to accommodate the Americans despite earlier U.S. Army attacks on his tribe and the retaliatory raiding of his own younger men. The cavalry's upcoming attack on the unsuspecting camp would be an important part of Sheridan's campaign, but, by chance, Captain Hamilton wasn't going to be among the men leading the charge. He was assigned instead to duty as officer of the day, a routine task that required him to stay behind and guard the supply wagons with eighty men, which took him out of the fight and placed him far to the rear of the action ahead. "To a soldier of Hamilton's pride and ambition," Custer wrote afterward, "to be left behind in this inglorious manner was galling in the extreme."[31] Officers rose to prominence in part from their role in action, and Hamilton "was greatly distressed because this duty fell to him," Godfrey explained, "and [he] begged to go along to command his squadron, but was refused unless he could get some other officer to exchange with him. Lieutenant E. G. Mathey, who was snowblind, agreed to take his place."[32]

Hamilton mounted his horse and headed to the front in the bare light of dawn. As the cavalrymen inched closer to the camp, a barking dog broke the bitterly cold silence, followed by the sudden crack of a gunshot. The regimental band immediately struck up the tune "Garry Owen" as a signal to start the fight, and the soldiers charged. Hamilton ordered his men to "keep cool, fire low, and not too rapidly" lest they lose their aim in the melee.[33] The shooting and commotion were intense. "It was early in the morning when the soldiers began the shooting," Kate Bighead recalled, as she was awakened in the village from the noise. "There had been a big storm, and there was snow on the ground. All of us jumped from our beds, and started running to get away. I was barefooted, as were almost all the others."³⁴ Black Kettle was killed by a shot in the stomach while others ran terrified along the stream, hoping to find some form of safety.³⁵ "The air was full of smoke from gunfire," recalled Moving Behind, "and it was almost impossible to flee, because bullets were flying everywhere."³⁶ In the rush of men and galloping horses, Hamilton was almost immediately shot. The ball entered the left side of his chest, passed diagonally through his body, and exited below his right shoulder blade, killing him instantly. "When struck," a reporter noted after interviewing Custer's men on their return, "he gave one convulsive start, stiffened in his stirrups, and was thus carried a corpse for a distance of several yards, when he fell from his horse, striking his face, which was from this cause terribly lacerated and disfigured."³⁷ When it was all over, some counts had as many as 103 Cheyenne men killed, while others tallied that between 13 and 16 men, 16 women, and 9 children had died that day. Fifty-three women and children were taken captive, eventually sent on to Fort Hays, Kansas, where the Laundress might have seen them. Everything in the village was burned and destroyed to keep it from being of use to others, an effort to cripple the Cheyennes. Twenty-two cavalrymen were killed, including Hamilton, who was made a hero and posthumously brevetted to the rank of major the same day.³⁸ He was one of two officers killed in that battle, and his remains were carried back to Camp Supply, the army's temporary camp at the confluence of Beaver River and Wolf Creek, where Sheridan was waiting to congratulate Custer on a job well done. Godfrey later recalled how they "buried Hamilton near the camp with all the formalities and solemnity of a military funeral, the Seventh Cavalry and the Third Infantry present in formation."³⁹ Hamilton's body on its bier was carried by General Sheridan, George Custer and his brother, Lieutenant Thomas Custer, along with four other officers in pomp and honor. His remains were later disinterred and placed aboard a train for a final trip to New York State, where he was buried with honors and a stone monument.⁴⁰

The bullet that pierced Hamilton's heart that November morning left behind an unusual widow. Transgender laundresses in distant forts without the protection of an influential officer inevitably find themselves in a difficult position. Godfrey already knew her reality, and, despite her efforts, some of the women she worked alongside were likely to find out as well, either by hunch or by accident. In fact, over time many of them would come to consider her "something" between a man and a woman, while distancing themselves in the process.[41] It was the perfect time to leave the military, but the Laundress chose instead to remain. Dangers aside, it was a potentially lucrative and relatively comfortable position: laundresses charged for their services at a rate fixed by the post; the average rate for soldiers to have laundry done was two dollars a month for enlisted men and five dollars a month for officers. In addition, they received several valuable benefits: a daily ration of food, fuel for the stove, the services of the post surgeon, and living quarters on the outer perimeters of a fort, a group of quarters often known as "sudsville" or "suds row."[42] At some posts officers complained that laundresses were nothing more than a contentious network of women raising illegitimate children and fighting among each other. Some fights grew so fierce that post guards were called to break up the conflicts. One laundress threatened to knife the officer who had used an especially cruel punishment on her husband, while laundresses at Fort Rice were nicknamed the "Modocs" for their "war-like propensities" and ferocious reputation.[43] General George Forsythe described them as "good, honest, industrious wives, usually well on in years, minutely familiar with their rights which they dared to maintain with acrimonious volubility."[44] "The [army] regulations provide that the commanding officer has complete control over all camp followers," Elizabeth Custer explained, "with power to put them off the reservation or detain them as he chooses. Nevertheless, though army women have no visible thrones or sceptres, nor any acknowledged rights according to military law, I never knew such queens as they, or saw more willing subjects [among the enlisted men] than they govern."[45]

The Laundress was resourceful enough to recognize the advantage of her appointment as laundress for Company A. She probably also understood that Godfrey's reluctance to talk about Hamilton offered little danger that he would betray her existence. She worked these links while becoming known for valuable and profitable skills. She nursed weak and weary soldiers, tended to her sister laundresses—and occasionally an officer's wife—as an emergency midwife, became an excellent cook and a tailor. There was money in this: a reputation for good cooking meant that soldiers would pay equally good money for pies and other foods. In 1867 a savvy post baker and his wife at Fort C. F. Smith in Montana Territory saved up enough money to buy a house by selling pies to soldiers for seventy-five cents apiece and doing officers' laundry.[46] Tailoring uniforms also filled in the Laundress's hours between washdays, led to her doing minor alterations that helped ambitious soldiers look their best for inspection or the parade ground, and placed her within a needle's reach of the rank-and-file, especially while on campaign or in distant posts far from professional tailors. She was "as handy with a needle as any woman in the garrison," her contemporaries recalled, "making all kinds of fine shirts" for the soldiers of the fort.[47] These skills allowed her to make money and work her way up, so to speak, a ladder that was, for laundresses and camp women, officially nonexistent.[48]

Even the Custers knew of the Laundress's skill. Elizabeth Custer—who enjoyed a reputation for being well dressed—employed her to care for her and her husband's personal clothing and household linens. This type of work was not immaterial. Clean undergarments of starched cotton and linen—shorts, drawers, shirts, and so on—formed a critical barrier between the body and outer garments and were essential in keeping outer garments clean. Starched shirts, cravats, and collars also gave an air of presentation that visually upheld the value of the person wearing them, as well as the society with which that person engaged. This was particularly important for military officers such as George Custer, whose bearing and form were visual denominators of the power of the military. It was necessary for his clothes to uphold and represent the power of American society, even in a fort on the plains and perhaps especially there. The same standards applied to an officer's wife, who bore the responsibility of upholding her family's dignity through propriety of dress at all times, avoiding any slovenly appearance that would cast doubt on her character or, by extension, her husband's fitness for duty. Middle-class women usually owned two or three good silk dresses, which made clean linen undergarments absolutely necessary, while rows of starched and pleated ruffles were typically slip-sewn into the trains of dresses to protect the lining from street dirt. Detachable collars and cuffs of lace, or pleated and embroidered lawn, were the final touch, protecting the neck and arm openings from sweat or stains while displaying their fine quality and careful pleating and upkeep. A company laundress who could manage these delicate affairs was soon in demand among the ranks of officers' wives.

Elizabeth Custer first hired the Laundress when part of the Seventh Cavalry was stationed in Elizabethtown, Kentucky, sometime between March 1871 and March 1873. "She was our laundress," Elizabeth Custer recalled, "and when she brought the linen home, it was fluted and frilled so daintily that I considered her a treasure." A talented laundress, cook, or housekeeper was a valuable commodity in the far outposts, sometimes kept a guarded secret lest another officer or his wife steal her away. The Laundress perhaps played her role as a well-kept secret to maintain her security, for although delivering laundry placed the Laundress upon the threshold of power, she also had to remain on guard lest her situation become known. "She always came at night," Elizabeth Custer added, "and when I went out to pay her she was very shy, and kept a veil pinned about the lower part of her face."[49]

Employment by officers' wives for personal laundry was only part of a military laundress's work, always conducted on the side. Their principal task was to wash the clothes and bedding of several hundred soldiers. In the 1870s, each military company had over eighty men, and with four laundresses per company, the Laundress had to handle the clothes and bedding of around twenty soldiers. Because of this, "wash day" was actually a several days' affair, held every week or two as necessary, a routine of laundry tubs and lye punctuated by the swearing among the sorority of washing days as they stoked the wood fires that kept water scalding hot. Field service took its toll and guaranteed more piles of clothes to be worked over washboards to pound out the dirt, blood, and dust of campaign and camp. Much of the work was in washing the wool flannel shirts the army insisted on making regulation despite hot weather in much of the West. Army contractors had cut costs by making up shirts straight from the bolt, which became notorious for shrinking with repeated washings and bursting apart at the seams with ordinary wear. Until the army finally issued preshrunk woolen shirts in the mid-1870s, many soldiers and cavalrymen opted for nonregulation shirts of various materials, including cotton for summer and "cassimere" for winter, all of which required the Laundress's attention. The irons used by the laundresses to press these shirts were of solid cast iron with a handle above; the irons were kept hot over open fires to press garments flat, which required skill to make shirts starched and stiff without scorching them.[50]

Laundresses were on the lowest rung of the social ladder, but such social prejudices worked in the Laundress's favor, primarily because she was not expected to be beautiful. "He was a masculine looking woman," recalled a Bismarck resident in 1878, "and would have made a poor belle. As a laundress, however, he got on finely."[51] This dismissive attitude applied to women working as laundresses as a whole. Nineteenth-century Americans readily considered laundresses as crude, socially inferior people. The army's Irish laundresses received the brunt of the discrimination, but Hispanic women also got their share of abuse, stereotyped for their imagined liberties of culture that mid-Victorian era society considered unacceptable; denigrated as part of some hoary tribe of unfamiliar, *cigaretta*-smoking creatures, these women represented the very opposite of the idealized images of feminine modesty and beauty.[52] A Mexican woman in Kansas or Dakota Territory was also something of a distinctive sight, providing an element of unfamiliarity: the Laundress's "coarse voice, and masculine looks all over" could be explained away, minimizing suspicion on its own.[53] As long as she kept her beard shaved and that green-colored veil eternally pinned about her face, things would be fine.[54] Only when she was away from the safety of a fort or when she was traveling in the confines of wagons was there a risk of exposure, as she discovered with Godfrey during her first year of feminine existence.[55]

Among all this the Laundress found new relationships, but the road was tough and initially heartbreaking. The first two husbands "didn't like the combination," remarked the *Bismarck Tribune* in 1878, but the third husband "seemed to enjoy it."[56] In fact, the first two men robbed her through marriage, gaining access to her savings before deserting her along with the cavalry. This was a hard experience for her. She was absolutely smitten by Harry Clifton, a twenty-seven-year-old sergeant of Company A and brown-eyed native of St. Louis who joined the Seventh Cavalry in 1866. After they married in June 1871, Clifton "lived with her about ten days, and then absconded with $500 of her earnings" and deserted on June 12, only months away from completing his term of service. By then the Seventh Cavalry had been transferred for two years' rotation to the Department of the South, with Company A stationed in Elizabethtown, Kentucky, just a few miles by rail from the large and prominent city of Louisville, the Seventh Cavalry's new headquarters. It was a relatively easy matter for Clifton to melt away into the world beyond, to any number of states via any number of steamboats or railroads, with Indiana just a bridge away and his hometown of St. Louis just a few days farther. She was recalled by people who knew her as being very much in love with the man, even to the point of searching for him after his desertion, despite his betrayal. Private James Nash was no better, "deserting her" a few days into their marriage "after getting possession of all her money" and leaving her with a nickname "known throughout the Seventh": "Old Jennie Nash."[57] Elizabeth Custer recalled how the Laundress bitterly complained to her about her first two husbands and how they had stolen her hard-earned savings before deserting her and the army. These relationships were predatory and brief, no longer than necessary to access her money and escape. They may have deliberately scoped her out to rob her, methodically courting her while plotting out the logistics of desertion. But ultimately there was nothing she could do: she could not raise charges without fear of being revealed and losing her hard-earned position and income. After two such husbands, she simply had to chalk it all up to experience.[58]

John Noonan was different. He was a career soldier, a man who saw the army as his life and the stability that it offered within its structure as central to his identity. By the time he joined the cavalry he was already an experienced soldier, originally signing up in Omaha, Nebraska, for a full term of enlistment with the Third Regiment of the U.S. Army Field Artillery. Just what brought a young Irish American man from his native Fort Wayne to Omaha is unknown, but a primary draw in Omaha at that time was employment on the Union Pacific Railroad's largely Irish construction crews. If so, his enlistment indicates that he liked the idea of military life better. The Union Pacific's main line was being built entirely by hand, promising only endless labor, while the genuine dangers of the military world were softened by glints and glamour of uniform brass and the assurance of stability and authority. Serving in the field artillery branch also offered a career with horses, which figure prominently in the careers Noonan chose for himself from this point on. Artillery horses were the second best in the army—big, strong animals that drew the gun carriages with artillery pieces into position on the battlefield. It was dedicated work to care for and train these animals, which had to perform their functions with skill and steadiness despite the noisy, crowded conditions of battle. He was assigned to the Third Artillery's Company C, which by 1871 had been sent to Charleston, South Carolina, and which boasted a stable for over eighty horses and a particularly fine military band.[59] When his term of enlistment was up, he changed units and reenlisted with the Seventh Cavalry, at that time stationed in the Southern District, noting his former occupation as "soldier" on the enlistment papers. Noonan's enlisting officer, Second Lieutenant Charles Braden, described him as a native of Fort Wayne, Indiana, twenty-five years old, five feet seven inches in height, with blue eyes and dark hair. Braden was a dedicated career soldier, spending his entire life in the army, and may have recognized something of the same dedication in Noonan. He assigned Noonan to his own company, Company L, under the command of First Lieutenant J. F. Weston.[60]

Cavalry horses were generally better ranked than artillery horses. By making the shift from artillery to cavalry, Noonan would work with the best horses in the army; he would employ the horse as a battle platform and engage the animal in a far more challenging manner, one critical to their military success. If a man on horseback was his own master, a cavalryman on horseback was a capable arm of a mighty force. The cavalry provided simultaneous feelings of independence and authority with the security of belonging and the safety of a vast military organization, allowing confidence and capacity along with more than a little pride. "You felt like you were somebody when you were on a good horse," a Seventh Cavalry member recalled. "You were a cavalryman of the Seventh Regiment. You were part of a proud outfit that had a fighting reputation, and you were ready for a fight or a frolic."[61] Good horsemanship was as critical to everyday survival as it was to war. Just days after Noonan enlisted, a fellow soldier with Company L battered himself badly when his horse reared up during morning drill and he fell on his saddle pommel. Even his commanders could be at risk: that fall, Lieutenant Weston stabbed himself in the armpit during drill when his horse reared up and the saddle slipped, pitching him onto the ground and his own saber.[62]

Noonan's first year with the Seventh Cavalry put him into the center of a national coming of age. In the aftermath of the Civil War, the administration of President Ulysses Grant undertook to further the work of the Lincoln administration in establishing and protecting the civil rights of Black Americans, often through a process known as Reconstruction. The newly ratified Fourteenth and Fifteenth Amendments to the Constitution were the most significant of these efforts, as they guaranteed the right to citizenship and equal protection and the right to vote, respectively, and for a time Black Americans newly recognized as citizens began to vote and enter politics. It was difficult work, especially in the states of the former Confederacy, where over two centuries of slavery and the relationship of enslavement to the southern plantation economy meant that segregation had deeply penetrated cultural and economic norms in the region. White southerners refused to consider or accept equality to those they had bought and sold only a few years earlier, and they imagined Black Americans as representing some subhuman state of existence that required and justified their cruelty. Some degree of that belief pervaded intellectual thought throughout Europe and other parts of the Americas, but it came to a head in the postwar South, especially regarding the mechanisms of political and cultural control. To support the U.S. Marshals in enforcing civil rights laws across the southeastern states, the Grant administration established military posts across the region they called the Department of the South. White southerners responded in turn by portraying themselves as victims of a federal menace: at Yorkville, South Carolina, Major Lewis Merrell of the Seventh Cavalry was popularly loathed as "a fit man to run down women and defenseless men with blood hounds at the bidding of Grant," while local judges made it nearly impossible for federal officers to successfully secure convictions for civil rights violations.[63] A Cincinnati man traveling to Yorkville in October 1871 was warned by resentful locals that Grant's marshals would arrest anyone they found, and he described Yorkville as a hive of furious activity with a "decidedly warlike atmosphere" and about four hundred soldiers. "Great army wagons came up to receive supplies," he remarked, "squads of infantry and cavalry were moving about, sentinels were pacing up and down, orderlies dashed through the streets, and there was a modified clamor of resounding arms to be heard on every side."[64] These efforts were not always local: in December 1872 Company L headed for New Orleans to keep peace in the tense and unsteady atmosphere that followed a contested gubernatorial election. They set up temporary barracks in a Treasury Department revenue warehouse on Magazine Street and watched as masses of men crowded St. Charles Street and Lafayette Square, but for the moment tensions subsided without need for the troops.[65]

Noonan got his first taste of western duty in 1873, when the Seventh Cavalry was reassigned to the northern plains for a planned expedition into the Yellowstone Valley. This move required a massive logistical effort, first to reassemble the previously scattered companies of the entire Seventh Cavalry in early April and then to move farther up the Missouri River to a temporary post at Fort Rice in Dakota Territory.[66] This offered Noonan his first view of Custer, and possibly his first sight of the Laundress, as she moved around the tents and washtubs. The Seventh Cavalry's final stop and ultimate headquarters was a few miles farther upriver at a fort that would be named Fort Abraham Lincoln, then under construction near the Northern Pacific Railroad tracks.

The West was the Laundress's lifelong home, but the northern plains would be bitterly different from the familiar southwestern landscape of her upbringing, and the test of the northern plains in winter would begin almost immediately. A late spring blizzard blew in while the Seventh Calvary was at Yankton, Dakota Territory, causing havoc for two days. Custer directed the cavalrymen to shelter their horses in local barns and stables where possible, and the higher-ranking officers and most of the soldiers were afforded emergency quarters at hotels and homes. The laundresses and their young children were left behind in the blizzard to shelter in "white tents half buried in snow," and they piled on blankets in their attempt to keep warm. One of the women gave birth to a child during the storm, and it is possible that the Laundress, given her later reputation as midwife, attended to the birth. The tents were miserable, but the women and children were lucky to have any shelter at all and even luckier that the temperature lingered around the twenties. "Ten degrees lower," Second Lieutenant Charles Larned wrote to family back home, and "few if any of those left in camp could have escaped."[67]

On May 7 the Seventh Cavalry resumed its journey, marching four hundred miles northward along the Missouri River toward Fort Rice. They traveled at a slow, four-miles-an-hour pace that stretched the travel time to several weeks. George Custer hired extra teamsters and wagons to move their supplies, along with a steamboat named the *Miner* to move the heavy baggage, the wives of the officers, and the laundresses.[68] While marching north along the upper reaches of the Missouri River, the cavalrymen could see an endless parade of steamboats with their tall black smokestacks passing by and sometimes heard their steam whistles sounding over the broad prairie. At this time of year, the Missouri River was in its glory, as spring runoff from winter snows brought high water and the year's best navigation. Steamboats ruled this landscape. The commerce and politics of an age were carried on their decks. Some of these boats were heading upstream toward forts and Indian agencies with cargoes of annuities promised Indian tribes by treaty. Other boats were pushing upstream into the gold regions of Montana Territory with cargoes of items ranging from champagne to shovels. Boats headed downstream carried buffalo hides and other furs from animals trapped and shot in the northern plains. At one point the cavalrymen saw the steamer *Far West* moving downstream in a hurry with one hundred tons of buffalo hides—an entire herd that had been shot down by commercial hunters and loaded onto the boat at Fort Benton.[69] The *Miner* simply paced the Seventh Cavalry as it moved upstream, lazily anchoring every afternoon at points along the river where they would rendezvous for the night's camp. The steamer's whitewashed woodwork and slow-paced comfort provided a rare moment of luxury for the Laundress, a moment of painted walls and swept floors, as well as boilers and a stove that kept the main deck and upper cabin warm. Whatever rudimentary comforts the laundresses found on the boat were probably better than those of the officers' wives, who were confined to a segregated ladies' cabin aft of the main cabin on the upper deck, farthest from the danger of boiler explosions and well out of reach of unfamiliar men. They had "all been more or less sick," Larned wrote, "cooped up in the small cabin of a rear wheel boat, living on the most atrocious of boat fare for 34 days. During that time they have succeeded in discovering each other's failings with astonishing distinctness, and, from all I hear, have made the atmosphere pretty warm."[70]

By early June, the Seventh Cavalry and its steamer consort had reached Fort Rice, built a decade earlier by the Thirtieth Wisconsin Infantry to contain the Sioux. Fort Rice was a major depot for all points west and was packed with people. "Three large steamboats lay at the wharf," wrote Larned, noting that "soldiers, officers, Indians, scouts and guides throng about the post and keep up quite a metropolitan bustle and excitement."[71] From there, the troopers would head out into the field for the summer to guard railroad surveyors as they moved toward the Yellowstone River, while the remaining staff and laundresses would head about twenty-five miles farther upstream to Fort Abraham Lincoln, at that time still under construction. The officers' wives were sent back East by train to wait out the summer while their officer-husbands were in the field.

In the political climate of the 1870s, railroad and military policies were interlinked. Western railroad construction proved a far more effective means of settling the "Indian problem" than armies alone, but railroads needed armies to protect the laying of track into contested lands. The Seventh Cavalry had already guarded railroad construction through the southern plains. Now it would repeat this work by guarding the Northern Pacific Railroad's construction crews as they built track directly into the northern plains territories of the Lakota Sioux and Northern Cheyenne Nations. This enormous railroad project was being built in two segments, each side building to the other, with an expected completion date of 1876.[72] Nearly two thousand miles of hostile territory separated the two sections. The Lakota Sioux, at the apogee of their power and territorial extent, considered the Americans an irritant and yet only one of several opponents to deal with that year, and they were prepared to trade with or fight them all. They were also fully conscious of what Custer was doing there and even more conscious of what they would lose if the railroad was built. The Northern Pacific effectively promised them nothing less than a total disruption of life, "evils amounting almost to extermination, from the extinction of the vast herds of buffalo which roam the Northern prairies and the pre-emption of all the valuable tracts of land" that served as home and hunting ground.[73]

The military base for this effort would be Fort Abraham Lincoln, a new fort on the Northern Pacific line at Bismarck, Dakota Territory. From there, military forces would spread westward wherever needed to protect construction of the railroad or to perform any other duty required of it. But Fort Lincoln was still under construction that spring, and it was necessary to use Fort Rice instead, until Lincoln could be completed. That summer the cavalry would protect the Northern Pacific Railroad's surveyors westward toward the Yellowstone River, guarding them from attack as they plotted out the necessary cuts, grades, and fills for miles of track in advance of actual construction. The cavalry was joined by nineteen companies of infantry under the command of Colonel David Stanley of the Twenty-Second Infantry, with Custer and the Seventh Cavalry supporting the infantry columns with horse capacity.[74] The expedition moved into the field during July. "We make an imposing show on these rolling prairies," Larned wrote in a letter, with "1500 men, 250 teamsters, 40 scouts, 250 wagons, 800 horses, 600 head of cattle and 1500 mules—too imposing in fact, for the Indians[,] who have not yet made an appearance."[75] The Northern Pacific surveyors cut nearly a straight line across the plains until they reached the Yellowstone River. At that point they began to follow the course of the Yellowstone farther west, taking advantage of the natural contours of the land to do so. A chartered steamboat met them at the Yellowstone with food, forage, and supplies for the next section of the survey before following the surveyors and troops as far up the Yellowstone as practicable.

The survey went well enough and even included two minor skirmishes, the first somewhat comical. On August 4 George Custer rode ahead of the regiment with a small detachment of men to scout out trails. After riding some distance, they paused for a noon rest by the banks of the Yellowstone. They had just kicked off their boots and were "disposing themselves on the grass" when they realized they were surrounded by a party of Lakotas and completely cut off from the rest of their men.[76] The Lakota men were led by Gall, a Hunkpapa in his early thirties who enjoyed a powerful reputation as a fighter and absolutely refused to accept living on an agency. He was a keen man whose "great natural ability [and] force of character" impressed all those who encountered him.[77] Over the next few hours Gall's men laid one trap after another for the cavalry detachment, but the Crow scouts accompanying Custer recognized the traps and advised him on how to avoid danger. Custer managed instead to fight it out in a holding pattern, relieved only when the rest of the regiment arrived, thereby shifting the balance of power and driving off Gall and his now outnumbered force.

A second encounter came six days later, after Custer followed Gall's trail to a point on the Yellowstone River not far from the mouth of the Bighorn River. The trail signs in the earth indicated a large force of several hundred or more men, who rapidly became visible on the opposite riverbank as the Seventh Cavalry troops approached. No less than the great chief Sitting Bull was among them; the powerfully built man of forty sat high up on a nearby bluff to watch the impending fight. Gall's men had been reinforced over the previous days by additional men from neighboring villages, making an imposing and impressive display. As their families watched from nearby bluffs, Gall's men "opened a brisk fire from the opposite side of the river" while sending small groups of other men to cross the river and attack the cavalrymen directly.[78] Gall himself, dressed in full war regalia and bright red colors, boldly rode his horse up and down the riverbank, taunting the cavalrymen to try and hit him. During the battle, men from Company L headed upstream onto on a narrow ridge, which they held despite a "hot time" from approaching Indians. Around the same time, Stanley arrived with the infantry, which began setting up their big artillery guns and lobbing artillery shells over the river into the forest where Lakota sharpshooters waited to pick off targets. The artillery's impact shifted the fight completely to the army's advantage. "Halloo!" the soldiers shouted. "Stanley's talking Dutch to them. Look at that!"[79]

The battle, barely thirty minutes long and fought to music from the cavalry band, wasn't particularly big or great—only two sides shooting at each other from across a river—but it was tactically useful for the army and narratively dramatic, and it burnished George Custer's reputation while demonstrating the strength and determination of the Lakota leadership. But just as the Yellowstone expedition was returning from the field, news came that the Northern Pacific's overextended financier had collapsed. The railroad had been built on the gamble that a profitable, fully equipped transcontinental railroad could be built through commercially undeveloped land on the strength of faith and finance alone, and it had placed this gamble in the hands of Jay Cook & Company of New York. Over the fall of 1873 Cook's financial implosion sent out economic shock waves that spread throughout the country, leading to a national financial depression. It would take years for the Northern Pacific to recover its finances, and the final spike in the line would not be driven until 1883, seven years late. Because of this, the war against the Sioux would also be slowed down for several years. For the moment, the town of Bismarck, which served as the Northern Pacific's railhead on the Missouri River opposite Fort Lincoln, became the farthest outpost of railroad civilization on the northern plains.

Bismarck's name honored Otto von Bismarck, the German chancellor who had just unified the German states, deliberately chosen by Northern Pacific Railroad officials to attract German immigrants into settling there and populating the upper plains, eventually providing the railroad with necessary traffic along the way.[80] A more immediate source of income was generated by lines of steamboats that ran between Bismarck and the upper reaches of the Missouri River, thereby taking advantage of the hundred-mile cutoff that the Northern Pacific's tracks into Bismarck offered for reaching Montana's gold mines. Boosters are perennial optimists, and by late 1873 Bismarck's set of boosters were already boasting how the "frontier roughs" had been overwhelmed by the promise of civilization and a newly built "Sabbath school."[81] While their boasts were premature, the railroad company along with the U.S. Army nonetheless had a significant interest in keeping Bismarck active and stable. Bismarck served as a depot for food and supplies, not only for the fort but for all westward commerce; it fostered a modest but growing domestic business, a roundhouse, shops, and railroad yards for the Northern Pacific, seasonal steamboat traffic, summer rushes of teamsters, and in 1877 the imposing three-story Sheridan House, a glory of clapboard lumber and whitewashed pilasters offering running water and drawn baths.

Across the river from Bismarck and slightly downstream was Fort Abraham Lincoln. Fort Lincoln, as everyone called it, was in effect two separate but linked posts made up of two distinct clusters of buildings: an infantry post to the north and a cavalry post to the south. All of the long, low, one-story cavalry buildings were built in perfect alignment, like a martial drill. From the Missouri River westward, the buildings increased with rank and purpose, allowing the officers on the far western edge of the fort the metaphoric glory of leading the charge into the wilderness beyond. Nearer to the river were six stables, arranged in a rectangle, with two pairs of buildings on the east and west sides, where horses could be fed, worked, and exercised. Laundresses and their soldier husbands occupied apartments in one of three row houses, with shared walls punctuated by chimneys, all facing north, toward the stables. Their houses were "easily traced by the swinging clotheslines in front," Elizabeth Custer later recalled. These row houses were together known as "suds row."[82] To the north of the stables were additional quarters for scouts. Three massive barracks, arranged parallel to the parade ground, were west of the stables. The kitchens and mess halls of each faced the stables, while the porches presented a united front to the parade ground itself. Flanking them on either side were storehouses, a dispensary, a guardhouse, and commissary stores. On the western side of the parade ground stood several officers' houses with broad porches that created a socially conspicuous setting where officers could view the post, review troops, and, for the Custers, pose with the other officers and their families on the wide steps that faced the field.

Noonan and the Laundress might have first encountered each other in the spring of 1873, when the cavalry reassembled for the trip into Dakota Territory, and they had definitely met by that fall, following the Yellowstone expedition. The catalyst for their meeting might have been Noonan's quest for an excellent tailor, because the precision and perfection of the uniform required to compete for orderly duty demanded the work of an experienced hand. An introduction might even have occurred through the Custer circle, as Elizabeth Custer already employed the Laundress, while Noonan was rising up the ladder and frequently chosen as orderly to Thomas Custer and occasionally George Custer. Elizabeth Custer certainly knew of Noonan and might have made the introduction, either herself or through intermediaries who had tailoring to be done. When fully tailored up, Noonan cut an attractive figure, so much so that Elizabeth Custer (who knew a thing or two about the male form) considered him "the handsomest soldier in the company" and "often admired the admirably fitting uniform his wife had made over, and which displayed to advantage his well proportioned figure."[83] Arranging these connections provided advantages all around, by keeping things within the circle, tethering the services of a valued laundress to the household through favors and connections, and providing officers with the best turned out orderlies possible.

The full dress uniform of the 1870s U.S. Army was spectacular, practically Teutonic: the Model 1872 dress coats of deep blue twilled wool were impressively padded at the chest, trimmed with contrasting piping of a color according to service branch, and fastened with brass buttons embellished with the United States' familiar eagle. A polished brass buckle fastened the black leather belt, from which a sword, pistol, and cartridge belt hung. Cavalrymen like Noonan were issued slightly shorter coats with side vents for ease when riding horseback, and their trousers of sky-blue wool were reinforced at the seat to withstand days in the saddle. By 1876 men in the Seventh Cavalry were reinforcing their riding trousers with white canvas instead of wool, which later spread in use among other cavalry units. (The Laundress may have tailored more than a few of these practical modifications.) On dress occasions the cavalrymen wore cords of woven cavalry yellow silk that looped onto the coat's buttons and draped over the chest, complete with yellow tassels. The 1870s full dress helmet was the most impressive of all—a stiff Teutonic dome of black wool and black leather, topped by a brass spike and yellow horsehair plume, draped in yellow cords, and embellished with a formidable brass eagle. For less formal occasions, the Seventh Cavalry's "regulation garrison uniform" included a short five-button coat of dark blue wool called a "fatigue blouse," a forage cap, sky-blue trousers, and, when truly dressed up, a sword.[84]

The men with whom Noonan served, and the soldiers they became, made up a large and distinct culture. They were generally but not always young, with the physical stamina to drill as required and fight if necessary, and they were adaptable to the requirements of military life both arbitrary and genuine. They had all signed up for a position that would take them away from freedoms of civilian life in exchange for service within a larger organization that promised principle and order, and for this they were willing to serve for five years. The average age of a Seventh Cavalryman in the 1870s was about twenty-five, although more than a few were in their late twenties, and some were occasionally as old as forty. Some of these men sought the security and foundation of military life or became enamored with the ideals of military service, which led some to make the army a lifelong career. Other men simply saw the army as a convenient option, with food and board thrown in, while still others were described by contemporaries as little more than "human driftwood," unable to deal with society, searching for structure, looking for a job or to escape from another life.[85]

John Noonan's own drive indicates someone keen on the stability, order, and principle of military life, coupled with ambition to rise within a set of clearly defined and understandable rules, which he followed and enforced with vigor. He appears to have been detached from the larger world and people within it, relying instead on rules and form to give his life substance, and for this the army, maybe more than anything else, provided what Noonan needed: a home. An officer who knew Noonan recalled him as "a temperate, well behaved man, of good ordinary intelligence," not too unlike many of the career soldiers who surrounded him. Yet he was also determined, and forceful about it; the same officer added that Noonan was "a rigid disciplinarian, soldiering being the trade of his life."[86] His relatively quick rise from private to corporal and ultimately to sergeant showed clear signs of a dedicated and professional soldier. This was especially true in the 1870s, when officers inched their way up the postwar ranks over the years of their career. This devotion to military order was rewarded by plum assignments as orderly to the Custer command. Orderlies are chosen for the day based on their competitive attention to detail and absolute precision of white-gloved cleanliness; in this contest the slightest advantage can put a soldier into the service of the highest-ranking officers and gain him proximity to power, prestige, and recognition. Common soldiers without a West Point background or military commission had little entry to the halls of power, but in competing for orderly duty Noonan found himself in the center of operations, which placed him directly within the Custer circle.

Just what Noonan thought of George Custer is unknown. At that time Custer was just another officer, although he was beginning to develop a national reputation. The consensus among Custer's fellow officers was that he was indisputably brave but had risen quickly without the necessary benefit of seasoning or temper. Lieutenant Larned thought that Custer lived up to his reputation as "a man selfishly indifferent to others, and ruthlessly determined to make himself conspicuous at all hazards," yet he was undoubtedly willing to take risks or try strategies that were otherwise daunting to his fellows.[87] The rank-and-file who served under him were generally impressed by Custer's hunting dogs and private cook, but they also called him "Hard Ass." He was "not used to being thwarted," one soldier remarked, "even by nature."[88] "He was too hard on the men and horses," another member of the Seventh Cavalry recalled. "He changed his mind too often. He was always right."[89] Noonan's fairly rapid rise to orderly within Custer's circle of officers, as well as his reputation for rigid devotion to military principles, indicates that he was prepared to spend as much time within that circle as possible. This devotion to his career paid off: Thomas Custer chose Noonan as orderly so often that he became "Colonel Tom's own man," as Elizabeth Custer recalled, gaining an aura of intimacy and fidelity as a right arm to the ranking officer, thus proving himself to be a trusted aide Thomas Custer could count on.[90] When Elizabeth Custer went riding, Noonan rode ahead of her on escort duty. He stood at attention in the inner sanctum, in rooms decorated with mounted trophies and tables covered in maps, newspapers, books, papers, and even an impressive "Rogers group" of cast plaster depicting two soldiers in war, titled *Wounded to the Rear—One More Shot*, placed upon the table in a position of honor, while guarding the doors of rooms where policies were made and history created, silently watching the inner workings of a family command both divisive and unifying. The journalist William Curtis might have seen Noonan when he visited George Custer in his study, "surrounded by adjutants and orderlies, to whom he gave his military directions" during the summer of 1874.[91] That fall Noonan could also see his own likeness as orderly in a framed photograph; hanging on a wall in Custer's study, it showed Noonan standing beside Custer and a trophy bear. This meant that Noonan's image, however incidental, was part of the everyday life of the Custer household and something that the household looked upon every day.

Noonan and the Laundress shared a good deal in common: dedication to a career, gumption to get there, and the willingness to go the extra length to succeed. They might have first begun to understand each other while the latter was tailoring the officer's uniform, in moments spent with chalk and pins, and they were later reported to have married in late 1873. They were fortunate: the army discouraged marriages among noncommissioned officers, refused to enlist married men, and made it as difficult as possible to marry once enlisted. From the army's perspective, marriage divided a soldier's attention and occupied his time with family concerns instead of military ones. If his wife was sick, a soldier looked after their children while officers fumed. Even so, military posts recognized reality and erected housing separate from company barracks to accommodate married soldiers, even permitting them privileges such as eating at home with their wives instead of having to attend the company mess. The Seventh Cavalry had no shortage of married soldiers, and in 1873 a reporter counted "twenty women[,] wives of soldiers, and as many children accompanying them."[92] Like Mrs. Noonan, enlisted men's wives often contributed to the family income by working as laundresses.

The Noonans' marriage, as well as their domestic world, was by every contemporary account genuine, affectionate, steady, intimate, and lasting. It was also omnivorous on Noonan's part. Just where he appeared on the scale of human orientation is unknown, but it appears that he stood somewhere between the absolutes and that he enjoyed his wife as she was, both socially and intimately. "Noonan called her Rose," Emma Klawitter, a neighboring laundress later recalled, "but how he could think of such a pet name for a woman without any womanly features is beyond me."[93] Their devotion was evident in letters they wrote to each other while Noonan was away on duty in the field; they kept in touch even when separated by hundreds of miles, chatting about the comforting and incidental trivialities of life. "It is 'Dear Husband,' 'loving wife,' and the common-place gossip of post and camp life," remarked a Bismarck resident who in 1878 read the letters Mrs. Noonan had written to her husband. Noonan's letters to her in return were just as affectionate, addressed to his "Dear wife" and signed "Your Darling Hubby."[94] For all this, though, she was not beyond upholding a fierce reputation held by some laundresses. "Nobody dared cross her path without her permission," recalled Klawitter. "I saw her drunk one time bending over Sergeant Noonan with a big butcher knife; and I just know his head would have rolled if Sergeant Hill hadn't intervened."[95]

With each year Mrs. Noonan's sense of a woman's life became more innate. The initial novelty of experiences in a new life, even small ones like hanging up a skirt or arranging long hair with its attendant combs and pins, subsides over time into familiarity. A man entering into a woman's life requires at least a year to assume anything approaching interior understandings of the role, and only with subsequent years does the sense of a woman's life develop more dimensionally, with an imagination and philosophy reflected through the practical experience of seeing the world through a woman's eyes. Much of this was mirrored by the way she kept house and decorated her quarters. "Her house was as neat and clean as it could be," an observer later remarked, "and the walls were ornamented with some very beautiful pictures."[96] Elizabeth Custer agreed, later recalling an impressively neat and tidy house, even if the furniture was improvised from packing crates. In this space, a simple room in the laundresses' quarters on the Dakota prairies, the Laundress created a domestic and intensely personal paradise.[97]

The clothing worn by Mrs. Noonan reflected a deeply interior part of Mrs. Noonan's world. Fashion was serious business in distant forts: for an officer's wife, it meant being in touch with the outside world and upholding its standards, even in the West; for a company laundress, it meant aspiring to be a "leddy," or at least its imitation. Sturdy cotton wash dresses were a staple of her working world, and she probably regularly wore corsets, even while working at the washtubs: working women of that era in every occupation, from factory girls to fishwives, depended on their corsets as a foundation garment throughout the day. She also had several "good" dresses; Elizabeth Custer recalled seeing stockpiles of "silk and woolen stuffs for gowns" neatly kept in her quarters at Fort Lincoln. Mrs. Noonan appears to have loved clothes and actively engaged in making and wearing them, even working briefly as a milliner at Fort Leavenworth in 1869. Silk dresses might seem surprising for a military laundress, but Mrs. Noonan was demonstrably fond of fashion and engaged the dream-like fantasy of stylish living whenever possible. In this she was not alone. A favored story among Seventh Cavalry members stationed at Fort Rice during the winter of 1876–77 told of a sartorial rivalry between a well-dressed laundress and an equally fashionable officer's wife who encountered each other on the field. "Both ladies were togged in their finest fixings," a soldier remarked, "were equally proud and dignified, and they passed each other with eyes front and nose up, as if each thought she owned the whole reservation, with the troops thrown in." The Fort Rice laundress in this story kept her wits and strolled steadily on, while the officer's wife gave in to jealous curiosity and looked back, only to trip over "a plebian [sic] wheelbarrow, which had no respect of class or caste," in full view of the entire fort. She untangled herself, kicked the wheelbarrow for its insolence, and strode off.[98]

Fashion and society merged in glittering military balls—the social highlights of life on a military fort. They punctuated the winter season like bright stars and offered welcome pleasure to an often difficult life. For Mrs. Noonan and other laundresses, they were as close to genuine glitter as a laundress could get. The most impressive of these were company balls, hosted by the different military companies over the winter season in what was essentially a sporting contest of social dominance. The success of a company ball reflected the strength and capacity of the company itself, and each company sought to outdo its rivals in splendor and hospitality. "Military balls are the rage," reported the *Bismarck Tribune* in the winter of 1878, as Companies G, L, K, E, and M lined up in competition.[99] This kind of sporting hospitality could cost serious money. For example, Company F under George Yates spent "several hundred dollars" on food and decorations for an especially rich ball in January 1876.[100] In February 1878 Noonan's Company L put on a "pleasant and enjoyable" ball that featured evergreens and the national flag for decorations; a table set for sixty couples boasted "one of the finest spreads ever seen at the post" when it hosted its annual ball. "Colonel Tilford[,] commander of the post, and Lieutenant Wilke[n]son, the company commander, led the grand march of 38 couple[s]" to open the dancing to string and brass band music provided by the fort's bands.[101] An evening's dancing traditionally opened with a grand march, followed by intricate quadrilles interspersed with quicksteps, schottisches, and polkas. The dances were complex, and the music was sumptuous. By the 1870s, brass instrumental music had reached a breathtaking richness in tone and tempo that ranged from pounding time to deft interludes of a variety popular tunes (including opera) that ordinary people hummed by heart. The first dance sets were reserved for officers and their wives who "complimented" the soldiers by attending. These extensions of ceremonial invitations and compliments between officers and the rank-and-file were part of a larger, well-oiled system of social courtesies that upheld the ideal of military life: enlisted men entered the dance only after the officers and their wives had finished dancing and gone to supper, thus allowing the effect of hospitality while maintaining the strict hierarchy between officers and the rank-and-file.

With so few women on a military reservation, common soldiers held laundresses in particularly high regard during dances. Their presence helped them forget the reality of a wooden barracks floor and imagine themselves as social lions at the fashionable society balls of the eastern states. Elizabeth Custer, reminded by her husband not to openly laugh at the homemade dresses of the various company laundresses, remembered Mrs. Noonan "going to soldier's [sic] balls dressed in gauzy, low-necked gowns" that copied the fashionable ball dresses of Paris and the paintings of James Tissot. "Even the tall Mexican laundress" she recalled, "would deck herself in pink tarlatan and false curls, and not withstanding her height and colossal anatomy she had constant partners."[102] By the early 1870s Mrs. Noonan had begun wearing a frisette of false curls to create a fashionable cascade of ringlets down the back of her neck, together with that ever-present veil, which concealed her masculine features, merging sultana with coquette. Her passion for ball dresses and the fantasy life they evoked edged to the point of becoming theater: at military balls in 1877 and again in 1878 she "at all times was arrayed in the finest of the land" and distinctly remembered for changing her ball dresses "as often as three times" in a single evening.[103]

The ritual of wearing three different dresses over the course of a single evening opens a unique and significant door to understanding Mrs. Noonan's interior life, one that indicates a part of her world where all she wanted was to be admired. It required leaving the cozy warmth of the music-filled barracks for the bitter cold of a Dakota winter, walking across the fort grounds to her quarters in the middle of the night and in the dark, a shivering mass of gauzy tarlatan, and doing this no fewer than six times, back and forth, during the night. Once at her own quarters, the match was struck and the lamp lit, the old dress was rapidly unhooked and thrown aside, a quick decision made of which new dress to wear, the new dress pulled on and fastened up, bodice adjusted, bustle refastened, skirt and overskirt checked to be sure they lay correctly over petticoats for the fashionable shape, hair checked in the mirror, lamp extinguished. She was excited and ready to go, ready for the theater of the next magnificent grand entrance upon the ballroom floor, more attention, and more pleasure in dancing. There is a kind of innocent, giddy determination in this that drew Mrs. Noonan perpetually across the military grounds in the middle of the night during cold Dakota winters for the fantasy of social triumph, a moment to shine that was hers alone.[104]

Fashion sense and domestic frills offered pleasant distractions but could not penetrate the absolute social barrier that existed beyond the walls of Mrs. Noonan's quarters. Laundresses occupied the lower rungs of the social ladder, and an army caste system discouraged the mixing of officers' wives and laundresses beyond necessity. It reinforced the social hierarchy that infused the military system and incidentally served to keep at a safe distance those women with time on their hands who were inquisitive and prone to gossip. Officers' wives and other women sometimes did venture into the laundress quarters when they had to ask about their work, but the situation was akin to slumming, even when the woman placed herself at the behest of her social inferior. Yet here she pushed the limits and did so successfully. Elizabeth Custer recalled visiting Mrs. Noonan's quarters at least twice: first to see about her health, after Custer's cook told her that the Laundress was ill, and again to ask for her services as a midwife for Annie Yates, another officer's wife. Elizabeth Custer's visits suggest an interest in the Laundress's well-being as well as in her household services, and, while transactional, these occasions allowed Elizabeth Custer to see how well Mrs. Noonan cared for and kept house, which impressed Custer and influenced her later memories of Mrs. Noonan as a decent and respectable woman. In turn, Mrs. Noonan's association with the Custers reinforced this perception of respectability, allowing her to work under the umbrella of a large and systematic hierarchy that offered patronage, stability, and a sense of extended family.

The Custer system of command that touched the Noonans was a circle of related individuals whose chains of authority and recommendation formed a sort of protective structure, akin to patronage and familiarity. The Custers recognized loyalty and rewarded it. Where Mrs. Noonan had earned a reputation as an excellent laundress and loyal midwife to the Custers' circle where it counted, her husband earned an equally loyal reputation as orderly to Thomas Custer and on occasion to George Custer. Continued recognition for his excellent character upon promotion to the rank of corporal, and his likeness in the framed William Illingworth photograph of Custer and his bear that hung on the wall in Custer's study, placed Noonan's fidelity and duty more literally in Custer's everyday life. The Custers were linked to the Noonans. They wore the clothes she laundered and counted upon him to support their daily duties. Little Elizabeth Yates, playing with toys on the carpet of the Yates household, safely came into the world thanks to Mrs. Noonan.

A material measure of Mrs. Noonan's status within the Custer command became evident when she served as nurse and midwife to George and Annie Yates on the recommendation of Elizabeth Custer.[105] The recommendation was not casual, but it was conditional, mostly because they could not find anyone else. But it still made clear that she was considered of enough quality to do the work in the household of a lady, and an officer's wife at that. George Yates commanded the smart and snappy Company F, while Annie Yates was the daughter of a prominent civil engineer who included the Northern Pacific Railroad within his portfolio of clients; both counted themselves among the Custers' intimate circle of friends. But they turned to Mrs. Noonan only after a heavy snow blockade on the Northern Pacific tracks prevented Yates from hiring a professional midwife from St. Paul and after the other officers' wives declined from lack of experience or interest in trying.[106] Forced to turn to whomever they could find locally, Elizabeth Custer later claimed credit for remembering Mrs. Noonan from the Laundress's further reputation as a midwife, and she already employed her as a personal laundry worker. Writing of this incident a decade later, Elizabeth Custer was careful to mention Mrs. Noonan's experience, thoughtfully reassuring her middle-class Victorian readers that she did not normally project so liberal a sentiment as to hire transgender midwives to tend to the socially respectable and upstanding ladies in her circle unless *absolutely* necessary.

Elizabeth Custer's memories of Mrs. Noonan during this time also give another intimate glimpse into her personal world, beginning with a visit she and Annie Yates made to Mrs. Noonan's quarters on suds row to inquire about her midwifery services. They found her home "shining" and neatly kept, the bed "hung with pink cambric," and the house ornamented into as comfortable a home as she could manage. Mrs. Noonan claimed reluctance to leave her husband but agreed to care for Annie Yates with the provision that she be able to return home every evening and cook his supper and, unbeknown to Custer and Yates, shave her beard. This was the real reason for her request, which created a twofer: privately, she was able to protect herself by determining a regular schedule for shaving, while publicly, Custer and Yates were impressed by her devotion to her husband and her husband's well-being. It was part of a series of careful excuses she routinely employed to protect herself from discovery and interruption, which included her encounter with Godfrey seven years earlier in the wagons in Kansas when she claimed anger at noisy children as an excuse to ride alone in separate wagons, where her beard would not be as visible. She had a singsong manner of language, at least in Elizabeth Custer's account, that borders slightly on romantically playful camp. She called her husband her "manny manny" and insisted on cooking her "manny manny's supper" every day. When caring for Yates, she would lean over her bed to see if she was comfortable, asking her, "Are you comph?" They set up a bed for Mrs. Noonan, and she stayed within the Yates household for several days. Here she saw what her husband saw during orderly duty at the Custers', although one floor up and in a far more personal way. Within the Yates home, the steady nature of observation during interior moments, especially in domestic settings, reveals aspects of personality that are often hidden by the formalities of street dress and manners. Whether Yates or Custer actually understood this is unknown, although Custer was no fool and Yates had a clue: Custer recalled that Yates "used to whisper to me that when she watched her moving about the dim light of the sick room, she thought with a shiver how like a man she seemed." The image of Annie Yates in her bed whispering to Elizabeth Custer about the woman not far away and just out of hearing is striking. Yet Mrs. Noonan's skill and patience with Annie Yates during childbirth and the "gentle, dexterous manner in which she lifted and cared for" Yates won their respect and impressed them, especially Elizabeth Custer, with her qualities. Mrs. Noonan successfully delivered the infant into the world and took care of both mother and child for many days thereafter. As the danger of childbirth passed, Elizabeth Custer took over care for mother and child, leaving Mrs. Noonan "a richer woman by much gratitude and a great deal of money."[107]

Caring for Annie Yates, and especially at Elizabeth Custer's request, placed Mrs. Noonan in a valued position, not only within the immediate circle of Custer patronage but also within larger affairs at Fort Lincoln. Elizabeth Custer's recommendations and approval set the tone and tempo for domestic affairs within the fort. Her approval of Mrs. Noonan drew from and focused on shared internal ideals and possibly characteristics: while she considered Mrs. Noonan "tall, awkward and seemingly coarse," she also thought her "tender hearted" and, more critically, recognized that she led a "quiet, orderly life," which indicated a person of propriety, decency, and character. This made her suitable to serve a respectable household and identified her as a valued supporting member of the military environment.[108] More significantly, it influenced Elizabeth Custer's long-term memory, ultimately resulting in her later portrayal of Mrs. Noonan as a woman, a woman in alliance with her own society. She would never view her as her social equal but accepted her as part of a moment where "all classes and conditions" were thrown together by common experience and worked together for a common good, a moment of rough equality in the progress of civilization upon the plains.[109]

The halt in the progress of the Northern Pacific rail laying had led Sheridan and other army officials to consider another tactic. If railroad construction would not let them occupy the area, they could be required to do so by a sudden rush into the same region, particularly for gold. Scattered reports of the remote Black Hills had trickled back to the East as early as 1743, when a pair of French explorers and fur traders, François and Louis-Joseph Vérendrye, saw the Black Hills in the distance from the top of Bear Butte, a rocky laccolith resembling a small hilltop fortress about ten miles away. But those hills bore a forbidding reputation; the Indian men who guided the explorers refused to go nearer, describing the formidable nature of the tribes who claimed the Black Hills as their own.[110] At that time, a contest for dominance and possession raged over the territory, ultimately leading to Lakota ascendance by the 1770s and a century of Lakota control. Yet from the 1830s on, the Black Hills provided equally formidable rumors of gold. By the 1860s, several unsuccessful attempts had been made to exploit those hills for mining, but the Fort Laramie Treaty of 1868 officially gave the lands the to the Lakota Sioux "for the absolute and undisturbed use and occupation of the Indians" in exchange for handing over a much larger territory nearby, ending for the moment any other groups' attempts to claim them.[111]

Blocked by the treaty, General Sheridan proposed scouting locations near the Black Hills for a new fort that would give Custer a pretext to explore further. This would require an expedition, and an expedition that found gold, however incidentally, could bring pressure to alter or abandon the treaty and open the Black Hills for mining and settlement. Formally, the Black Hills Expedition of 1874 was a scientific reconnaissance, officially intended to provide information about the geography, wildlife, and other features of the mountains that rose in the southwestern corner of Dakota Territory.[112] A scientific corps had been assembled to give the expedition its official bearing. They were all "bug hunters" as far as the enlisted men were concerned, but the scientifically inclined team actually represented an array of skill and knowledge: two botanists, a geologist from Minnesota who was expected to take the "testimony of the rocks," and George Grinnell, a "young but interesting" naturalist who had come out from Yale at the suggestion of Othniel Marsh, the Yale paleontologist.[113] The expedition also carried William McKay and Horatio

Ross, two experienced miners from the Bismarck area, specifically to search for gold, provide an estimate of how much gold might be in the region, and report directly to Custer rather than to the geologist. They were "practical miners and explorers," the *Bismarck Tribune* exclaimed, "and are expected to find the gold."[114] They were also an open secret. Neither man was officially part the expedition, and both were consciously hidden from view. Despite this attempt at secrecy, their purpose was publicly featured in the pages of the *Bismarck Tribune*, which thought it "a burning shame that so vast a region, reputed so rich in minerals and agricultural resources . . . should so long remain unexplored."[115] Everyone knew what they were doing there and what they had to find in order for the expedition to be considered successful. While camped at the base of one of the great peaks, twenty-three-year-old reporter William Curtis of the *Chicago Inter-Ocean* acknowledged the following on July 23: "We have seen nothing remarkable; the miners have discovered no gold, the geologists have whacked in vain. . . . So far, the expedition, in a positive sense, has been unsuccessful."[116]

The expedition was enormous. Nearly eighty wagons in four parallel columns flanked with soldiers on horseback, ten companies of the Seventh Cavalry, two infantry companies (one company each of the Seventeenth and Twentieth Infantries), and an engineering detachment along with mules, men, supplies, forage, and food, plus even a civilian post trader, prepared to move into the Black Hills. There were civil engineers to map out distances and terrain, a civilian topographer, and an odometer cart, under the charge of Sergeant Charles Becker, that clicked off the miles.[117] More ominously, it carried a battery of artillery under First Lieutenant Josiah Chance of the Seventeenth Infantry, including a three-inch Rodman gun of the same type that lobbed shells over the Yellowstone the year before, and three ten-barreled, rapid-fire Gatling guns, whose inventor reportedly hoped that they would be tested in battle.[118] Several days' march led them through the Badlands of the Dakotas to the base of the Black Hills, on the Montana Territory side, and the expedition began its ascent into the hills themselves. The layered formations of weathered granite, limestone, and sandstone piled up into rumpled mountains provided a dramatically sublime feel to the landscape. Some of these weathered rocks were nearly two billion years old, absolutely inconceivable to the men who scrambled around them. The air was fragrant with spruce and ponderosa pines that stood interspersed among scattered pastures that formed pleasing parks along the way. Nearly everyone remarked about the abundant grass and clear water, wooded slopes, and spectacular array of wildlife. The soldiers staged a ball game, the officers had a champagne supper, and Company H formed a glee club. The brass band played music that thrummed and echoed off canyon walls.[119] Scattered buffalo bones were occasionally found, sometimes with fragments of skin still attached—signs of a recent and already changing antiquity when buffalo roamed the Black Hills as part of their grazing territory and vast herds dotted its slopes. The scattered coyotes that soldiers saw trotting along the lower slopes gave way to gray wolves; pronghorn antelope were so numerous that, although very hard to catch, they regularly fed the men, who found their meat "fresh and juicy, broiled on a bed of pine coals."[120] The herd of beef cattle brought along for food grew fat by virtue of simply being left alone.

John Noonan's image was preserved for posterity on August 7, the day George Custer shot a grizzly bear.[121] Signs of bear were reported as they ascended into the Black Hills in late July, but they did not actually see one until August, as the expedition made its way back out of the hills on the return journey. Custer rode ahead of the column, accompanied by Bloody Knife, acting as scout for the expedition, and thirty-one-year-old William Ludlow, who held the rank of colonel. While searching for a camping ground, Bloody Knife spotted a great mountain bear, ambling over a ridge only seventy-five yards distant. Custer immediately fired a shot, wounding the bear in the thigh, followed by a second shot. Bloody Knife and Ludlow also fired, securing the outcome with three more shots before Bloody Knife slit the animal's throat. Noonan was serving as Custer's orderly that day and helped move the bear to a rock, where the carcass was prominently laid out. It was a proud old bear, with teeth well worn and wrecked, scarred from many summers of life and ancient battles with rivals, felled on the edge of his prime.

"I have reached the hunter's highest round of fame," George Custer wrote to his wife Elizabeth. "I have killed my grizzly after a most exciting hunt & combat."[122] To mark the occasion, the expedition's photographer, William Illingworth, was brought over to take the trophy photo. The bear lay dead in the foreground while Custer was at the center, dramatically posing with his rifle and wearing his buckskin coat. Ludlow was to the right, slightly lower, while Bloody Knife sat to the left, his rifle at an angle, looking at the lens with a slightly resigned expression. Noonan stood behind Custer, farthest from the camera, practically as much a part of the landscape as he was part of Custer's command. He wore a dark slouch hat and loose-fitting field uniform of blue wool with brass buttons, and he held his rifle in his hands. He was twenty-seven years old, in the prime of life and bearded from months on campaign, a man weary of and resigned to the affairs of the world. For the second image Illingworth took, Noonan adjusted the brim of his hat upward, so his face was in the full light. The images were later printed in stereographs that lay on parlor tables from Boston to Cincinnati—three-dimensional glimpses of a frontier viewed in the comfort of an easy chair by the fire—and image No. 847 was of Custer's grizzly, with Noonan standing by. Illingworth later printed and formally framed an enlarged version of the image for George Custer, and it took a prominent place on the wall of Custer's study. This effectively placed Noonan's likeness there as well, a portrait of service the Custers would look upon every day.

Custer's grizzly capped a more important development. A week before, the two miners accompanying the expedition had found gold, and the find was promising. Custer wrote to Sheridan the next day, saying that "gold has been found in several places, and it is the belief of those that are giving their attention to this subject that it will be found in paying quantities."[123] Custer ordered a rider, Charlie Reynolds, to go ahead of the party and deliver the news in advance of the cavalry's return. Reynolds wasted no time, riding four days south to Fort Laramie, from where the gold strike was quickly announced to the world. "Gold!" shouted the editors of the *Bismarck Tribune* as they detailed the "rich gold and silver mines" that would make the Black Hills the "El Dorado of America."[124]

The expedition returned to Fort Lincoln on the afternoon of August 30. After three months and nearly nine hundred miles in the field, and with a good many more miles than that traversed on side trips, the worn and tired band played "Garry Owen" as the troops marched back onto the parade ground that separated the barracks from the officers' houses. The civilians and what soldiers had been left behind gathered immediately to welcome the returning men. Elizabeth Custer fainted in the arms of her husband (Private Theodore Ewert thought that a very nice piece of work), officers turned out to greet their own wives, and Mrs. Noonan found her "manny manny" safely home again for the winter.[125]

In March 1876, Private Noonan was promoted to the rank of corporal.[126] Two months later Corporal Noonan bid his wife good-bye as the Seventh Cavalry rode out of Fort Lincoln, bound for war against the Sioux and Cheyenne tribes. The war had started the previous spring. In the aftermath of the Black Hills Expedition, the U.S. government attempted to gain the Black Hills for settlement by offering to purchase the territory, then by changing the terms of the 1868 treaty. The Lakotas refused to accept the altered conditions or any other offers and continued to live along the Yellowstone and its tributaries as they had previously agreed. But miners were already swarming the Black Hills, and by November 1875 the Grant administration had realized it was necessary to find a pretext for war to compel the revised terms, which, once found, would set into place military plans to force the Lakotas onto smaller reservations.[127] After several delayed attempts for a winter campaign, war plans finally got underway in early 1876. They involved a coordinated, multipronged effort of different military forces in the wider region surrounding the Yellowstone, all marching toward and converging upon the general area of the Yellowstone River and its tributaries to control the area and starve the tribes out. The nontreaties, as the Americans called the Indians in question, were assumed to be somewhere on their hunting grounds south of the Yellowstone River, possibly along the tributary rivers of the Tongue, Rosebud, or Little Bighorn, not far from where the U.S. Cavalry had fought them in 1873. General George Crook would make his way north from Fort Fetterman on the North Platte River, while General John Gibbon would advance eastward from Fort Ellis along the upper waters of the Yellowstone. General Alfred Terry along with Custer would advance westward from Fort Lincoln toward the Yellowstone and the Rosebud Rivers, eventually moving toward the Bighorn.[128]

Noonan marched with his company as far as the mouth of the Powder River, where a supply depot had been set up not far from where the Powder flowed into the Yellowstone. The chartered steamer *Far West* joined them there with supplies. Its modest white-and-gold saloon on the upper deck was transformed into temporary officers' quarters, a snug but comfortable demonstration of gilded civilization within the lean wooden flanks of a shallow draft mountain boat, lost among the winding rivers of the northern plains. For a few days Custer and Terry's soldiers carried medicines, food, furniture, tents, and even useless ceremonial sabers on and off the boat in the preparations for the big battles to come. "The troops are so thoroughly organized," wrote *Bismarck Tribune* reporter Mark Kellogg in a letter from the field, "and so disposed that if the Indians can be found they will be taught a lesson that will be a lasting one to them."[129] A sutler who had come along set up a two-tent emporium of sorts staffed with several employees, while Kellogg described "an amusing scene" as the soldiers lined up to purchase everything from drinks to supplies at ruinous prices. Kellogg would be killed a few days later along with many of the soldiers, but for the moment they were set up with drinks, a band, and several days of preparation for the coming campaign. On June 15 Custer and Terry broke camp, and their combined troops marched off as far as the Rosebud with the *Far West* steaming alongside before the two commanders split into separate groups. Custer followed the Rosebud toward the Bighorn, while Terry continued along the Yellowstone before heading south along the Bighorn to the same point. The *Far West* steamed along with Terry, eventually moving ahead to a berth on the Bighorn River, not far from the battle to come.[130]

Noonan wasn't among Custer and Terry's men. Instead of joining his army's march to battle he was detailed to remain at the Powder River supply depot, where he was to look after a herd of beef cattle brought along to feed the soldiers. It turned him into something of a cowboy, riding his horse among the cattle as they were grazed within safe distance of the guarding soldiers. Keeping him company were 150 cavalrymen, stationed there for protection, along with the cavalry band and an even larger number of infantrymen. The potential of Indian raids was thought low, but the depot's supplies were critical and worth protecting. Bags of grain and corn, forage for the horses, tools and repair equipment, weaponry and materials, plus tents and other niceties of life too heavy for an active campaign, were all kept under the watchful eye of Seventeenth Infantry quartermaster Josiah Chance.[131]

A few weeks later the *Far West* returned, with wounded soldiers and the nearly unimaginable news of the cavalry's complete defeat at the Little Bighorn on June 25. That morning, George Custer had put on a dark blue shirt, which Mrs. Noonan had likely laundered a few weeks earlier, and moved quickly toward a combined Lakota and Cheyenne encampment. Without realizing or appreciating its size, he took action a day earlier than planned on the mistaken belief they had been spotted while passing up on calling in reinforcements, which his contemporaries thought was because of a desire to lead the cavalry into the fight on his own, for personal glory. The news came back that Custer and everyone in his immediate command had been wiped out, as well as 60 percent of the men in Noonan's Company L. Most of these men died with Lieutenant James Calhoun on what would be called Calhoun Hill, while a few others died a half mile distant, with Custer, on what would later be called Last Stand Hill. What cavalry troops did survive did so only after prolonged fighting on a distant ridge, in what would later be called the "hilltop fight." There, a more fortunate 18 percent of Company L's men joined the other surviving troops for two days of fighting under the leadership of Major Marcus Reno and Captain Frederick Benteen, saved only by the arrival of Terry and fresh troops on the morning of June 27. "Our young men," Sitting Bull later explained, "rained lead across the river and drove the white braves back."[132]

By the chance assignment to guard cattle over one hundred miles away at the Powder River, Corporal Noonan avoided the fate of his company. This survival reflected in part the divergent rules for climbing the ladder of success offered to commissioned and noncommissioned officers in the nineteenth-century U.S. military. Commissioned officers such as Captain Louis Hamilton climbed the ranks in part by making names for themselves through demonstrations of ability and success in battle. For Hamilton, staying behind guarding the supplies at Washita would have denied him an opportunity to show this strength at a critical time in a young officer's career. He was within his rights to request a change in order to enter the fight and would have been admired or at least respected for it. His immediate loss in battle was not so much the result of his ambition but the system that guided it. Noncommissioned officers such as Noonan climbed the ladder differently, by following orders as smartly and efficiently as possible, never claiming more than what they were granted, and working ahead of their command and entirely in its service. This ladder of rank had room for pride and snap but rewarded duty and starch, allowing soldiers to rise within the seamless confluence of the noncommissioned officer and the commands of his superiors. If ordered to stay with cattle, he did so, and as efficiently as possible. The muster roll of Company L later recorded Corporal Noonan as "absent in charge of cattle herd at Powder River," with ten years' continuous service, and that he was drawing on his allotted ration of tobacco. He was also noted as the only corporal who survived the Battle of the Little Bighorn.

The *Far West* steamed into Bismarck late in the evening of July 5, docking at both Bismarck and Fort Lincoln to relay the terrible news and unload the wounded men for care. As the news spread through the fort, Mrs. Noonan may have feared for the worst, and at least one early report held that all of Company L had been lost. Seventh Cavalry laundress Emma Klawitter recalled being "panic stricken" as men were unloaded off the steamboat, thinking her soldier husband might be among them.[133] Over the next few weeks Mrs. Noonan watched the muffled deconstruction of the Custer patronage system as the women she worked for put on the black clothes of deep mourning, packed their belongings, and left the fort for good, possibly with Mrs. Noonan's help in getting their clothes ready for the trip and possibly with a few words of condolence on Mrs. Noonan's part. For Elizabeth Custer, it was the start of a lifetime career as George Custer's widow. For Mrs. Noonan, it meant the closing of the Custer opportunity window that she had carefully developed over several years, as well as the requirement of setting up a new one and starting fresh.[134] In the Custers' absence, and within the new and unfamiliar command of Colonel Samuel Sturgis, Corporal Noonan would have little chance to gain an impression through competing for orderly duty, and the new command would have little idea of who he was otherwise. He would follow the rules and rise up the ladder through the best duty he could manage despite the limited opportunities offered to noncommissioned officers. Mrs. Noonan had it a little better, as a fresh set of officers' wives would be quick to take advantage of her services in the start of new patronage systems. She was also quick to assert her territory among the laundresses; Emma Klawitter, now happily reunited with her husband, recalled that during the arrival of Sturgis, "soldiers with families were to have the biggest rooms" in the laundress quarters, which did not sit well with Mrs. Noonan. "General Custer let me pick out the quarters I wanted," Mrs. Noonan said, pounding her fist on the table, "and no soldier, no officer, and not even General [sic] Sturgis is going to put me out of here. I'd like to see them try. I have lived here since I came to Fort Lincoln and I'm going to die here." She kept her quarters.[135]

The Battle of the Greasy Grass, as the Lakotas and Cheyennes called the Battle of the Little Bighorn, was a powerful success for them, but a persistent American military presence pushed the war of attrition relentlessly past the momentary shock of Custer's loss. Terry stayed in the field, Sheridan sent in more troops, and the *Far West* immediately steamed back upriver with fresh supplies. Over the winter of 1876–77 most Indian families began to realize it was impossible to fight on with any success. Many moved onto reservations, where their guns and ponies would be taken from them, while a few fled north to Canada before eventually surrendering. A final detail in that chapter came with a series of running battles with a band of Nez Perce men over the summer and fall of 1877. The Nez Perces had as a whole avoided the conflicts that raged elsewhere, even as their own lands in the Pacific Northwest were being steadily reduced by treaties and mining claims. But while some bands were making their way to a reservation, some of their younger men killed four settlers while drunk and angry. Fearing retribution, the entire band fled, attempting first to find refuge with the Crows before turning north toward Canada, passing through the newly formed Yellowstone Park, and engaging with the Second and Seventh Cavalries in a series of escapes and battles before surrendering to General Nelson Miles just short of the Canadian border.[136] Mrs. Noonan may have watched as Chief Joseph and his tribe passed through Fort Lincoln on their way to Bismarck, where General Miles was offered an honorary banquet and toasts at the Sheridan House for his triumph. The next day a group of Nez Perce chiefs were invited to dinner at the same place by several Bismarck citizens, led by "Colonel" George Sweet, who introduced them to several silk-dressed women in the Sheridan House parlors before giving a speech about the superiority of white civilization while standing over a table laden with roast beef and salmon. Become farmers, Sweet said to his guests, or die like the buffalo. There was very little Shaved Head and Chief Joseph could say in reply to hospitality like that, and they focused instead on the importance of good sentiments. "I expect what I speak will be said throughout the land," Chief Joseph said through an interpreter, "and I only want to speak good."[137]

With scattered exceptions, what the Americans called the Indian Wars were essentially over. Military duties shifted to managing the new landscape. John Noonan had reached the rank of sergeant by the time his term of enlistment was up on January 14, 1877, and he immediately reenlisted the following day, continuing his commitment to both his career and his wife. Rank did not continue for reenlistments, and at thirty-one years old Noonan reentered the army as a private and set his path up the ladder once again, and he had risen to corporal by 1878. Yet for all their hard work, the Noonans' good life was set up on a delicate chain, where any broken link could send their world tumbling. The very worst thing that could happen was the death and exposure of Mrs. Noonan while John was away from the fort. They seem to have had no plan to protect them in case this happened, and this is exactly what happened during the fall of 1878. In that year, Corporal Noonan "broke camp" on July 25 for a four-month duty escorting Cheyenne captives southward along the Deadwood stage route. As summer merged into fall, the last good days of Noonan's life were spent around the Black Hills and climbing Bear Butte for the view of the surrounding landscape, much like the Vérendrye brothers had done over a century earlier. From Bear Butte's peaks Noonan probably saw the Black Hills in the distance, the endless moving freight wagons with their canvas covers looking like white specks. As the weather grew colder, he was assigned to scouting crossings along the Niobrara River, just as his greatest fear became reality.[138]

In the cold October air, Mrs. Noonan had contracted a case of pneumonia that developed into pleurisy. Pleurisy inflames the lining around the lungs, which can become dry, creating a sandpaper-like sound when linings rub harshly with every breath. Infection makes breathing even more difficult. A momentary relief from chest pain only indicates the condition is worsening; in fact, it means fluid is filling the pleural lining. For several days she lay in quarters, surrounded by sister laundresses who kept her fever as low as possible with damp towels and hushing words. She was probably no older than thirty or thirty-five, yet she realized she was facing death and began to make arrangements, setting aside "a bag of money," hidden inside her mattress, for the Catholic Church.[139] Catholicism was her link with her origins, a spiritual heritage and fidelity to the former Spanish lands and territories that now made up the American Southwest. Catholicism also formed a potential bond with many of the Irish laundresses with whom she worked. When the end became inevitable, the Reverend John Foffa, the pastor of Bismarck's Catholic parish, was sent for to hear her confession. Foffa listened to whatever small things she may have mentioned and returned across the river to Bismarck, where he was supervising the installation of a new bell at St. Mary's. Her caution with Foffa was prudent: upon news of her death, Foffa absolutely refused to provide services for her burial in light of the discovery. But while Foffa refused her soul, he embraced her money, which she had so carefully saved for the Catholic Church and hidden within her mattress, and he cut open the mattress himself.[140]

Corporal Noonan was over three hundred miles away when Mrs. Noonan died at four thirty in the morning of October 30, 1878. There was absolutely nothing he could do to protect her, nor had there been anything she could effectively do to protect him. She had tried, though, attempting to avoid detection one last time by asking the other laundresses to bury her "in the clothes she had on" to avoid the discovery of her anatomy.[141] But to them this request was improper and inconceivable; she required a decent burial, and that required washing the body followed by redressing in clean, respectable clothes. The news she worked so hard to avoid in life became inevitable in death. After waiting in silence for ten years, Godfrey saw the story finally emerge when "one of the laundresses volunteered to 'lay her out.' Soon after she commenced the ordeal," he recalled, "she came out of the quarters screaming 'Holy Mither of Moses, Holy Mither of Moses, etc.' The families rushed out to see what was the matter. She replied 'She's got balls as big as a bull, she's a man.'"[142]

The startling news swept across Fort Lincoln. It was shouted down the barracks halls, discussed in small groups upon the field ground, joked about during stable duties. The entire military post, from enlistees to officers, their wives, servants, laundresses, cooks, blacksmiths, lieutenants, captains, and privates all knew within hours, probably less. Laundresses who had long considered her "something" between a woman and a man saw their hunch confirmed, while others were astonished, curious, shocked, and confused.[143] Before long the news had spread across the river to Bismarck, and from there it spread by telegraph to the rest of the world. The *Bismarck Tribune* later reported on how "all Lincoln with Bismarck thrown in was plunged into a pleasurable curiosity to know the particulars," adding that other laundresses had reported that "Mrs. Noonan made the dying request that she be buried as she was then dressed. The request was disregarded, and the secret came out."[144] The death of the "supposed Mexican laundress" became a minor sensation, confirmed by the official report of W. D. Wolverton, the post surgeon, who wrote to the post's commander, "I examined the deceased in question assisted by A. A. Surgeon C. C. Miller U. S. A. and found the body that of a fully developed male in all that makes the difference in sex, without any abnormal condition that could cause doubt on the subject."[145]

"Corporal Noonan is in the field with the Seventh Cavalry," added the *Bismarck Tribune* somewhat jocularly, "and will probably swear when he hears the sad news."[146] In fact, Noonan's detachment was already preparing to return to Fort Lincoln. They left Nebraska's Niobrara River on November 2, moving northward in the brisk fall weather toward Camp Ruhlen, just fourteen miles from the new town of Deadwood and a few miles west of Bear Butte Creek in Dakota Territory, where the outpost guarded the bustling freight routes to the Black Hills. Four days later, they left for the final leg of the return trip to Fort Lincoln. If news of Mrs. Noonan's death had not already reached them, it would soon. The news had been telegraphed across the country and carried by newspapers and word of mouth wherever telegraphs had yet to go. The cavalry was moving north toward Fort Lincoln along the bustling "Bismarck Route" used by the North Western Stage & Express Company, whose stage wagons regularly carried the latest newspapers, the mail, and passengers between Bismarck and the Black Hills. News of interest was regularly hurled at passersby as the stages drove past, and Mrs. Noonan was a hot topic, leaving Noonan to mourn for his wife while suffering the abuse of his comrades on the march back. All eyes looked for him when his detachment finally entered Fort Lincoln on November 20.[147] Two days later, on November 22, First Lieutenant John W. Wilkenson, the commander of Company L, requested Noonan's discharge "for having been married to and cohabitated with a *man* as his wife." Wilkenson explained that "this man Noonan is looked upon by the members of his Company with feelings of repugnance, and detestation, and for the good of the service I earnestly recommend his discharge."[148]

The bias against living with "a *man* as his wife" was one count of many, all critical. Military life often blunted the latitude that individuals in both civilian and frontier worlds sometimes enjoyed, instead imposing strict regimentation that echoed and enforced the march of civilization with its intricate hierarchy of rules. Momentary encounters with distinctly nonmasculine individuals might not ordinarily have threatened a man's sense of personal masculinity, but Noonan's involvement and more importantly his commitment—especially his commitment to, and by implication, love for this partner, and within the military structure and environment—set up the intense visceral reaction among his former comrades. It wasn't about him but them. The reputation of a company was the reputation of its men. Noonan's actions placed every man in Company L directly in the firing line of jokes and innuendo hurled by every other soldier at the fort and were thus taken personally by every man in his company. Their own reputation was at stake. Noonan's former comrades probably also felt that he had deserted them for the good life of a married man, taking on privileges they did not share and living it up in comfort while they suffered in the barracks before he ultimately embarrassed the company—and by extension the entire army—by that conceit. This would have been seen as selfish and rude. But far worse, he was a noncommissioned officer, one of the rank-and-file who rose in the ranks to gain authority over his fellows. Noncommissioned officers, a Fort Lincoln officer wrote that December, were required to "personally see to the execution of the orders of the despotic officers over them, and are more or less obnoxious to privates" as a result of that duty. The same officer added that Noonan was "a rigid disciplinarian," which only made matters worse, indicating that he stubbornly stuck to the letter of the law in enforcing orders.[149] This last detail made this turnabout especially harsh. Every soldier he ordered, punished, or reprimanded seethed with loathing for him, no matter whether he was in the right or not or made the decisions or not. As far as the men of Company L were concerned, Noonan was the officer who gave them orders and was strict about them while living a comfortable life in private quarters with the wife and carpets and home-cooked meals; he was that noncommissioned officer who had the house and all the privileges they did not have. Discovering he had achieved this luxury and position from what they thought of as a fake wife struck them as a trick, and it was bitterly resented.

John Noonan's career and self-image collapsed in a matter of days, and in the worst way possible. His chosen profession of a career soldier was to be stripped away, his comrades jeered him, and his wife was gone. Six years of service with the cavalry, ten years of service with the army, an excellent military reputation, public standing, and private companionship were all destroyed in an instant. His very bearings upon the world as he had known it had traumatically shifted. There was not even privacy in his grief, for his trunk and personal belongings were unceremoniously removed from his old quarters to the barracks. In that one large room, lined with beds, trunks, and former comrades, and likely in the worst bed in the room, the farthest from the stove and coldest at night, he could not escape the angry repudiation heaped upon him by his company. "Aren't you lonely without your wife?" Company L soldier John Burkman reportedly recalled jeering at Noonan.[150]

The timing could not have been worse. The military brass were already dealing with dents upon their public image, and they did not need any other, especially something as unexpectedly curious as Mrs. Noonan. Some were largely nuisances, such as Captain Thomas French of Company M, Seventh Calvary, charged with public drunkenness, debauchery with laundresses, and periodic absence without leave; he would be "too drunk to appear" at his court-martial in Bismarck the following January.[151] Situations like that of French could be addressed carefully, and local newspaper reports of the hearings never mentioned French's name, allowing the army to handle the situation as smoothly as possible. But other situations made national news, and one of these was gearing up at that very moment. Mrs. Noonan died just two months before a military court of inquiry opened in Chicago to examine charges of cowardice against one of the Seventh Cavalry's ranking officers, Major Marcus Reno, for his actions during the Battle of the Little Bighorn. During the battle, Reno found himself forced into a defensive position, unable to reinforce George Custer's troops, and subsequently blamed for Custer's defeat. Although Reno had requested the hearing in hopes of clearing his name, the embarrassing public association of a Seventh Cavalry officer with incompetence and cowardice informed the general feeling of frustration and anger that influenced the circumstances in which Noonan found himself.[152]

The minor sensation of Mrs. Noonan paled in comparison to the implications of the Reno hearing, but the public nature of Noonan's story, along with the trespass against social convention and military honor felt by his associates, required an equally demonstrative and public punishment to save face. News of Mrs. Noonan's death had reached Chicago by November 1 and Washington the following day. Washington was most critical; in the halls of government, every ally or opponent of the cavalry and the military program would now be aware of the story. Colonel Sturgis endorsed Wilkenson's request for a dishonorable discharge on November 23, 1878, with a damning request of his own: "If there is any law by which this man could be sent to the penitentiary," Sturgis stated, "I would respectfully suggest that it be called into requisition in his case."[153] Sturgis was already suffering from dents to his own reputation, primarily for his criticism of Custer and his subsequent mediocre performance during the Nez Perce campaign. It appears he wanted Noonan to be punished as severely as possible, as well as sent to prison for as long as necessary, to protect his own reputation. At the headquarters for the Military Department of Dakota in St. Paul, military brass concurred, and Sturgis was "instructed to bring the case to the attention of the U.S. District Attorney."[154]

Noonan's record suggests a man so devoted and accustomed to the military environment and so aligned with its principles of honor with obedience that the thought of desertion at this point appears to have been inconceivable. Yet even if he had wanted to, running away would have been nearly impossible. The fastest and most efficient way out of Bismarck was by rail, and a daily Northern Pacific passenger train left Bismarck for Duluth and all points east every evening at 7:10. But in such a small community as Bismarck, where the fort was an anchor and every soldier a familiar face, Noonan could not walk down Bismarck's streets without being recognized, much less purchase a train ticket or travel out of town in anonymity. He might have stowed away on a freight train, but without a ferry to get him across the river to Bismarck, the point was moot. The other way out of Bismarck was by the river itself, on a steamboat. But river traffic was seasonal, and boats on the upper reaches of the Missouri could run only from mid-April to early November, when water ran high and free of ice. The last of the Bismarck traffic was already dashing for their winter berths by the time Mrs. Noonan died on October 30. The steamboat *F. Y. Batchelor* arrived into Bismarck around November 5, marking the last boat in and the end of that season's navigation.[155] By the time Noonan had returned with his detachment to Fort Lincoln on November 20, the river was closed, and Bismarck's riverbanks were dotted with dormant steamboats with empty boilers and greased-over machinery, silently waiting for the coming spring. Noonan might alternately have taken one of the stage lines out of the city, or even a teamster's wagon, but like everything else in Bismarck, even with one thousand teams freighting out of Bismarck to points west, its businesses were local, and everyone would have recognized him, if not immediately, then before a few miles were gained, when he would inevitably be reported missing. Then again, Noonan might simply have walked away, alone into the wilderness, but here he would inevitably meet his death by freezing in the snow or slow starvation. The situation crushed him. Unable to run, surrounded by jeers and insults, and threatened with prison and hard labor, he kept as much out of the way as possible but ultimately succumbed. On November 30, exactly one month after his wife's death and ten days after returning to the fort, he walked into a Fort Lincoln stable and shot himself in the head, surrounded by the horses that had made his life's career. By that point, the horses were the only forms of life on the military post not deriding or making fun of him.[156]

With both Noonans dead, whatever remained of their household effectively vanished. Whatever personal belongings they had, whatever letters, keepsakes, or mementos, whatever tools and household supplies, were scattered to the winds after their trunks were opened. Their furniture, rugs, and pictures disappeared. Their chickens were instantly claimed by their neighbors, and their polished tins were taken away. John Noonan's clothes and equipment were distributed among the soldiers, while his saddle, arms, and military furnishings went to others. The Laundress's prized dresses and bolts of fabric were scattered among the other laundresses, altered or cut apart, and remade to suit new owners.

Their marriage certificate, along with the ones that Mrs. Noonan had saved from her two previous marriages, were noted by a Bismarck correspondent for the *Chicago Tribune*. "Her letters have been unearthed," he remarked, "and the only plausible theory of her marriage to a man was her horrid immorality."[157] Corporal Noonan's letters to his wife, from Mrs. Noonan's ransacked trunk, were read almost immediately, even while Noonan was still in the field. Addressed "Dear Wife" and signed "Your Darling Hubby," they offered an affection unfathomable to his contemporaries.[158]

Corporal Noonan's portrayal as an implied sodomist became embarrassingly problematic for the cavalry, for if an excellent soldier such as Noonan could have done such a thing, the theory went, any outstanding officer or soldier could. The entire army was therefore suspect. As long as Noonan lived, the path to regaining the cavalry's honor was through prosecuting Noonan to the fullest extent, through the authority of the military in a public demonstration of indignation, outrage, and principle. But his death absolutely halted any chance of public prosecution, while the problem of the public image persistently remained. A solution unexpectedly came a few days later on December 2 with the first of two works of lurid satirical fiction from the renegade pen of the *Bismarck Tribune*'s sensational new editor, Stanley Huntley. Huntley was a thirty-three-year-old journalist of "long experience and varied accomplishments" from the *Chicago Times* who agreed to take over the *Bismarck Tribune* from its founding editor, Clement Lounsberry. He was also a satirist, famous for writing comedic stories with titles such as "The Lost Collar Button" and "Opening the Sardines" along with a popular humor series he later wrote about a fictional couple he named the Spoopendykes.[159] Huntley traveled to Bismarck in company with Marshall Jewell, a twenty-one-year-old associate from the *Chicago Telegraph*, and the two reporters settled into the *Tribune*'s Bismarck offices just weeks before Mrs. Noonan's death offered the scoop of a lifetime.[160]

Under Huntley, the *Bismarck Tribune* had initially reported Mrs. Noonan's death and Corporal Noonan's subsequent suicide with dutiful accuracy and minimal fuss. But on December 2 Huntley changed his tack with the first of two entirely invented fictional stories. In the first, a fictional "Noonan" would insist he never knew about his wife's body and was wholly innocent (while nonetheless helping her with one of her many abortions), while in the second, the Laundress would be brought back from the dead through a "séance" to take the blame and declare him innocent. The "interview" and "séance" were more than attempts at winter humor; they were critical parts of the effort to exonerate Noonan for the good of the cavalry and society. As long as Noonan lived, he was to be made guilty and punished to the full extent of the law. But Noonan's death made punishment impossible and forced this effort into the civilian hands of the *Bismarck Tribune* editorship, from which the full blame of the situation could be tossed directly onto the Laundress's lap. Noonan himself was immaterial; he was persecuted or saved as required or convenient to achieve the larger goal of restoring the cavalry's public reputation.

The fictional Noonan's "interview" began with some genuine information: that the real Noonan had laid low for a few days, that his comrades gave him the cold shoulder, and that his suicide caused a lot of excitement at the fort. But that was as far as it went. Huntley then launched into a series of jokes that cast lurid titillation upon the tragedy: "When I married her sir," the fictional Noonan was made to claim, "I believed her to be a woman, and I never knew to the contrary until I heard of the *post mortem*." "You were a husband to her, were you not," the fictional reporter asks, "a husband in all that the name implies?" In other words, the fictional reporter asks the fictional Noonan if he was having sex with his wife. "I was," the fictional Noonan replies, "so help me God, but the later revelations mystify me. I can't understand it." Huntley repeated this sensational, dirty joke for a second round, this time adding purpose and suggestive misalignment. The fictional Noonan innocently insisted that they "longed for children, but there seemed to be something I could not understand that prevented the full fruition of our hopes." He then verged into the fantasy of tragic motherhood: "she told me of the coming footsteps pattering on the clouds, but it resulted in nothing but pain and sickness." With this joke finished, Huntley turned to a new and contradictory sensation, claiming that the fictional Mrs. Noonan had several abortions as a result of "heavy burdens" that had "relax[ed] her muscles" and was helped in one case by the fictional Noonan. The final pitch attributed Mrs. Noonan's transgender life to "some dark mystery," which always played better when left open to speculation and was the literary equivalent of stagehands shaking sheets of metal to create the sound of an ominous thunderstorm. The fictional Mrs. Noonan "must have done something terribly wrong which demanded a disguise of her sex," although the fictional Noonan could not "understand how the alteration could benefit her."[161]

Huntley was using the personal tragedy of a dedicated soldier to build a pathetic, burlesque picture of a man fumbling in the dark around his supposed wife. He either did not care about the opinions of the military when writing about a soldier or was only exaggerating feelings that they and others already felt; in turning Noonan into a joke, Huntley was doing on the literary stage what many among the post's rank-and-file were already doing personally. In this he summarized the real Noonan's situation succinctly, if melodramatically. "They can pronounce her man, woman, God or devil as they see fit," the fictional Noonan declares, "but I am doomed to the infamy and can find no relief."[162]

Huntley's "interview" became a minor national sensation. Stacks of the *Bismarck Tribune* were routinely loaded onto Northern Pacific trains for delivery to each significant city and depot point, where they made their way into local newspaper offices hungry for national news. The story's route across the country can be traced through railroad timetables and its reprinting in the press of the nation: six days to reach Chicago, nine to reach New York and Washington. From there, newspapers in St. Paul, Minnesota; Jackson, Mississippi; Deer Lodge, Montana Territory; and Gold Hill, Nevada, all printed the fictitious interview within two weeks. It was ludicrous but effective, cleaning up the story for the public eye, establishing an image of an innocent Noonan in the national mind, or at least placing doubt upon his complicity. Noonan was unaware, the nation read, and the Laundress had tricked him. Huntley's story and its media presence in the newspapers of a nation effectively reined in the narrative and returned the cavalry and its soldiers to a respectable position.

Like all good professionals, Huntley left the story open for an even more sensational sequel. "There is something beyond my wife's grave," the fictional Noonan vows, "that must be settled at some time, and there will be a time when the mystery will be cleared up." Huntley was already thinking ahead. But the only way to take the story further was to invoke the departed laundress herself, and for this Huntley needed a specialist. A "French trance medium" promptly materialized at Bismarck, ready to flush the Laundress back from the mist and declare Noonan innocent. As "Madame La Secher" called the spirits, "Mrs. Noonan" arrived with a wild story of improbable actions: she was, or at least had been, living in disguise because she had drugged and slaughtered an entire family in Washington. She then practiced medicine in New Orleans but was discovered. To escape prosecution, there was naturally no other option but to change identities and start a career as a military laundress. But in death, however, life caught up with her, and she was "surrounded by the damned" and paying penance. "Oh!" she cried, "This is hell! The dead stare at me in the face!! The worst of it is all the little ones I strangled." The windup then led to the pitch: "Corporal Noonan is not with me," the departed laundress proclaims. "He is better off than I am. I deceived him from the time of our marriage. He always believed me to be a woman, and I was afraid to reveal my sex or name, for fear he would drive me from him or tell what I had done. He was a man of fine honor and integrity, and I knew he would abandon me if he knew I had ever been guilty of crime."[163] "Madame La Secher" appeared in the newspaper three or so times over several weeks, each report describing a séance that had supposedly occurred in some discreet location among select guests. Over time, her levitating levies revived Mrs. Noonan, a woman called Morphine Liz, and finally a floating parlor table that simply rambled about a room bumping into people. "I don't want no trouble myself," the fictional medium assured the *Tribune*'s readers in January 1879, "but I can get there as quick as any one if it once commences."[164]

Huntley's creation of Madam La Secher probably referenced the genuine spiritual interests of Colonel George Sweet, who had hosted Chief Joseph the year before at the Sheridan House dinner. Sweet wasn't alone in believing in spiritualism, but he risked becoming a crank in embracing it to the extent that he did. The spiritualism craze in America had begun thirty years earlier, when a prank played by two girls caught the national imagination. Few people really took it seriously. The majority of it was parlor work—simple tricks to amuse guests and while away the hours of an evening. But for Sweet, spiritualism seemed to be a new form of religious faith, and in early 1878 he gave a lecture, "Spiritualism, the Religion of the Future," before an audience of patient but weary friends.[165] Huntley ridiculed Sweet for this by reporting that Sweet was underwriting Madame La Secher as a sort of spiritual mistress to the tune of fifty dollars a month and that the fifty-five-year-old Sweet was watching his diet and taking up an interest in exercise.[166] But the joke was wearing thin, and Huntley had other things on his mind. He married Florence Chance in January 1879, only days after dodging Madame La Secher's parlor table, and left Bismarck for a career in the East writing articles and humorous stories, which Florence Huntley continued after his death in the 1880s.[167]

By the spring of 1879, Corporal and Mrs. Noonan had largely been forgotten. The winter's ice began to break up along the Missouri River as dormant steamers began to swarm with men, preparing for the coming season's navigation. The first successful crops were sowed on the farms surrounding Bismarck. That summer, Father John Foffa briefly traveled up the Yellowstone River before returning to Bismarck to celebrate mass, while George Sweet rambled west to explore and speculate. Madame La Secher simply disappeared into the mist. The Northern Pacific Railroad recovered its finances and resumed construction westward. For the first time, graders began turning over earth for the railroad's roadbed on the western bank of the Missouri, followed by construction of a massive trestle of steel girders spanning the Missouri with its metallic web, and finally the whistles of locomotives. Bismarck no longer stood on the edge of the frontier. Instead, it stood on the cusp of a new dawn, having become a bustling center of supply between river and rail, a farming region and a commercial center, a prosperous city crowded with wagons and freight. Marshall Jewell was a keeper: he took over the *Bismarck Tribune* with the assistance of its original founder and stayed on as editor for over thirty years.[168] In the summer of 1883, he noted how "one success after another has crowned the efforts of our people to build up their city and make it attractive, and to-day its people are in the height of their prosperity."[169]

The final arc of the story would come six years later, from the most unassailably civilized, respectable, and proper of voices, when Elizabeth Custer included her memories of Mrs. Noonan in her published memoirs. Released in the spring of 1885, her book *"Boots and Saddles"* portrayed the faithful devotion and sacrifice of military wives in following the flag while she defended and glorified her late husband's military reputation. By including Mrs. Noonan in her narrative, she shifted that story's course to an entirely new path. It was a woman's time now, and this time the soldiers would be tossed to the dogs and the Laundress would be made innocent.

Elizabeth Custer described Mrs. Noonan as a peculiarly innocent soul. She was one of the team, a sister worker in the army of women supporting the military's role in bringing civilization to the plains. Custer was one of the very few people able to make this statement from an informed perspective: she had known Mrs. Noonan personally and relied on her regularly for the support of her own household. She also valued the dedication and loyalty Mrs. Noonan offered, "considered her a treasure," and appears to have respected her, within the standard social stratifications of the era, or possibly even admired her. The most striking element is her portrayal of Mrs. Noonan as a woman, despite the fame of Mrs. Noonan after her death and the role of that fame in encouraging Elizabeth Custer's own retelling. She related the discovery of Mrs. Noonan's anatomy as male, yet she continued to describe her as a woman and emphasize her virtues as a woman. This perspective was calculated, but it also seems to have been somewhat sincere. Her personal and extended experience with Mrs. Noonan in the Yates household was probably critical to developing this sense of understanding, allowing her to intimately observe the compassion, care, and devotion that Mrs. Noonan offered to Annie Yates during the difficulties of childbirth. As a result, she described Mrs. Noonan as sharing her own values, writing that Mrs. Noonan led a "quiet, orderly life" and that she "knew her to be tender-hearted."[170] That is, while she lived the rough life of camp women, she upheld principles of hard work, decorum, and decency and was personally kind and thoughtful. Elizabeth Custer never attempted to explain Mrs. Noonan but simply depicted her as a benign oddity, as a sweet but curious creature with moral principles, as someone who lived poorly but in the most respectable way possible. "The bed was hung with pink cambric," she recalled of Mrs. Noonan's home on suds row, "and on some shelves she showed us silk and woolen stuffs for gowns; bits of carpet were on the floor, and the dresser, improvised out of a packing box, shone with polished tins."[171]

In Elizabeth Custer's world, these polished tins were critical: they were the markers of a charming step toward realizing the advance of civilization. Mrs. Noonan didn't let her humble tins tarnish or dull; she kept them polished, as one would the family silver, and displayed them to their glory upon an improvised dresser. This was a demonstration of personal dignity and an imitation of the grandeur of respectable houses in the civilized world, as well as a sign of her character as the loyal, industrious, and dutiful wife. Elizabeth Custer saw Mrs. Noonan's carpets, pictures, and proud little garden as emblems of civilization on the frontier and Mrs. Noonan's activity creating such a home a civilizing element itself, which would uphold and advance nineteenth-century standards regardless of condition or environment, especially in this case. This notion was a projection: Mrs. Noonan appears to have had little concern for larger affairs of civilization or its advance into a wilderness and was more likely simply imitating the grandeur and glory of the great houses for an imaginary life, much as she did with her ball gowns.

The result of this experience was telling. In Elizabeth Custer's account, the Laundress is never vilified or even derided apart from being part of the laundress class. Instead, she was simply one of the odd aspects of human nature one encounters in life on the far-flung reaches of human existence. Mrs. Noonan was the human frontier, in a frontier landscape, actively working to boost civilization while retaining her personal frontier in doing so through simple delights such as making dresses, dancing, baking pies, carefully tending to the laundry, fussing over starched pleats, or carefully pounding the dust of campaign from George Custer's woolen shirts.

It was simple for Elizabeth Custer to portray Mrs. Noonan's first two husbands as scoundrels, courting her only long enough to gain possession of her savings before immediately deserting her. This avoided any issues of potential sexuality by emphasizing greed and thievery, allowing the husbands, while dishonest and corrupt, to remain what would later be considered masculine and heterosexual. Corporal Noonan then posed a quandary. Elizabeth Custer clearly remembered him and his handsome figure, as well as his loyal service to her family as an orderly and his excellent reputation as an experienced, dedicated soldier. Yet Noonan's name had also been prominently featured in Huntley's vulgar, sensational stories, cementing associations that socially proper ladies such as Elizabeth Custer went to great pains to avoid lest they become tainted by the association. This last point was critical: Custer's personal reputation, her professional goals, and her new career as George Custer's widow required an absolute quality of untouchability. To solve this problem, Elizabeth Custer employed a careful stratagem: removing the Noonan name entirely, while simultaneously gliding over any issues of intimacy by describing the Noonans' dedicated and intimately loving marriage as nothing more than a "*mariage de convenance*."[172] To advance this new picture, she deliberately renamed Mrs. Noonan, calling her "Mrs. Nash," after one of the earlier deserter-husbands, the dishonorable cads whose story was sufficiently distant to escape any critical observation. If Mrs. Noonan once carried the name "Old Jennie Nash" for a few distant days, she had been Mrs. Noonan for nearly three years by the time Elizabeth Custer left the fort and had been Mrs. Noonan for five years at the time of her death, and she carried that name in all press accounts of her death. By changing the name, Elizabeth Custer protected herself, the army's reputation, and even Corporal Noonan's memory. It was a purely political and calculated invention, a simple rebranding of a problematic property.

To this end, Elizabeth Custer's portrayal of Mrs. Noonan turned a potentially embarrassing story into a remarkable advantage. She was able to mold the account in the popular mind to her own requirements while maintaining and emphasizing the glory and bravery of her husband and the military society that surrounded her husband. She recognized Mrs. Noonan as a subtle ally: a loyal, hardworking woman tirelessly supporting the military and its goals. But far more than this, Elizabeth Custer implicitly recognized Mrs. Noonan as a transgender woman and presented her as a supporting member of the metaphoric chorus surrounding the cavalry as it led the charge of civilization into the open frontier, where transgender laundresses were simply benign oddities in the grand sweep of culture and civilization. In its own hierarchical and demure, shrewdly calculated way, it echoed the magnificent tumult of the American scene in Walt Whitman's poems. Roustabouts, teamsters, dogs, warriors, and laundresses all took part in this big picture, an inevitable movement toward American supremacy upon the continent, one made up of innumerable people and stories, harnessed by moral and cultural bonds, where "all classes and conditions" came together in a singular moment of the American experience. In this way, she made Mrs. Noonan part of a larger American pantheon of heroes dutifully enacting their parts in what nineteenth-century Americans were already calling American Progress.[173]

So who was the Laundress? Where did she come from? At first, he was likely a Hispanic man who enjoyed dresses and dressing up and liked being in the company of men, especially soldiers, along with the associative sense of security, stability, and family that the military structure offered. He was literate, bilingual, and a skilled worker with a strong work ethic that covered a diversity of roles, from teamster to army laundress. He was probably born in the 1840s, possibly in what would become or already was New Mexico Territory, and was Catholic, as evidenced by the request for a Catholic priest for confession at the end and leaving a bequest for the Catholic Church. His life as a teamster for the U.S. Army of the 1860s regularly put him on the open road with small groups of men, for whom he tended the wagons and their teams for weeks at a time and which taught him to rely on these men for security, sociability, and protection from the dangers of the trail. His transition to the identity of a women occurred at Fort Leavenworth, Kansas, during the first three months of 1868 under the protection of a particularly willing and well-placed military officer, possibly guided by the model of Two-Spirit people he might have encountered among the New Mexican pueblos and on the southern plains. In the women's world she remained and flourished as a laundress, tailor, cook, and midwife, effectively diversifying her portfolio of skills under the protective but simultaneously dangerous wing of army service. She was married three times, was victimized by the first two marriages and successful in the third, and dealt with the realities of life through a cushion of internal fantasy and a carefully imagined external identity. In so doing, she effectively created a woman's life not only in her present but also in an imaginary past. This identity allowed her to live within the broad and stable structure of military hierarchy that allowed a dependable foundation for her life and helped minimize the chances of being discovered or interrupted. Those disruptions that did occur were effectively handled save the last, which also cost the life of her third husband. In this last relationship both parties clearly took a significant risk. Yet they did so while pursuing mutually exemplary careers in military service, as a well-regarded laundress and career soldier, respectively, and succeeded in doing so for five years.

FIG. 1. The hundred-mile Stockton-to-Mariposa run had been the longest of Charley Parkhurst's three stage routes, a day-long jaunt from the Central Valley to the Sierra foothills. He had moved to the coastal community of Monterey by 1859, about the same time this stage was photographed at the Oso House, along his former Mariposa run. Carleton Watkins, *Oso House, Bear Valley, Mariposa County*, about 1859–60. The J. Paul Getty Museum, Los Angeles.

FIG. 2. Private John Noonan (*upper right*) was serving as George Custer's orderly the day Custer shot a grizzly bear in the Black Hills, inadvertently preserving his image for posterity. This copy was owned by Elizabeth Custer, who wrote Noonan's name on the back along with her husband's name plus the others. W. H. Illingworth, *Bloody Knife, General George Armstrong Custer, Private John Noonan and Colonel William Ludlow, with a Bear*, 1874. National Park Service, Little Bighorn National Monument, Big Horn County, Montana.

FIG. 3. Elizabeth Custer (*standing, center*) relied on Mrs. Noonan's laundering skills to uphold and reinforce the standards of civilization in both military and domestic ideals, consciously recorded in photographs like this, taken at Fort Abraham Lincoln in 1875. A white-gloved orderly, possibly John Noonan, stands on the porch in attendance. Long after Mrs. Noonan's death in 1878, Elizabeth Custer purposefully continued to describe her as a woman, even while describing the discovery of Mrs. Noonan's male anatomy, effectively placing her among a pantheon of determined women advancing the cause of civilization across the West. *Group on the Front Steps of the Custer Home, Fort Abraham Lincoln, Dakota Territory*, 1874. National Park Service, Little Bighorn Battlefield National Monument.

FIG. 4. At the time William Breakenridge served there in law enforcement, the mining town of Tombstone, Arizona Territory, existed on the borders of civilization. Breakenridge thought it perfectly peaceful, but its citizens nonetheless lined the streets to eagerly watch a "desperate street fight" between the Earp brothers and their cowboy-rustler foes. Carleton Watkins, *Street in Tombstone, Arizona*, 1880. California State Library.

FIG. 5. William Breakenridge (*second from right*) spent a lifetime negotiating the borders of frontier and civilization. Much of this time was spent in surveying and law enforcement, balanced with an impossible passion for a charismatic cattle rustler. He was photographed here among a group of early Arizona settlers, conscious of their posterity and influence. *Arizona Pioneers (Six men, two of whom are identified as Marcus Smith and William Breakenridge, early settlers of Arizona)*, about 1890. State Archives, Arizona State Library and Public Records.

FIG. 6. Ora Chatfield (*far left*) was back with her family when they posed for this photograph on the Colorado Midland tracks near Basalt, in the Roaring Fork Valley, possibly for a wedding in December 1900. Her parents, Mary and Clark Chatfield, are on the right. *Ora Chatfield and Family*, courtesy of Catherine Seveneau.

FIG. 7. A 1914 study found that homosexuality was common and "developed" within California lumber camps, while a retired lumberman later remarked that nearly all the men he encountered in a Colorado lumber camp, and about half of the fifty or so men at his California mining camp, engaged each other (and him) to various degrees. *Logging Camp*, Pacific Lumber Company, Scotia, California, about 1910. California State Library.

4

William Breakenridge and the Human Borderlands

Twenty-seven years after the Scotsman William Stewart made his last trip across the prairies and just as Captain Louis Hamilton was guarding the Kansas Pacific Railway's construction across them, a party of Union Pacific Railroad surveyors and their military guard stood at attention on a low hill in present-day Wyoming, on the banks of Crow Creek, not far from the Rocky Mountains. It was July 4, 1867, and General Grenville Dodge, along with his officers and soldiers and the Union Pacific survey crew they were there to protect, looked out from a hillside the general had named Cheyenne. "I was called upon to recite the Declaration of Independence," recalled one of the men present, a railroad consulting engineer named Silas Seymour, but as "no one present had an authentic copy, I was obliged to improvise the following for the occasion":

> When in the course of human events it becomes necessary for a community composed of military Officers, with 350 rank and file, Government Directors, and civil Engineers of the Union Pacific Railroad, with their friends, to sever their social relations with the people of the United States and all the rest of mankind, it seems eminently proper that they should publish to the world the reasons which have induced them to emigrate to, and establish this goodly city of Cheyenne, at the Eastern base of the Rocky Mountains, of the Western half of the American continent, six thousand miles above

the level of the sea, within the shadows and beneath the summits of Long's Peak and of the great Snowy and Black Hills Ranges.[1]

They were joking, but only barely. Time in the field surveying a route for a railroad had placed them in daily contact with an open wilderness, far from the rituals of civilization that they complained about. There was no need for white starched shirts on the slopes of the Rockies, or the elaborate rituals of etiquette demanded in Long Branch or Saratoga Springs. Nor was there the sufferance of humid summer business weeks in Washington or New York City, at least where the Platte River ran clear and cold. They had discovered what was for them a kind of endless summer among the plains and mountains, where they could live week after week in plain, comfortable clothes and speak their plain, comfortable language.

> And generally, to do just about as we please at all times and under all circumstances, with due regard and gentlemanly respect to our companions, and a proper observance of the laws of Nature and Nature's God, which reign supreme throughout all this vast and beautiful country.[2]

The irony they well knew and commented on was cruel. Every sighting of the surveyor's theodolite brought the rails that much farther into the West and that much farther into the frontier. Their work in surveying and engineering a railroad right-of-way was making it possible to destroy the very world they had only recently come to know and love, a landscape shaped and scooped by teams of graders along the surveys of their own making.

> Although we are now so far from the Westerly confines of civilization, we expect within a few short months to be broken in upon by the shrill whistle of the locomotive upon the Great Union Pacific Railroad, which is now making such rapid progress through these beautiful plains, and necessarily bringing with it all the evils, as

well as many of the blessings of the very civilization which we have renounced and endeavoured to escape.[3]

Among the men working on the Union Pacific Railroad that summer of 1867 was a twenty-one-year-old Wisconsin man named William Breakenridge. In later years, his old associates would joke about him as a gay man: "You know Billy and I know Billy," one of them wrote to another. "He was in those days a nice girl, and in his declining years should be a nice old lady," they joked. In the summer of 1867, however, that "nice young girl" Breakenridge was employed as a brakeman, the single most dangerous job in railroading. At that time, automatic air brakes did not yet exist, and all trains, whether long or short, had to be braked by hand. That meant stopping tons of steel, iron, and wood, and men charged with that task forcefully turned brake wheels attached to chains, levers, and brake shoes that gradually fought momentum and brought the train to a halt. It was a dangerous job, remarked Joseph Taylor in 1874, a "game of 'catch who can' with death" or certain injury.[4] The brakemen on passenger cars could conveniently stand on the end platforms and turn the brake wheels, but the brake wheels on freight cars were extended up to the roof, where brakemen stood, exposed to the worst of it; as many as five men could be found running along the top of a single freight train, especially on mountain grades, jumping from car to car to work the brake wheels. In bad weather they stood through rain or snow, but in good weather they had the finest view in the world, and in the West, this view was nothing less than a vast, grand, and spectacular panorama of open blue skies above fields of tawny green. It's the same world that William Stewart saw, but from a platform a few feet higher and a good deal faster. In July 1867 brakemen like Breakenridge were regularly seeing herds of antelope, buffalo, and even, on very rare occasions, a plains grizzly.

Breakenridge didn't come for the nature, at least in the educated, upper-class way that General Dodge's officers and their civil engineer compatriots had come to love. Nor did he look with respect and appreciation to the Native peoples who already lived there, as Stewart had done. He was instead, like many of his day, all for the rush of civilization and the suppression of any obstacle, native or otherwise, that got in its way. For him, the West was opportunity to live as he wanted and the call of manifest destiny only a ticket to claim and justify that prospect. He was not sentimental; he appears instead to have been an opportunist, grandiose about his minor place in the world, perpetually cloaking himself time after time in the authority of the railroad, or civilization, or law, or whatever happened to be convenient. Yet while he rode the coattails of civilization to get to the West and clung to civilization for the security and righteousness of its authority, he perpetually sought its outer edges, where he could enjoy these things with minimal burden or obligation of conformity and restriction. He also found himself strongly drawn to men who thwarted these works through their easy disregard of civilization. This was his own irony, as inherent to his own life as that of the men on Cheyenne Hill. He was surfing the waves of civilization into the frontier, while simultaneously seeking a life without its restrictive boundaries.

The life to which he appears to have been perpetually drawn existed along civilization's outer edges, offering a life of free and easy opportunity, short-term contracts building this, moving that, always granting freedom of movement afterward, always with an out if he didn't like it. A whole class of men came of age in this world, with dispositions and trades that would only work on the edges of civilization and in half-built towns that placed this state of life in a physical stage for them to, as a nineteenth-century saying went, "run the place to suit themselves." Frontier towns thrived in this half-built nature, but as they came into their own and inevitably became more or less fully civilized, this generation of men would inevitably move on to the next town, slightly rougher and slightly newer. They were camp followers of civilization's move westward, except they looked for the best part of the forward wave. Throughout the nineteenth century, they embraced this self-imposed netherworld, enforcing and creating that which they themselves would run from when completed, surfing the frontier, looking for the next undiscovered waves. Boomtown after boomtown drew them in like moths, only to drive them out after things changed and civilization became too restrictive. By the 1890s there was nowhere else to go but Alaska.

Breakenridge was born in December 1846 in Wisconsin, where he later worked as a newsboy on the cars of a local railroad before moving west as a teenager and signing up as a teamster for the U.S. Army Quartermaster Department in Missouri. A year later he followed his older brother George across the Great Plains to the newly established city of Denver, in Colorado Territory, where they ran freight wagons supplying miners during the Pikes Peak gold rush of 1859.[5] In those days, Denver served as a supply station on the way to the Rocky Mountain mines, and Breakenridge recalled its population as "largely transient," a city of strangers, perpetually moving in, then on.[6] Yet even then, as isolated as it was, hundreds of miles from the Missouri River, it was being built up in brick, every piece of which was transported by teams of freight wagons across the plains and through the Native nations. Less than a year earlier, boasted one of Denver's earliest newspapers, "there was not a frame building in Denver City, a fact, which, when we survey the town to day, with its seven hundred edifices of brick and wood, with its large stores and spacious warehouses, stocked with the necessaries and luxuries of life, appears to be incredible . . . we have actually eclipsed all previous advances in civilization."[7]

Commerce was the handmaid of progress, and Denver's boosters emphasized that with progress, "the laws and customs of enlightened and civilized communities maintain undisputed sway" in that place, where "but a few months since was an unbroken wilderness."[8] The brick and gumption of the young municipality of Denver was an instant demonstration of its ambition, faith, and confidence in its future. The log houses soon disappeared, save for a tiny few, hidden from sight and forgotten, one of which was found by accident a century later and ceremoniously hauled into a museum for safekeeping as a pioneer relic.[9] By the time Breakenridge arrived, Denver had evolved so quickly that the log structures were already relics. He worked briefly as a page for the Colorado Territorial Legislature, a prime job for a teenager and one that put him into the halls of power and provided potential access to a political career as well as the attention of Denver's young ladies, but he left to work wagon teams once again, this time for a telegraph company linking Central

City to Denver by telegraph wire. "When the line was completed," he recalled, "I went to work as a messenger boy at that place and, as the mine managers were very generous, and always paid me well for delivering their messages promptly, I made good wages."[10]

Denver's early years were interrupted at two points by emergencies—one real, one imagined—that appeared to threaten the city. The real emergency came in 1862, with an approach of Texans under the Confederate flag seeking to capture Denver. They had already captured Santa Fe and were looking toward a larger push to control territory across the West. The Colorado Volunteers rapidly formed in response to the threat and found a new hero in a burly, aggressive man named John Chivington, a Methodist preacher who discovered a passion for mayhem that war granted, along with carte blanche.[11] In March 1862 the Coloradans marched south to meet the Texans, confronting them at a place now known as Glorieta Pass, where they fought for several hours to the point of standstill. The tide turned only when the Coloradans managed to destroy the Texan supply train, burning "their wagons, eighty in number, containing all their ammunition and supplies," effectively preventing them from advancing any farther and placing Denver completely beyond their grasp.[12]

The imagined emergency came two years later, when Indian fever struck Denver, prodded by resentment toward the Cheyennes and Arapahos that increased directly in proportion to the commercial value of the land and the length of the trip across the plains necessary for the Americans to reach it. By the early 1860s the attitude in Denver and its surrounding regions had become violently anti-Indian. Once again Chivington sought reasons to fight, this time with the righteous potential of no quarter given, which erupted into a brutal massacre of Indians gathered for treaty at Sand Creek on November 29, 1864. In the melee, the old notions of plains traditions and Indian manners were shot to pieces by the new; 133 Cheyennes and Arapahos were killed, including 105 women and their children. Black Kettle, who later died during Captain Louis Hamilton's charge at Washita, had supported peace and thought that an array of American flags raised over the camp would protect them, but Chivington wanted a fight, and nothing would stop him. The massacre broke this sense of the world, infuriated Indians throughout the plains, and prompted the Cheyennes and Arapahos into a war alliance with the Lakotas in retaliation. Over the following years reprisals exploded as the Platte River valley became a grassy wasteland of burned wagons, dead bodies, and ruined stage stations, which the Americans in turn used to justify further action. It brought a court-martial for Chivington, who resigned his post to avoid punishment, and the rise of a stubborn new point of contention between westerners and easterners regarding the moral high ground.[13]

Breakenridge made no secret of his contempt for Indians and claimed as early as 1875 to have taken part in the massacre. A party of Kansans who met him that summer wrote approvingly of "that young fellow, Mr. Breakenridge," who had been "one of Col. Chivington's soldiers in that famous massacre of 1864."[14] Breakenridge was eighteen years old at Sand Creek and seems to have taken it somewhat as an adventure. "It is rather hard to express the sensation we felt as we came in sight of the battlefield," he later recalled. "While I had been close to several Indian skirmishes, I never had been in a real fight with them, but my feeling of antipathy towards the Indians was so strong that I forgot all fear and was only anxious to get into a fight with them. The idea that I might get hurt never entered my head." He later claimed that he had only killed someone in self-defense after the man shot at him first but refused to reconsider the larger action. "I had no conscientious scruples in regard to killing an Indian," he later boasted, "but, I did draw the line at scalping or mutilating them after they were dead."[15] This did not stop him from trading with another soldier for two Indian scalps, carved out by the soldiers as they went among the dead bodies in the aftermath. He sent them to his sister back in Wisconsin as a prank.[16]

By 1870 the war on the southern plains had nearly ended. Rails had replaced the old wagon roads that served as Denver's lifeline, bringing a new and dramatically accelerated rate of change. The old Kansas Pacific had finally breached the Kansas-Colorado border and reached Denver, while a new railroad, the Denver Pacific, ran north to Cheyenne, linking with the Union Pacific and effectively connecting Denver by rail with nearly every city in eastern America and more than a few farther west. Boxcars loaded with freight packed in Baltimore, New York, or San Francisco now rolled directly into Denver's railroad yards, while passenger trains disgorged steady streams of curious easterners, startled by the mix of ox teams and fine hotels that marked Denver's place as the shifting border between two and often more worlds. In 1871 Breakenridge signed on as surveyor for the construction of a rather novel narrow-gauge railroad named the Denver & Rio Grande, chartered to build south from Denver and reaching Colorado Springs only a few months after construction began.

All of this meant that Colorado was safe for tourists, who flocked on "the cars" to see the scenery at exotic new resorts such as Manitou Springs, nestled into the mountains just below Pikes Peak. By the summer of 1872 Manitou Springs had become absolutely packed with eastern tourists, every bed and more than a few tents occupied by people coming from as far as Cleveland and Philadelphia, even Switzerland, to climb the mountains and test the properties of its hot mineral springs. The tourists who rambled about Manitou in the 1870s were, in effect, rambling through two worlds occupying the same space at the same time: the constructed one, safe from Indians and ornamented with rustic gazebos and ceremonial mineral springs where people in starched shirts and frock coats could sample the waters, and the unconstructed one, of hotel clerks and stage operators, packers and carpenters—men and women who made all this function, in their plain, comfortable clothes and speaking a plain, comfortable language. They ran the hot springs and bath houses, as well as the trains of pack mules that took the tourists up to Pikes Peak, generally making this entire way of life possible. These two worlds coexisted, separated mostly by layers of perception and, to a greater degree, consideration. The starched shirts went where life had been prepared for them to enjoy; the wool shirts cut the trails and did the lifting before drifting, largely invisible, into the background.

Breakenridge was working among these latter, unconstructed men in Manitou when he met Cornelius Vanderbilt Jr., the gay son of Cornelius "Commodore" Vanderbilt. The younger Vanderbilt was touring the West with his partner, the hotelier George Terry, in the summer of 1872.[17] Vanderbilt's family connections were nothing less than formidable: his father was one of the richest men in America, with a fortune built from shipping and railroads, including the California steamers that Charley Parkhurst traveled on. The senior "Commodore" was brisk and brutally businesslike, expected his family members to be the same, and had long battled to force his son Cornelius Jr. into the same mold. Cornelius Jr. did not possess the temperament his father demanded, but his father did at least succeed in getting his son to marry, thus conforming to the expectations of both his family and their society, even if the union proved childless. It was not until after his wife's unexpected death of pneumonia in early 1872 that the newly unencumbered Vanderbilt was finally free to travel and engage the world on something like his own terms, and with his own genuine and enduring companion, Terry, who appears to have served as a patient governor to the temperamentally impetuous Vanderbilt.[18] Their trip to the Rocky Mountain West was among the better times in Vanderbilt's life; in the West he may have felt momentarily free from the obligations and restraints of the East Coast and its established civilization, an experience perhaps not too dissimilar to William Stewart's time with Antoine Clement in the same lands only thirty-five years earlier.

At Manitou, Vanderbilt had approached Breakenridge and requested a buggy ride to see the sights. Breakenridge recalled him as a "good-looking young stranger" and later boasted about having pranked Vanderbilt by pretending not to know who his father was. Over the following days Breakenridge socialized with Vanderbilt and Terry somewhat constantly, apparently testing the fancy greenhorn and leveling rank. He seems to have recalled Vanderbilt as genial and somewhat vulnerable, especially when Breakenridge cheated Vanderbilt over climbing a mountain to win a bet. He later wrote that "Vanderbilt, who was a good sport, paid the bet, but said that it was a regular Yankee trick." Breakenridge's trick was not necessarily for lack of principle as Vanderbilt had been unduly rude and inconsiderate in boasting of beating a local man during a previous day's climb.[19] "I took him and his companion on several trips," he recalled.[20] Their drive through Colorado took several days, with a concluding dip in the hot mineral waters at a bath house in Idaho Springs. Breakenridge probably enjoyed the time he spent in their company, guiding them through the impressive scenery of the Rocky Mountain West before they moved on.

Breakenridge's contests with Vanderbilt suggest something of a competitive streak combined with genuine appreciation, something he would repeat in Tombstone, Arizona, nearly ten years later. He did so by making himself Vanderbilt's equal within the western landscape, through his earned knowledge of the area and its ways together with his ability (and willingness) to pull a few fast ones. He was in effect placing himself as equal to Vanderbilt's gilt-edged social company by mentally raising himself up while knocking Vanderbilt down a few pegs. This was a habit he would periodically enact during his life, displaying an almost smug opportunism to even out people he admired by placing himself at their level and making them meet him there. But these efforts also suggest a sense of loneliness and desire for companionship, expressed through forthright socializing that placed Breakenridge within a position of intimate address with the two men. Vanderbilt invited him to come to New York, this time to turn the tables. "Young Vanderbilt invited me to return to New York with him as his guest," Breakenridge later recalled, "and told me that if I would go with him he would show me more of New York in two weeks than I could find myself in two years, but I thought I could not afford it. He said he wanted to show me that I was as big a tenderfoot in New York as he was in Colorado. I have always regretted," he admitted, in one of the few elements of his recollections that reveal something like genuine personal feelings, "that I did not go with him."[21]

In truth he was fortunate that he did not go. For all his glamour, Vanderbilt suffered from gambling addictions that placed him in perennial cycles of debt, leading Terry to hold him up—the traditional suffering of all men who have found their love in a flawed hero. Vanderbilt was also considerably older than Breakenridge remembered, a memory possibly adjusted by his desire to think of Vanderbilt in a golden and idealized light. Had Breakenridge traveled with the two men to New York, he would have rapidly realized the true situation and grown disillusioned. Instead, he remembered and cherished a few weeks' flirtation in the Manitou with two wonderfully rich men, for the moment frontier comrades who were not only like him, with all the recognized secret signs and symbols, but who offered the example that people like Breakenridge could rise above their world if they wished and live a wonderful life.

Breakenridge conducted himself not as a gentleman, with all the strict social requirements of the role, nor as a "gent," the well-dressed sporting men who thronged the boxing rings and saloons of the Victorian world. He was something else: skilled and educated in the surveyor's trade, combined with the outdoor labor of the freighting teamster—in effect a human borderland between the civilized and the wilderness, equally capable of functioning in each setting. For the rest of the decade, Breakenridge followed his familiar pattern of railroad construction interspersed with freighting. His railroad work was spent surveying with the Orman brothers, a pair of contractors involved in the construction of nearly every railroad in Colorado Territory, from the Denver Pacific and Colorado Central to the Denver & Rio Grande and the Atchison, Topeka & Santa Fe. The brothers were full of "energy and pluck," remarked observers, and were "just the men to build western railroads." Breakenridge recalled surveying the Denver & Rio Grande as it built from Denver southward toward Pueblo and beyond.[22] Breakenridge was building the railroad but living in the wilderness to do it, thus mirroring the human borderlands experienced by the men on Cheyenne Hill seven years earlier. The work took him among an interesting group of men: a visitor to the Denver & Rio Grande's extension to Pueblo in October 1872 found several crews at work, stationed at seven camps four to six miles apart, each run by a different contractor. "The workmen at the various camps number about six hundred," remarked the visitor, adding that they earned "from $2.50 to $3.00 a day, owing to the kind of labor they perform, and are boarded [provided with meals] at $6.00 per week, and good board at that." The life and society of the construction crews were like those of teamsters and freighters, living in camps among their own kind in the open air— far, at least for the moment, from settled towns. They were a curious group: one camp had "two broken down preachers, a former professor of mathematics in an Indiana educational institute, two graduates of Yale, and forty or fifty witty, jolly, blarneying Irishmen, with so many patches all over them that the original stuff of their breeches would defy the researches of science." They all went to bed early, and by evening the camp was "silent and almost lightless."[23] Breakenridge's own surveying work was sometimes interrupted by incidents, as when he spent a few weeks in the prairie rounding up a number of the Ormans' mules that had strayed from Pueblo, probably the animals James Orman advertised as missing in May 1873. After following their tracks, Breakenridge discovered that the mules had integrated into herds of wild horses, splitting further into groups around individual stallions, which he shot so as to recover the mules. "We were able to shoot most of the stallions," he remembered, "but it took about two weeks to recover all of the stock."[24]

In 1874 the Ormans began work for the Atchison, Topeka & Santa Fe, which was extending its main railroad line westward toward Pueblo. At that time, the Santa Fe and the Rio Grande railroad companies were not yet angry rivals, and the Ormans along with Breakenridge moved easily from one railroad project to another in pursuit of contracts and financing. By the summer of 1875 the Ormans' construction crews were close to completing the Santa Fe's grade between Las Animas and Pueblo, a distance of 83.5 miles. Between those two points, the *Atchison Champion* remarked that May, "work has been in progress for some time, the road is partially graded and bridged, and track-laying is to be completed by the middle of July." They expected trains to be running from Atchison west to Pueblo by the first of August, a distance of 620 miles.[25]

This work was momentarily threatened by the Kansas Pacific, which was also grading a railroad line toward Las Animas on the same route. The Kansas Pacific plans were not new, but by the time its graders approached just west of Las Animas in May 1875, the Santa Fe right-of-way was well established and lay directly in its path. "The Kansas Pacific men are now seven and a half miles west," reported the *Las Animas Leader*, adding that within that distance, its planned route would cross the Santa Fe line in no less than three places. "They have not as yet interfered with that grade," the newspaper report added, and were "notified by Messrs.

Orman, Moore & Carlile not to do so. Whenever they reach the grade of that road they skip over and resume work beyond."[26] Breakenridge later claimed credit for personally blocking the Kansas Pacific, taking the initiative in Orman's absence to occupy the contested ground with Orman's graders overnight before the Kansas Pacific men realized what had happened. "Orman, the contractor, was in Pueblo over Sunday," he recalled, "but I took authority in my own hands" while sending word to Orman about his actions. "When the other camp began to stir," he wrote, they "at once hitched up their teams and started to grade also. I stopped the first team as it came on the right-of-way and told them they could come no farther. It looked serious for a short time, but their men said they came there to work and not to fight."[27] Possession of the right-of-way was later decided in the courts in the Santa Fe's favor.

If he told this story to the party of Kansans he met two months later, they made no mention of it. Breakenridge was working as a timekeeper for the Santa Fe when he encountered them in August 1875, in a Santa Fe railroad office car parked at a railroad construction camp west of Las Animas. The Kansans were returning home from a trip through the Rocky Mountains, but as regular train service was not yet running to that point on the newly laid rails, they had been forced to wait overnight at Orman's camp for the next construction train eastward. Their brief account of Breakenridge survives as the earliest description of him in the press, an evening inside a railroad car where, ensconced amid the oil lamp–lit woodwork, Breakenridge told them of his adventures. He told them of his service with Chivington, along with an anecdote about how the old mountain man Jim Bridger called hotel rooms "tepes" and hotel hallways "canyons" during a trip to St. Louis, flummoxing the hotel clerk until an army officer offered to translate. Both stories focused on the material advance of civilization over an old, quaint, and primitive West, reflecting his ability to use (and alternately raise or diminish) prominent figures to project, through their name, an implied endorsement of his own ideas.

In the spring of 1876 Breakenridge stepped aside from his railroad work to lead a party of colonists six hundred miles, from Colorado into Arizona Territory, only to be cheated twice in a row, first by the group's organizers themselves and then by the party's leader, a tubercular man from Boston named Samuel Hunt, who went into partnership with Breakenridge on an Arizona ranch. The Arizona Colonization Company was the work of a Boston promoter who published glowing reports of a new paradise while pocketing most of the transportation fees. He was also a man criticized as a reckless opportunist even by Arizonans, normally interested in promoting settlement. The company treasurer was the charming but slippery Hunt, who headed west for his health but also took advantage of Breakenridge in the process. The colonists themselves were decent enough, mostly young men from New England, "clerks, mechanic and school teachers," Breakenridge recalled, but they had arrived at the La Junta rail station in Colorado on May 8 without any experience in handling the wagons and livestock they had shipped there and would need to manage for the next six hundred miles of their trip. A local freight forwarder first asked Breakenridge to "unload the stock" from the railroad cars, "match it up into teams, and put it into shape for the road," which took a few days.[28] He was very proud of this work, especially in matching the best horses for each team and type of wagon, and made a point to describe it in his later autobiography. Hunt then asked if Breakenridge would drive them the rest of the way, promising good wages and stage fare back to Pueblo once they arrived. Breakenridge agreed, asked for time off from the railroad in Colorado, and set off for a few weeks' adventure. At first it went well enough, but halfway through the trip troubles arose in the heart of New Mexico Territory when two disaffected colonists began to advocate for mutiny, proposing to seize the stock and strike out on their own. To keep the group together and prevent them from being stranded, Breakenridge drove off and hid the stock at a ranch several miles away before returning to drive off the two men with the threat of a firearm. Only then did the animals reappear and the party continue after a day's delay. During the entire incident, Hunt was writing promotional letters from their camp to the Boston press, and, careful to disguise the trouble, he stated that the men had simply left "of their own accord" and that the animals had merely gotten lost during a thunderstorm.[29]

Had Breakenridge known of this reputation, or of Hunt's hand in it as the treasurer of this company, he might have reconsidered before accepting the job. Instead, he found himself deep in Arizona Territory, where he was promptly stiffed. "There was no money in the bank at Prescott to pay my salary and the money I had advanced," he later wrote. "I started to attach the outfit when Hunt showed me a bill of sale for the outfit," declaring the outfit (that is, the livestock and wagons) his own property, effectively preventing Breakenridge from getting paid. Yet with the supreme ease of all people accustomed to living by such means, Hunt glossed over the issue and proposed that Breakenridge go into partnership with him instead, leasing a ranch "where he would farm and I go freighting with the teams. . . . His idea was that by freighting we could pay for the expense of the ranch and have our own clear crop in the fall." As a colonist, the normally smooth and slippery Hunt seems to have made a genuine go of it. He "rented a farm belonging to Judge Tweed, to whom he was well known," registered to vote, joined the local farmers' grange, and became actively involved in community life. He made a point to volunteer as a theatrical director for a local benefit as a "man of culture and refinement" while writing a series of letters to the local and Boston presses promoting Arizona's "rapid strides of progress" toward civilization.[30] But when Hunt died of tuberculosis at the age of thirty-four in June 1877, Breakenridge found that their oral agreement of partnership was useless and that all of the money he had earned and forwarded to Hunt was gone, much of it sent to Boston. The ranch itself was gone: their crop had been sold and delivered off property, and their tools, implements, and furnishings had already been hauled away. Hunt appears to have realized he was dying and settled his affairs with his creditors in Massachusetts while ignoring his debts to Breakenridge, leaving him with only a team and wagon.[31] Why the normally savvy Breakenridge fell twice for this elegant young man is hard to say.

After a year or so of freighting to pay off debts, Breakenridge took up surveying work in Phoenix, advertising himself as a "civil engineer and county surveyor" through the summer of 1879. He shared office space with Hiram Linville, a commissions merchant and real estate agent on

Washington Street who had come to Phoenix for his health in 1876, bringing his large family along with him.³² Linville was looking to reproduce the familiar standards of home in the dry desert climate, while Breakenridge was joining the ranks of architects, attorneys, and physicians who made up the corps of professional men intent on developing, formalizing, and maintaining such a community. It was a responsible career, one that a man in his early thirties might find desirable as a path toward social respectability and community benefit. It worked to the extent that he was offered an appointment as a sheriff's deputy in Phoenix, which he accepted.

His first experience in law enforcement was brief but memorable. Over a matter of days in August 1879, a farmer and a businessman were killed in separate incidents, one from a grudge and the other randomly. Their respective murderers were subsequently hanged by a vigilance committee before a crowd of several hundred people in the city plaza, with speeches and a patina of social decorum.³³ One of the murdered men was John LeBarr, a popular businessman and IOOF lodge member who left behind a wife and children along with many friends and lodge brothers. LeBarr had lived in Phoenix for less than a year when he was murdered, and the community realized that their investments and future prosperity would suffer if Phoenix gained a sensational reputation as a dangerous place. Accordingly, the vigilance committees of Phoenix did not embellish themselves with elaborate hubris as similar vigilance committees had in San Francisco in the 1850s, nor were they wild and unruly. They conducted themselves instead with an almost methodist precision, presenting their actions as the very model of decorum and respectability while deliberately minimizing the affair for the public record. The captain of the vigilance committee simply "gave notice to all rough characters to leave town at once," ordered that saloons remain closed for the rest of the day, and announced that "the assembly should quietly disperse," which it did without question. "It has been a long time," remarked the press, "since Phoenix appeared as quiet and orderly as it did yesterday afternoon and evening." Breakenridge claimed to have been the one who arrested LeBarr's murderer, but he was not present for the hangings the following afternoon, thus minimizing his role in the event while simultaneously implying endorsement of the results. He recalled having been directed instead to take an elderly, unrelated prisoner out of town on a minor errand, which he later realized was intended to prevent the man from being caught up and hanged with the others. "I am satisfied that the sheriff knew what the Committee intended to do," he recalled, "and sent me off with the old man to get him out of the way."[34]

A stable Phoenix was a predictable Phoenix, and Breakenridge seems to have grown restless to explore the world again. As early as 1878, reports of mineral veins along the San Pedro River had been drifting into Arizona Territory newspapers, offering tantalizing hints of wealth hidden beneath the nearby ranges. This nascent fervor only grew stronger as investors began to investigate the claims seriously, setting up the necessary mining infrastructure over the course of 1879. The Tombstone region, as the new area was called, steadily evolved into a working mining district with mine hoists and stamp mills, fifteen stage arrivals per week, and even "four American ladies" who formed the nucleus of a social circle.[35] Tombstone's boosters looked forward to a promised land, the future home of "the sturdy miner, the happy farmer, the man of business, the mechanic, and happy homes with bright eyed, laughing children."[36] Tombstone's new mines were only thirty to forty miles from the Southern Pacific's new railroad line but still well within a wild country that required and rewarded caution, experience, and nerve, all elements that held appeal for Breakenridge.

In January 1880 Breakenridge left Phoenix to explore Tombstone's prospects with two associates, Frank Cox and G. W. Merald.[37] By that time, Tombstone had solidly embraced the unmistakable roar of industry: "the rumble of heavy freight teams," as a visitor remarked, with "their mammoth loads of ore from the Tough Nut mine; the rattle of light wagons, carriages, etc. in the streets of Tombstone; the rap-rap of numerous hammers on the many new buildings being erected in different parts of the city; and in fact all the rustle and bustle of a busy, wide-awake mining camp."[38] The *Colorado Miner* reported that while there were "but half a dozen first rate mines" in Tombstone, they were nonetheless valuable, worth from $250,000 to $2.5 million. "Several of them have steam hoisters," the newspaper added, and three had stamp mills: "Toughnut has two mills, the Contention one, and the Sunset one—all on the San Pedro river," about six or seven miles west of Tombstone, where the river water was used for processing the ore slurry.[39] In the stamp mills, rows of stamps—heavy cylindrical iron hammers used to crush ore for processing—were worked constantly, banging and smashing heavy chunks of ore into mineral pulp. "The sound of these twenty-five stamps in the Tombstone country will be music to the miner's ears," remarked an observer in the spring of 1879 and would undoubtedly spread word of "Arizona's greatness." Already an ocean liner named the *Arizona* had been launched in distant Scotland; this ship would later bring Oscar Wilde to North America for a tour of the United States.[40]

Prospecting is difficult work, often favored by those who find in the siren call of the rocks a lifelong thrill of the search and the associated way of life. Breakenridge was not among those who favored it, and he soon moved on to a job in Tombstone as a sheriff's deputy, a position that involved travel, authority, and a series of interesting short-term problems—a perfect mix for the restless and stubborn mind that lay within him. The work was fairly basic, even if mining towns were known to have more saloons than did agricultural towns. Breakenridge thought that Tombstone itself was quiet, orderly, and peaceful, that ladies and gentlemen could walk through town unmolested, and that no houses were ever burglarized. It was nonetheless a rudimentary settlement: nearly all of the buildings in the central district, including the firehouse, and more than a few outside of it were built of mud brick and fitted with imported doors and windows made of locally precious wood. Few of them were any better or worse than those in Tucson or even Phoenix, and nearly every town in Arizona Territory realized for the moment the necessity of earthen buildings as a temporary phase, something to be endured and wallpapered and forgotten as soon as possible on the grand march toward civilization.

Breakenridge settled in and began engaging in the mundane routine of Tombstone's civic housekeeping: serving a summons or two, taking inventory of a store that had gone out of business, occasionally making an arrest. But sometimes things heated up, and on one occasion in early 1882 he got into a gun battle against two rustler-outlaws who had holed up at a ranch, killing one of the men and injuring the other. Breakenridge's posse had pursued "Zwing" Hunt and "Billy" Grounds to Chandler's Ranch, a few miles outside of Tombstone, when Hunt and Grounds began to fire. In the battle that followed, Grounds was killed, along with one of the posse's men, while Hunt and two of the posse's men were injured. The *Tombstone Epitaph* reported that "Hunt must have fired several shots at Breakenridge," who was taking shelter behind a bullet-riddled oak, but "a few seconds after Hunt opened the battle, Grounds came out, and Breakenridge blazed away at him with his shot-gun, and was so fortunate as to put a full charge of buckshot into his head, which laid him out."[41]

Law enforcement work in Tombstone would also test Breakenridge's abilities to remain aloof: he found himself among a small but active group of men, mostly in their thirties, who were engaged in a perpetual war of attrition in a western desert. On one side lay a loose grouping of ranchers who rustled cattle on the sly—the Clantons, the McLaurys, and others; on the other side stood the five Earp brothers and their associates, engaged in law enforcement, investments, and gambling. The rustlers had it coming, and the Earps made it personal, a particularly vicious grand opera that opened with "a desperate street fight" in Tombstone on October 26, 1881, during which three of the rancher-rustlers were shot to death by the Earps on a street not far from Tombstone's OK Corral. The event was a spectacle before it even began. "Crowds of expectant men stood on the corner of Allen and Fourth streets," one newspaper reported. The "whole town watched the fight from the housetops," recalled another observer, "and it was sweet while it lasted."[42] The entire city immediately came to a halt: steam whistles blew alarm signals, neighboring mines shut down, and miners came up to the surface, where many of them formed armed vigilance committees that the Tombstone sheriff had to send away to keep what peace remained. Despite conflicting testimonies, a hearing resulted in an exoneration for the Earps, and over the following months the rustlers retaliated, killing Morgan Earp while badly injuring another.

This brought more retaliation from the Earps: a deadly rampage that culminated in a genuinely sensational public shooting at a Southern Pacific railroad depot in the city of Tucson. The Earps gunned down one of the rustlers, a man who had boasted of killing Morgan Earp, in full view of a Southern Pacific passenger train, whose engineer put on steam and raced to safety out of the station. "There must have been a dozen shots," the engineer testified. "Pulled out so fast they could not get on the train."[43] Rustlers or not, shooting outlaws in a civilized railroad depot was too much for Arizona society, as it threatened to justifiably tarnish Arizona's prospects with a lawless reputation in the national press. The cars in that train, and many of the passengers inside them, were booked through to Oakland and Sacramento, and their eyewitness accounts would rapidly spread tales of Arizona lawlessness far beyond its borders. The Earps were subsequently compelled to leave the territory and surf the frontier elsewhere.[44]

Breakenridge appears to have avoided this kind of drama, even as he walked his familiar line between factions. Officially he worked for the law, in common cause with the Earps; unofficially he got along with the rustlers and appears to have favored their temperament over that of his fellows. To negotiate between the two and accomplish his goals, he was described as having relied on sociability, combined with a firm but easygoing persuasion. "Mr. Breakenridge is a general favorite with all classes of people," remarked the *Tombstone Epitaph* in April 1882. "He is genial and social in private life and prompt but courteous in the discharge of official duty."[45] This approach did not materially reduce the extent of rustling within the region, but it did allow him to cool down heated moments, regain a stolen horse, or even collect taxes from the outlaws themselves. He was in effect *regulating* the outlaws, minimizing their extreme activities while maintaining and supporting the stability necessary for a broader community investment in the mining district.

All these talents came into play during the recovery of a stolen horse in 1881. A man named McMasters stole a prize saddle horse owned by Eliphalet Gage, general superintendent of the Grand Central mine, later trading it to a man named Milton Hicks.[46] Stealing a horse from

Tombstone directly, and from one of the most prominent mining figures especially, was bad form, and the established rustlers appear to have acted accordingly to reverse the damage that McMasters had unwisely created. Breakenridge was thus tipped off by one of the rancher-rustlers, thirty-four-year-old Ike Clanton, who "met me on the street and told me that if I wanted the horse to get to McLaury's ranch before dark and I should find him there." He rode to the ranch and advised thirty-two-year-old Frank McLaury that keeping the horse would endanger his ability to maintain the appearance of a common rancher, adding that "if I go back without the horse and tell that you will not give it up, you will have to quit ranching here and join the rest of the rustlers."[47] McLaury didn't steal the horse but knew the people who did and didn't think trouble at his ranch worth someone else's stolen horse. He told Breakenridge that the horse "would be there before morning; he would not [say] who stole it." The cowboy-rustlers "divided blankets with me," Breakenridge recalled, "and I slept on the floor with them all night. I was up at daylight and the horse was in the corral." As he prepared to leave with the horse in tow, McLaury cautioned him that the thieves were unhappy about losing such a prize animal and would set on Breakenridge once he left the safety of McLaury's ranch. This second tip-off allowed Breakenridge to evade the men (despite a few shots fired) and return to Tombstone with the recovered horse. Eliphalet Gage got his horse back, Breakenridge accomplished the job, and Clanton and McLaury preserved their ranches and, for the moment, their status quo. The only losers in the game were the men who had stolen the horse in the first place, but they had endangered their fellows by committing the faux pas of stealing directly from people in Tombstone itself and thus risking the larger rustling business, which thrived primarily on cattle stolen from across the nearby Mexican border and as such would be more easily overlooked.

The story of the horse became something of a tale among the rustlers, told among themselves over several days and as many campfires. It offered them a material measure of Breakenridge's capacity: he didn't race in with guns blazing or make a scene but instead worked quietly and persuasively, focusing on his goal while leaving others be and firing only after the actual horse thieves had fired on him first, then returning their fire, at least as he relates, effectively and conclusively. All of this helped build Breakenridge's reputation and contributed to the respect both parties held for each other, thus allowing him to work largely without serious incident among the roughest men and conditions. While riding through the Sulphur Springs Valley east of Tombstone not long after, Breakenridge came across two of the rancher-rustlers who "knew all about my getting the horse, and laughed and said, 'You had better look out or you will get caught the next time.'"[48]

During his time among the rustlers, Breakenridge developed a special feeling for one in particular, a man named William "Curly Bill" Brocius. The feeling was mutual: Brocius, "it would seem, had a friendly feeling for Breakenridge" in return.[49] The two men first saw each other in the spring of 1881, at a saloon outside of Tombstone. "I had never seen him before," Breakenridge recalled. "He was fully six feet tall, with black curly hair, freckled face, and well built." Brocius was reclining on a saloon table like a deadly odalisque, casually shooting a cup of water out of the bartender's hand, warning him that water was poison. For a man like Breakenridge, the sight of Brocius—languid, deadly, and magnificent—was unforgettable. He was immediately and understandably struck by the sight. The two men formally met some time later that spring, when Breakenridge was sent to collect taxes on properties east of Tombstone. He engaged Brocius to recover taxes from the outlaws, an audacious plan that let the two men size each other up and formed the beginning of a remarkable and nearly impossible relationship between lawman and outlaw.

The outlaw tax plan was both effective and emblematic of Breakenridge's reputed skill in law keeping. He knew that going into the outlaw hideouts on his own would be unsuccessful and possibly fatal. Instead, he asked for an introduction to Brocius, explained his purpose, and appointed Brocius as his deputy, with the power to collect taxes from his fellow outlaws. Fortunately, "asking the chief of all cattle rustlers in that part of the country to help collect taxes from them struck him as a good joke," for Brocius replied, "Yes, and we will make every one of those blank blank cow thieves pay his taxes." The following day, they set out into a series of "blind canyons and hiding places where the rustlers had a lot of stolen Mexican cattle" and collected taxes, including a few receipts that would be taken care of by the rustlers' banker. By the time he returned to Tombstone, he had collected nearly a thousand dollars.[50] The effectiveness of Breakenridge's proposal drew from its ability to place both men into a top position, a savvy win-win proposition that allowed Brocius as much of a feeling of authority as Breakenridge actually had, thus easing their path toward working in harmony. It was a particularly effective tactic that provided both men with the means to accomplish Breakenridge's goals in a friendly, efficient, and positive way and offered Brocius a warm and positive first impression of Breakenridge and his gitalong. Breakenridge got the county's taxes, and Brocius had the enjoyment of authority, over both the rustlers and Breakenridge's safety.

Breakenridge enjoyed the time they spent together. He recalled that he would "never want to travel with a better companion than Curly was on that trip. He was a remarkable shot with a pistol, and would hit a rabbit every time when it was running thirty or forty yards away. He whirled his pistol on his forefinger, and cocked it as it came up." Breakenridge also related some advice Brocius gave him: "He told me never to let a man give me his pistol butt end toward me, and showed me why. He handed me his gun that way, and as I reached to take it he whirled it on his finger, and it was cocked, staring me in the face, and ready to shoot. His advice was, that if I disarmed anyone to make him throw his pistol down." He added that "he would not lie to me. What he told me he believed, and his word to me was better than the oaths of some who were known as good citizens."[51]

If Breakenridge painted him in an idealized light, Brocius nonetheless had a dangerous reputation, one that Breakenridge could not have been unaware of. Already Brocius had been involved in and acquitted of the October 1880 shooting of Tombstone city marshal Frederick White, who had tried to disarm him late one evening for disturbing the peace. Although ruled an accident, the incident formed the backdrop for a series of menacing stories that followed Brocius like a shadow until he was finally shot to death by the Earp brothers over a year later.[52] One particularly sinister story described how Brocius and his gang set up one of their own members, a new man suspected of disloyalty, through complaints about his dancing while at a saloon, leading to a mock trial that ended in his "conviction" and sentence of death in a long and elaborate procedure that only gradually let the victim become aware of the genuine depth of his trouble and his final end. Another story, published in his lifetime, related how Brocius came across a fandango in progress one evening and forced the dancers at gunpoint to disrobe entirely, after which he watched them dance like this for half an hour before leaving.[53] Breakenridge personally relished a tale of how Brocius and his men "went to church" on their own terms, demanding at gunpoint that a terrified preacher either dance before them, as some accounts related, or, as Breakenridge recalled, read them a sermon and lead them into hymns before they departed, as he filled his hat with gold coins on their way out. Either way, Brocius was arrested the following morning for disturbing the peace and fined $250, which he paid on the spot, remarking that church was too expensive for him.[54]

It may have been this bad reputation that appealed to Breakenridge as much as Brocius's physical presence, the alluring image of unbridled freedom often projected onto outlaws and the idea of the outlaw as a surrogate for the observer in thumbing their nose at society's institutions. Brocius also appears to have had a particular charisma in both personality and gait that impressed Breakenridge, enabling him to command a leadership role among the men with whom he associated. Breakenridge may also have shared, or imagined himself sharing, a common gumption or temperament through the construction of their gitalong, a dynamic similar to what he may have had with Vanderbilt but on a far more robust and equitable platform, with a similar dose of vanity by association. His interest in both Vanderbilt and Brocius may have spurred him to pursue the same end, ironically through people on opposite sides of society, reflecting problems that Breakenridge and many other middle-class gay men experienced in the nineteenth century.[55] Preoccupied and confined by reputation and the safety of its preservation, they could only look to and idealize people who, by their sheer wealth or absolute lack of it, could circumvent and disregard middle-class social concerns. As a literal outlaw, Brocius possessed freedoms (even if at a price) that Breakenridge, employed in the public eye and concerned with protecting his increasingly public reputation, could not have attained without great cost, or at least the fear of a cost, to his way of living.

Brocius's soft spot for Breakenridge may have contributed to a near-fatal argument between Brocius and his own partner, Jim Wallace, in May 1881. For some time, Brocius and Wallace had been "thicker 'n spatter," but when Brocius developed a liking for Breakenridge, his partner, for some reason, did not.[56] At a saloon one evening outside of Tombstone, Wallace first "pulled his pistol on Deputy Sheriff Breakenridge," but "'Curly Bill,' who, it would seem, had a friendly feeling for Breakenridge, insisted that Wallace should go find him and apologize for the insult given."[57] Breakenridge personally recalled that while outside a saloon, Wallace had attempted to provoke him and even pulled his weapon on him, which Breakenridge easily handled before telling Wallace to stop "making a fool of himself." Later that evening, Breakenridge recalled, Wallace explained how "Curly was very angry with him, and told him he had to apologize to me. He wanted me to go to the saloon with him so that he could square himself with Curly." This was done, but trouble lay ahead: Brocius left to get his horse "and said he was going to camp. Wallace followed him and they had some words. Curly told him to keep away and not bother him anymore or he would shoot," but while mounting his horse to leave, "Wallace stepped up behind him and shot him. The bullet hit Brocius in the cheek and knocked out a tooth coming out through his neck without hitting an artery." In the turmoil, Brocius asked Breakenridge, "Billy, someone shot me; who was it?" The fight was a surprise all around. "Wallace and 'Curly Bill' have been partners and fast friends for the past five or six months," reported the *Arizona Weekly Star*, "and so far as is known, there was no cause for the quarrel, it being simply a drunken brawl." The *Arizona Weekly Star* continued that while "the wound is considered very dangerous, congratulations at being freed from this dangerous character are now rather premature, as men of his class usually have a wonderful tenacity of life."[58]

Brocius pulled through after a few weeks, but Wallace was done. There was no place for him in Tombstone anymore: he had ruined his relationship with Brocius in the most dramatic, immature, and unnecessary manner and was coming to the broken-hearted realization of having completely messed up in life, losing both his partner and his place within their society. As Breakenridge escorted him out of town, Wallace asked how Brocius was doing and if he would die, recalled Breakenridge, then the man "told me he was broke, and I paid for his supper and gave him ten dollars. I never did see him again, but he mailed me the money soon after I got to Tombstone. Later, I heard that he was killed in a fight near Roswell, New Mexico."[59]

Brocius did not have long either. He was shot to death by the Earp brothers during a gun battle outside of Tombstone in March 1882, only days after they shot Frank Stilwell alongside the passenger train at Tucson in the final moments of the ongoing war between the Earps and the cowboy-rustlers. "The cowboys ambushed the Earps as they were approaching the Springs," reported the press, "and poured a volley into them, wounding one man and killing a horse. The Earps returned the fire and charged upon the cowboys, who ran, leaving Curly Bill dead upon the field." It was a splendid showing for the Earps and devastating for Brocius. The following morning his body was taken back to one of the mill towns along the San Pedro River, where the remains were attended to by his old comrades. While Brocius was dead, it is notable and telling that Breakenridge seemed to prefer the idea that Brocius might still be alive, perhaps in Mexico instead, perhaps in Wyoming and then Texas, perhaps in the hope of seeing him again when the time was right.[60]

As Tombstone's mining fortunes waned and the place grew dull, Breakenridge moved to Tucson, where he balanced law enforcement with occasional surveying work, initially as a U.S. deputy marshal in the 1880s, then as a county surveyor evaluating potential water systems in the Tonto Basin and confirming the border between Yuma and Maricopa Counties, and then as a railroad detective for the Southern Pacific Railroad, a stable job that lasted the rest of his career. Most of this work focused on mundane thefts from boxcars in railroad yards, but occasionally things would heat up when he went after train robbers. He took custody of two men in 1894, the first having been responsible for a sensational robbery of a Southern Pacific express train north of Los Angeles in February 1894, while the second was caught by ranchers on the Gila River that fall and turned over to Breakenridge for trial. In the spring of 1895, a group held up a Southern Pacific train near Wilcox, New Mexico Territory, blowing up the express car with dynamite. Armed with a tip and a reported sighting, Breakenridge searched for several weeks before he cornered one of the men, who shot himself to avoid capture.[61] When Breakenridge traveled to Los Angeles on business, he usually chose to stay at the four-story Hollenbeck Hotel, which was also favored by Wyatt Earp.[62] By 1910 Breakenridge was living in Tucson with another unmarried man, fifty-two-year-old Francis Munguia, on East Sixteenth Street. The two men had independent incomes, were eleven years apart in age, and shared Munguia's modest but comfortable home with Munguia's elderly mother.

As he grew older, he became nostalgic, reflecting on his life and the changes he saw in Tombstone and similar towns during the 1870s and 1880s. Nearly all the people he once knew had moved to more stable climes: the Earps together with former Tombstone mayor John Clum and wife moved to Southern California, while Fred Dodge, who ran a Tombstone saloon while working undercover for Wells, Fargo & Company, now lived on a ranch in Texas with his own wife. Even John "Doc" Holliday, who, of all people, miraculously managed to die in his sleep, was respectably buried in Glenwood Springs, at the foot of the Roaring Fork Valley. As time passed and the street fight at Tombstone approached its half-century anniversary, many people began to reconsider the period, an era once considered too modern and vulgar to be respectable. Now somewhat sentimental, they had a growing nostalgia for an age of bowler hats, oiled hair, and walrus mustaches. Memories of gunfights and stage robberies, the Lincoln County Wars, the streets of Dodge City and Tombstone had grown rosy among the memories of elderly men who once lived them and now began to reconnect with each other, bound by common experience. Into this era swarmed a phalanx of writers who busied themselves popularizing and embellishing these accounts for public consumption, nurturing the seeds of the western myths and legends to follow. Among the more notable of these was a book luridly written by Walter Burns in the best pulp adventure magazine style: *The Saga of Billy the Kid*, which hit the bookstores in 1925. Breakenridge completed his own memoirs in 1928 under the title *Helldorado*. Stuart Lake's *Wyatt Earp, Frontier Marshal*, followed in 1931, weaving the "gunfight era" firmly into American legend. In this process, the street fight in Tombstone, now rebranded as the "gunfight at the OK Corral," became universally emblematic in popular culture as the "Wild West."

Yet for all his strengths, Breakenridge's aversion to street fights, perhaps coupled to a tolerance for rustlers, set him to the side of romantic history in favor of the dramatic, clear-cut, and bloodthirsty fights between the Earp brothers and their cowboy-rustler foes. Even so, Breakenridge's book helped spur a series of early reenactment events at Tombstone dubbed Helldorado Days that began to define a genre. Apart from the rows of Ford and Dodge Brothers cars parked on the dirt streets, the Tombstone of 1929 was nearly unchanged from its appearance in the mid-1880s, and the film cameras that recorded a reenactment of the street fight at Tombstone that year preserved a haunting image of what the original event may have looked like, performed by people who were alive when the original occurred, with the sounds and images of the original still present in more than a few of their memories.

Just as persistent were the ancient divisions between the respective associates of the Earp brothers and the cowboy-rustlers, made worse by a breach of decorum on Breakenridge's part, in meeting with the elderly Wyatt Earp before writing of him in his book in a way that struck Earp's friends as ungrateful and rude. In December 1930, two Earp associates, Fred Dodge and John Clum, exchanged Christmas greetings along with opinions on the new books coming out, especially on Breakenridge's *Helldorado*. They knocked Breakenridge down a bit before Dodge wrote something remarkable, an indication that everyone in Tombstone, from the rustlers to the Earps, from Dodge to Clum, knew that Breakenridge was gay and that they all accepted him as such, even if Dodge later dismissed Breakenridge with diminutive phrasing. "You know Billy and I know Billy," Dodge wrote knowingly. "He was in those days a nice girl, and in his declining years should be a nice old lady, instead of trying to make himself a hero of 'Helldorado.'"[63]

5

The "Lady Lovers" of Victorian Aspen

The western slopes of the mountain ranges of the West bear the full brunt of winter storms, and the Rocky Mountain winter of 1889 was especially long, cold, and bitter. Eight inches of snow fell across the Roaring Fork Valley as late as May 9, and the night previous three inches of ice had dragged down newly installed telephone wires. The Roaring Fork River cuts through the Colorado Rockies for some fifty miles, gouging and spreading with indifferent majesty a course along the western slopes of the Continental Divide. On some spring days, the valley was an intoxicating mix of cold, crisp, brilliant blue skies; the icy downstream rush of the Roaring Fork River; the snort and breath of any number of horses straining to move wagons, sledges, sleds, or sleighs between the mines and smelters; and wood smoke from a dozen nearby cabins and ranch houses.

At the upper end of the valley lay the mining town of Aspen, a silver gilt stamp of civilization surrounded by mountains engulfed in snow and the drifting blue haze of several hundred chimneys that marked mine shafts, stamp mills, and boiler works.[1] Relentlessly modern and electrically lit, Aspen was an industrial town but one with opera houses, morality, and attitude. Aspen's boosters imagined that their town rivaled any contemporary eastern city in the United States, and it was, they modestly felt, the finest in Colorado, a place where respectability, progress, and order would prevail.

In the nineteenth century, morality was firmly linked with progress. It was not the idea of progressive politics as it has come to be understood today but rather the idea that mechanical and technological progress would become a handmaiden to the enforcement of morality. To this end, communications between the isolated silver camps and established Victorian society were indispensable. Telegraph lines arrived in Aspen in 1882, an "electric spark connecting us with the busy multitude across the range," while electric lighting followed in 1885 and telephones in 1889, all providing mines, homes, and businesses with efficient, instantaneous communication.[2] Aspen's newspapers reported on world events telegraphed almost instantly from across the globe; its store windows displayed pineapples and bananas, brought by steamer and railroad from across the South Pacific and up from South America.[3] Its churches, opera house, and brand-new Jerome Hotel were built of cut stone in the Romanesque style; its better homes were of respectable brick, graced with porches and eaves. "The frontier atmosphere," remarked the *Rocky Mountain Sun*, "has long since departed, and Aspen presents the cultivation and order of old settled communities."[4]

Aspen's supreme triumph came in 1887, when no less than two railroads entered the Roaring Fork Valley within months of each other, building track along opposite sides of the valley in a sort of commercial forbearance as they raced toward the silver mines. The Denver & Rio Grande was the first, going directly past the valley's ranching communities as it sneaked its narrow-gauge rails along a three-foot path into Aspen and most of the Rocky Mountains.[5] The Colorado Midland Railway arrived just three months later and established a station on the opposite side of town, at the base of present-day ski lifts on Aspen Mountain. The "Midland Road" was of standard-gauge construction, with larger locomotives and cars, which offered faster service to Denver than its narrow-gauge rival.[6] Mountains echoed with the whistles of shifting locomotives working the spurs of its mines and the hustling express trains that brought Aspen within hours of the rest of the world.

Aspen's social patterns extended far beyond its city limits, embracing many living in the smaller satellite towns and ranches. Emma, about twenty miles down the Roaring Fork, along the Denver & Rio Grande line, was the "garden spot of the Roaring Fork Valley," where each spring and summer thousands of broad, green acres produced hay, oats, and potatoes.[7] Over the winter of 1889 Emma lay semidormant under snow and ice, while teams of horses snorted and struggled along frozen roads against the icy breath of winter. The Emma School had closed, and eight inches of new snow fell around Valentine's Day. Despite this, families and friends on horses and in sleighs made their way to a Valentine dance at the Emma ranch home of Clark Chatfield, where the carpet was rolled up, music played, and sentimental trifles were exchanged in the form of chromolithographed Valentine's Day cards from Germany. Hospitality is everything in places like this, and one of the guests thought "the supper, under the supervision of Mrs. Chatfield and her affable daughters, was first class."[8] No one then knew that one of these affable daughters, Ora Chatfield, was in love, or soon would be, or that the object of her affection was the Emma postmistress. Nor did Ora Chatfield and postmistress Clara Dietrich realize or anticipate the extent to which the society they eventually sought to escape would work to bring them back into harness.[9]

Ora Chatfield's extended family was drawn into the Roaring Fork Valley by any number of promising business opportunities that surrounded its silver veins in the early 1880s. They were not necessarily sophisticated in the manner of William Stewart, nor were they aggressively devoted to duty, as John Noonan was. Instead, they sought whatever opportunities came their way while maintaining a respectable, upper middle-class lifestyle. Their dignity, while genuine, was shaped and influenced by popular middle-class authorities; they perpetually sought to represent and enact the social pantheon of the "most approved" fashions, manners, or materials, rarely questioning just where such approval came from. They were not innovators. They sought to climb ladders that were already well established in search of power, propriety, and opportunity, like wanderers in tailored wool and silk.

The patriarch of the family was Ora's uncle, the Honorable Isaac Chatfield, who had been elected to the Colorado General Assembly the previous year while still pursuing his mining and ranching interests throughout Colorado.[10] In 1883 Isaac Chatfield purchased a lot and a house in Aspen at the corner of South Monarch and East Hopkins Streets, and he bought an interest in the Bonanza, Little Jimmy, and other mining claims. By the spring of 1889, the Chatfields were prosperous enough to have several properties, including ranches in the Roaring Fork Valley near the small town of Emma, Pitkin County, to which they had moved, and Isaac Chatfield had a cattle ranch in Las Animas County. Clark Chatfield purchased four lots at the corner of Third and Gillespie Streets in Aspen, while Isaac Chatfield was reported to have bought a lot on nearby Hallam Street. Even so, Isaac's wife, Eliza, "refused to remain in that wilderness wholly devoid of social attractions" and insisted on returning to the whirl of fashionable Denver, remarking that she "could no longer subject herself to the inconveniences and misery entailed upon one accustomed to the social attractions of the metropolis, merely to gratify the political aspirations of a spouse to whom she was in every other conceivable way devoted."[11] Either way, the Chatfields' prominence was sufficient to warrant routine notice in the columns of Aspen's three newspapers, and Isaac Chatfield's political opinion was occasionally sought after by reporters—and deftly dodged.[12] With Isaac leading and Clark content to follow along, the Chatfield brothers moved through their world, engaging any number of ranches, farms, or business contracts, perpetually attempting to climb the ladder toward prominence and meritorious position among the important and progressive men of Colorado.[13]

Both brothers had large families, each with nine children, most of whom reached adulthood. Clark and his wife, Mary, raised Della, Ora, Clark Jr., Arthur, Willard, Mabel, and Jacqueline. Their eighth child, Levi, would be born that fall, followed by Margaret four years later, in 1893. The families' pursuit of respectability was almost a given. "The attendance at church and school," explained the *Rocky Mountain Sun* in 1886, "is generally accepted by modern thinkers as a fair index of material, moral and intellectual standing."[14] The Chatfield daughters were accordingly raised in a world of Sunday school, socials, and curfews, all calculated to cultivate and introduce eligible young ladies to Aspen's social register while reinforcing their families' social and moral status.[15] The Chatfields belonged to Christ Episcopal Church in Aspen, where Clark's daughter Jacqueline and Isaac's daughter Ella would be confirmed that August.[16]

Ora Chatfield's life, as society intended it, would be a world of virtue and duty within a vast interlocking network of social mores and courtesies, all intended to grace their civilization with a harmonious and prosperous whole.[17] Her cousin Ella married Josiah Small, the Aspen postmaster, in 1887, while Jacqueline spoke vows at the altar in 1891.[18] Ora's older sister Della even married her cousin Elmer, Isaac's son, who managed the family ranch at Emma and would live to the age of ninety-nine. Accordingly, Ora would take her future place in Aspen society alongside an appropriate husband and continue to the carry the magnificent torch of Victorian civilization.

The village of Emma stood on the old stage road that passed from Carbondale and the lower valley to the endless array of silver mines and smelters scattered about Aspen and the upper valley. A side road headed south to coal and coke ovens on the slopes of Mount Sopris, where freight wagons and teams loaded with processed coke passed by constantly. In this world, progress was literally tangible, measurable in moments, something people in Emma were acutely aware of—the fresh wood of a new barn on Emma Road, telegraph wires tapping to the entire world through the brass keys on the desk at the Emma Store, and the world tapping back. Not even ten years earlier, the arrival of stage service was considered a miracle, but now locomotives had rendered them obsolete: the last of the Kit Carson stagecoaches had already departed Emma three years before, their stage drivers lining their rigs up in a row for memorial photographs before taking their final trot up to Aspen while a locomotive, one of the Rio Grande line's big Baldwin consolidation types, loomed in the background. The Denver & Rio Grande line had built directly through Emma on its way to Aspen's silver mines. Aspen business was flourishing, and in May 1889 two passenger trains passed Emma each way daily.[19] But Emma itself was a flag stop; the express typically hustled through, but even the local would stop only if flagged down, when someone wanted to either get on the train or disembark. The Emma Store, which included a post office, was accordingly built by a Mr. Morrison the year before to handle increased business on the Rio Grande; it opened for business on February 15, 1888, four months after the railroad was built.[20]

The women of Emma dreamed of Iowa in the Rockies: civilization in the wilderness, virtue and harvest, decent morals and honest hard work. They ran its post office, raised its families, and tended its farms. They supported Christian temperance societies, made preserves, would *never* wear a Mother Hubbard in public, and read with approval of the "great moral wave" that threatened to "beat against the beach of immorality in Aspen" and flush out the saloon keepers of Cooper Avenue.[21] Their goddesses, if they had any, were temperance poster Amazons, furiously hacking apart whiskey barrels in indignation, or the sweetly smiling allegory of Progress shown on the cover of a railroad timetable, floating majestically westward across the continent. Its community namesake was the town matriarch, Emma Garrison, whose "hospitality and fine meals" had fed the region's miners in the hectic silver strike era years earlier. "I helped name [the place] Emma," recalled an Aspen old-timer, "naming it after Mrs Emma Garrison, who kept a 'half-way' house there where we bachelors of the time stayed. We built a log school house near Emma, the first school house in the valley."[22] In Emma Garrison's time, frontier was something to be put up with as long as necessary and put down as rapidly and forcibly as possible. When the place was new and raw and named Texas Creek, she pioneered it, sticking it out in the cold winters as best she could, having logs cut to build a hotel, then a chimney. She appears to have been both entrepreneurial and traditional, turning a woman's social role of housekeeper into a business, building the log hotel at Emma, and leasing a much finer hotel in Aspen, constructed of sawn lumber and actually decorated with wallpaper. At a fancy dress ball in Aspen in 1883, she appeared as Martha Washington, the mother of her country; two years later she was named postmaster of Glenwood and then of Emma.[23] "The government," remarked the *Aspen Times*, "never makes a person postmistress."[24] Now she gazed over a settled community, with farms and railroads, and dominated the local kitchens, dining rooms, and parlors with an absolute morality: domestic, maternal, unassailable, and clear to any man who walked into her public dining room. The old name of Texas Creek just wore away. Everyone called it Emma, and Emma it was.

Clara Dietrich was rising into this world by circumstance and gumption. Unmarried women are obliged to support themselves, and at twenty-six Dietrich had invested her savings into half ownership in the Emma Store and post office, a position that placed her in daily contact with the Roaring Fork Valley's populace. Everyone knew her: she was the functional center of Emma, the mildly determined woman who handled their mail, packaged their groceries, and watched as they traveled past on the Denver & Rio Grande. Passenger and mail trains hustled past the store four times a day, two in each direction, and four times a day Clara went out to meet the passing trains, walking across the ruts of the wagon road to stand by the railroad tracks with a canvas mailbag, waiting for the Denver & Rio Grande's Leadville & Aspen Mail & Express, tossing outbound mail at the moving cars and dodging mailbags tossed at her in return. It was a ritual of life, a means to an end, and a measure of her importance within the surrounding community; she was just one of many women in rural communities who found prominent and responsible employment where everyone pitched in.

People who knew Dietrich considered her a contributor to their society, a "clear headed, clever and undemonstrative" woman praised for her "education, business training and the position she sees herself in the world," a woman fully capable of fulfilling the practical work of her community within a proper and appropriate sphere.[25] However, her inner fires and furies appear to have been channeled toward something far beyond such ordinary alignments and suggest a simmering idealism effectively beyond any rational or realistic hope of acceptance—dreams of a future that ought to be but was not, nor could be, at least in Emma. Her goddesses, if she had any, were Amazons or viragoes—powerful women who cared little for the intemperance of men, or men at all for that matter. They charged about on white horses, fierce with armor and wavy hair, eyes steel cut, motivated, and strong, while beneath them ran a pantheon of terrestrial women, freethinkers, and free lovers daring to challenge conventions and living to their word. But in practical reality, Clara would have been grasping at straws at best, presumably conscious that a driven, independently thinking woman in a valley of potato farmers had little social purchase. She treaded water instead, selling goods, keeping the books, and walking outside every afternoon at three o'clock, in the snow, bundled in wool, with mail bags, to wait for the passing express.

Dietrich was connected to the Chatfield families through the marriage of relatives: her mother, Susan Dietrich, was the sister of Eliza Chatfield, Isaac Chatfield's wife. This connection offered her an important introduction to, and place within, the local community social sphere. It also brought the use of one of the ranch houses on the Chatfield properties, a house she shared with Clark Chatfield's daughter Ora, who had requested the arrangement. This situation was both entirely practical, providing living quarters for Clara, and entirely suitable, providing Ora the company of her older, unmarried cousin. Mid-nineteenth-century Americans looked upon a certain degree of romantic love between women as entirely appropriate to the perceived sentimentality of the female mind, a closeness cultivating charming bonds of loyalty within the sphere of the woman's world. This conception was entirely removed from any notion of true romance, which apparently only a man could provide. It was inconceivable to them that Ora and Clara could desire anything else, or develop, in Clara Dietrich's words, a "passion grand" for the hearts or souls of each other.[26]

They did, and their passionately romantic relationship became evident in either late April or early May 1889, when their "curious conduct attracted public attention, and they were separated."[27] The *Denver Times* later explained that "Ora Chatfield was suffering so from nervous prostration that the matter was investigated, and it was ascertained that she was madly in love with Miss Dietrich, with whom she was living."[28] Ora Chatfield was thrilled, but her family was alarmed: relationships between two women were unheard of, much less socially respectable. They concluded that Clara Dietrich was becoming insane, the only reason imaginable to them that would account for the circumstances. Bystanders thought that the feelings of probable insanity were mutual: "it is thought that the older one is not of sound mind, and a medical examination would probably establish the fact that the younger one was open to suspicion in the same direction."[29]

Clara Dietrich defended herself before the Chatfields, writing several letters in what would ultimately and inevitably become a futile attempt to prove the worth of her love. She wrote in words stunningly modern, demonstrating that her self-perception as what would today be called a lesbian was fully formed and accomplished at a time when very little was known publicly about relationships among women. Her letters, as reprinted in the press, show that an ordinary Colorado postmistress had developed, recognized, and defended a conscious sense of self-identity as a lesbian woman and that she viewed this identity as not just inherent to her person but necessary to its fulfillment as her "being's destiny." Stating that "I am in full possession of my reasoning faculties," she went on to say that she "was never more sincere in my life. I tell you I love your daughter as she never was loved and will never be loved again. I know it is out of the usual order of things for one woman to have the passion grand for another, but in all coolness and candor let me assure you that with me it is no ephemeral dream of fancy, but my being's destiny. You can't understand it; of course you can't, and I don't expect you to. The fact that my love for your daughter exists, however, just as strong as the love of man ever was for woman is beyond question, and I am ready to prove it with my heart's blood."[30] Clara Dietrich's self-realization as a lesbian woman shows that ordinary nineteenth-century Americans were capable and effective at realizing themselves as well as their differences in comprehension with the societies that surrounded them. It also shows that people who met her and others like her were occasionally encountering these statements of identity, even if they did not fully comprehend, recognize, or understand their meaning.

She wrote to Ora every day; her letters were "full of the strongest and apparently most heartfelt and ardent expressions of affection" and "showed that the love that existed between them was of no ephemeral nature, but as strong as that of a strong man for his sweetheart."[31] One of Clara's letters went past concepts of self-identity toward taking action in realizing the same. She proposed elopement: meeting by horseback at Woody Creek, then riding to Aspen for a marriage before a justice of the peace. "I will dress as a man," she wrote, "and as I am somewhat masculine in appearance and figure, I think we can carry the plan to perfection."[32] This plan was at best symbolic, offering no real benefits, while possessing and actively presenting several genuine dangers, not least the recognition, suspicion, and action by any curious justice of the peace. The plan appears instead to be more of a statement of desire between the two, a romantic and imaginary course of fulfillment and perhaps a kind of dry run for some future action. But while couched in fantasy terms, it nonetheless represented calculated intentions, and this appears to have forced Isaac Chatfield to act against Dietrich to protect his family's interests, as well as his social and political reputation.

These actions were not necessarily for saving face or career or due to prejudice alone. They drew as well upon a genuine family tragedy that had occurred a few years earlier, in 1886, when Ora Chatfield's older sister Ida stepped out one evening from their uncle's Aspen house and never returned. While Ida's father Clark grew ill and distraught, Isaac Chatfield took the lead, organizing search-and-rescue efforts, offering a reward for information, and representing the face of his family to the community and speaking to the press. "All day Saturday and Sunday Mr. I. W. Chatfield, joined at times by many others, searched the banks of the Roaring Forks, Castle and Maroon creeks," reported the *Rocky Mountain Sun*. "The sheriff's office has had men out in every direction searching the hills, gulches, old cabins, shafts, tunnels, the river banks, and everywhere there was a chance for concealment; but without reaching any clue." Isaac Chatfield even went to Denver to see if she had gone there. The search brought overwhelming fears she had been "abducted and destroyed" and at least one false and rather cruel lead, before her hat was ultimately found in the Roaring Fork River, followed by the discovery of her remains shortly thereafter, washed onto an entangled bank of the Roaring Fork, near its confluence with Woody Creek. It was an enormous and very personal tragedy. Isaac and Eliza Chatfield had lost two children in infancy, another as a toddler, and a fourth in his teens several years earlier. This was the first time his brother Clark and his wife Mary had experienced such a loss, and both families took it hard. Ida was nineteen years old, with every promise of life before her, as her family can only have felt. She was instead buried in the Aspen Grove Cemetery, where the Roaring Fork Valley begins to rise toward Independence Pass.[33] As far as the Chatfields were concerned, whatever was going on with Ora Chatfield and Clara Dietrich had awakened a visceral terror of something similarly awful.

Accordingly, Isaac Chatfield took Ora Chatfield with him to Aspen on May 9. He brought a letter of complaint against Dietrich, written by his brother Clark under the barely concealed pseudonym "C. S. Smith." He called upon the Pitkin County sheriff, John White, a handsome bachelor of forty-two with oiled hair and a walrus mustache, to take action against her. Sheriff White was a longtime resident elected, noted the *Aspen Daily Times*, in 1887 with an "unusually large majority of votes" that reflected his social standing within both the community and Republican politics. "He has succeeded in giving universal satisfaction," the *Aspen Daily Times* continued, "while faithfully guarding every public interest. He enjoys the entire confidence of the people of the county and all feel that in his official position, as in his private life, he reflects credit upon the community that has honored him."[34] In Aspen, Isaac Chatfield compelled Ora Chatfield to hand over her personal letters to the sheriff as evidence of Clara Dietrich's apparent delusion. Although the letters made clear that both parties had equally invested in the relationship and that Ora Chatfield's letters to Dietrich were signed "hubby," Isaac Chatfield was interested in saving his family's reputation by shrewdly characterizing the relationship as entirely one-sided on Clara's part. His business with the sheriff was to arrange "a warrant . . . sworn out at Aspen for Clara for the purpose of investigating her sanity."[35] Besides the public necessity of avoiding embarrassment, the uncle's motivation may have included sincere concern for his niece. He could not conceive of her truly happy with such a "monstrous, unnatural affection," nor would he allow it.[36] He saw the whole affair as a form of insanity and a perplexing one at that, a mental Nova Zembla—mysterious, distant, and forbidding. In 1889 psychology was in its infancy, Freud's couch freshly upholstered, and the workings of human life were just beginning to be understood. A long road lay ahead.

"Insanity" was a plastic term, loosely applied to virtually anything that extended beyond the nineteenth-century sense of stability and propriety. Insane asylums were coveted municipal moneymakers, and people were recorded as having become insane over religion or even the moon, like someone who had stumbled rather than walked along the path of life.

Clara Dietrich's troubles increased with a subsequently biased *Aspen Daily Times* article appearing on May 11 that portrayed the younger Ora as an innocent victim, apparently an effort to publicly exonerate the Chatfield name by tossing the blame on Dietrich. Titled "Curious Cupid Drives His Arrows into the Wrong Place" but ominously subtitled "Mad Infatuation," the article appeared before the likelihood of an impending public trial, likely to sway opinion in advance. Using pseudonyms to protect the family, the *Times* explained that "the younger lady, who for the purposes of this article will be called 'Belle' [Ora], said to her father that she would not have anything to do with her cousin 'Blanche' [Clara] and that 'Belle' complained that 'If I don't marry her she will kill me, and talks so strange I have grown afraid of her. Papa, she is killing me by inches.'" The newspaper remarked that the "ladies both live on farms below this city on the Roaring Fork river, and the oldest one [Clara] has always been considered a practical, well informed and extremely sensible woman. More than that, she holds a responsible position, and is far above the ordinary woman in point of education, business training, and position she sees herself in the world. She was never even accused of morbid sentimentality before, and while not strong-minded in the least, she is clear-headed, clever and undemonstrative. What this mad infatuation is or why it has arisen in her mind to the exclusion of everything else, not the slightest explanation can be given. That it exists in a degree beyond that ordinarily shown by man for woman there is no room for doubt after reading her letters and hearing Miss Belle [Ora] tell how her cousin cuddled her up, hugged her and even bit her."[37]

The *Times* provided an excerpt from a poem Clara had sent Ora: "The older lady insists she is in love with the younger one, not as one lady usually loves another, but

> More than words can wield the matter,
> Beyond all that is valued rich and rare,
> Dearer than eyesight, liberty or space,
> As much as child ere loved, or parent fond,
> Beyond all manner of such loves,
> I do love thee

"Or at least," continued the newspaper, "that's the way she put it, in the words of the immortal poet."[38] Dietrich was quoting from Shakespeare's play *King Lear*, but the words she used to profess her devotion were in Shakespeare's play nothing more than hollow flattery, offered by one of Lear's daughters simply to get the old man's loot. Dietrich may not have seen the play and evidently did not understand their original context. Like many nineteenth-century people, she reinforced her social position by appropriating elements of culture, whether in Shakespearean literature or the current fashions, that superficially seemed to support or advance her desires and worldview, fitting them in wherever they seemed to work. Shakespeare was authoritative and official; by quoting him, Dietrich perhaps believed her love for Ora Chatfield would take on the same qualities, strengthening itself through the same cultural appropriation that the society around them would use to tear them apart. They were mental moments of a lonely life in a valley of potato farmers where handsome Amazons were waiting in every corner to alternately play both chorus and advance guard to Clara Dietrich's world. She seems to have done so in imaginary moments of glory without any evident or serious consideration for the actual effects of these glories, much less the repercussions of their fulfillment. It was easier to quote Shakespeare out of context than it was to write original love poems and likewise easier to plot grandiose escapes than rational alternatives.

Dietrich became risky stock. "Opinion among the friends of both ladies," reported the newspaper, "seems to be undividedly in favor of the younger, all of them seeming to think that there is not the slightest excuse for such monstrous, unnatural affection. One lady suggested a dose of cowhide as the best way of curing such thoughts." The impression given by the article was a pathetic story of a spinster grown delusional from years of loneliness, made appalling by her advances upon a young lady entering prime marrying age. In this environment Dietrich could not possibly have defended herself successfully and appears to have realized the necessity of agreeing to the sheriff's demands in order to walk free. Had she defended herself to Sheriff White in the same way as she had before the Chatfield family, detention, jail, or time in an insane asylum at Pueblo would have awaited her. By renouncing her affection to the sheriff, Dietrich was able to buy time, taking advantage of the pseudonyms of the Aspen newspaper article to remove herself from the critical public eye. She may also have been aware that the Chatfields were equally interested in avoiding legal action and in fact only wanted the situation to go away, which allowed her deference to the sheriff greater purchase in obtaining her freedom on his receipt of her tearful promises. The only public notice of her trip to Aspen was an innocuous item in the *Aspen Daily Times* that "Miss Clare [sic] Dietrich, postmistress and storekeeper, at Emma, was in the city Tuesday."[39] A hearing had been avoided, the Chatfield name kept out of further newspaper reporting on the situation; the Chatfield family's interests had been served, and the matter could be let to rest.[40] The women's letters were presumably burned.

By mid-June the "romance" had long faded from the headlines and become a mere curiosity. Ora was firmly ensconced in the Chatfield family home, a life of daily chores and parlor recitals or, when in Aspen, perhaps taking piano lessons under Mrs. Stormer on East Hallam Street or being fitted for spring dresses at Shillings' Department Store.[41] Isaac Chatfield had business to attend to, mine shares to negotiate, cattle and property to manage. He was reported in Aspen on May 25, and on June 1 he purchased property in Aspen's Hallam's Addition, as he planned to build a house on Hallam Street. Talk turned to the exceptionally heavy and late snowfall and how Aspen's "ball boys" went to Denver to "cross bats" with the Denver baseball team, winning hands down, 18–0, and giving Denver a grand "goose egg" in the state league season.[42] Aspen society attended the Grand Presentation Society Ball at the Rink Opera

House and hosted both President Moffat of the Denver & Rio Grande and President Scott of the Colorado Midland as they arrived on special trains for inspection tours of their respective railroads.[43] Decoration Day was marked by a parade led by Grand Army of the Republic veterans with speeches and band music, and the first floor of Aspen's ambitious Jerome Hotel was nearly completed. The Palace Theater presented the "great moral drama" of *Ten Nights in a Bar Room*, while Wheeler's Opera House offered lighter fare with the "picturesque Irish drama" of *The Ivy Leaf*, a production as famous for its scenery as it was for its plot. But had the Chatfields attended a performance of *The Ivy Leaf*, they might have taken heed and observed the play's forbidden lovers secretly communicating with each other through the titular device, thwarting the opposition of their families.[44]

Six weeks passed during which Ora Chatfield and Clara Dietrich lived apart and, like *The Ivy Leaf*'s lovers, supposedly incommunicado. There were no more love letters, nor was Dietrich any longer in Emma. She left her position as Emma postmistress on June 15 when she and her business partner, Mr. Morrison, sold the store to Charles Mather, who assumed the role of Emma's postmaster.[45] If her departure was obligatory, no mention survived in the newspapers. When Isaac Chatfield returned from a trip to his cattle ranch in Las Animas County on June 27, she had already left Emma for good; the *Aspen Daily Chronicle* reported that Clara was "visiting in Aspen."[46] There was thus some shock when the *Denver Times* reported on July 6 that instead "the lady lovers went to Aspen, Miss Dietrich with the avowed intention of marrying a gentleman who lives not far from this place, and Miss Chatfield to visit relatives. From here they went to Denver and, as soon as they were missed, and their elopement suspected Hon. I. W. Chatfield was communicated with and requested to bring Miss Ora back from Denver."[47]

The story of the "lady lovers"—a description coined by the *Denver Times*—triggered no end of curiosity; the community was "rent from center to circumference" over the "sensational love affair."[48] Despite appearances, Clara Dietrich and Ora Chatfield had secretly planned an elopement. Their options were limited, and they had to be careful: while two steam railroads connected Aspen to the outside world, one of them, the Denver & Rio Grande, ran directly through Emma, where Dietrich and Chatfield were known to everyone. They appear to have prudently avoided this danger by taking the other railroad, the Colorado Midland, instead. The Chatfields never took the Midland line, Clara never slung mailbags at its express cars, and no Midland crewman would have any remote reason to know her face. On a Midland train, the two women would simply be polite strangers. Even better, the Colorado Midland's "Denver Express" left Aspen daily at four thirty in the afternoon, on a timetable much faster than the Denver & Rio Grande.[49] They planned separate excuses (visiting relatives, and a "traditional" marriage) that allowed them to pack a small amount of luggage and rendezvous in Aspen.

At the Colorado Midland's railroad station in Aspen, passengers scurried to board the cars as the last of the mail and express was loaded into the baggage and mail cars ahead. In approaching the cars, Dietrich and Chatfield reached a point of life where the full measure and attendant risks of a plan became dangerously evident, a point where one could step back and reverse course with minimal repercussion, if at all. If they walked away from each other, if they did not board the cars, or if they boarded the cars but thought twice and got off again, if they obeyed the laws of society, no one would notice, much less care. They could go on as if nothing had happened: Ora Chatfield could hurry back plausibly and without suspicion, while Clara Dietrich would have the rest of her life to find another woman, preferably closer to her own age and without an aggressive family. They stayed on the cars instead. After only a few moments they were crossing the Maroon Creek trestle outside of Aspen, moving through the valley to pause momentarily and dangerously at Aspen Junction, the present-day Basalt, only two miles from Emma, before burrowing instantly into the mountains toward the safety of Leadville and beyond.[50] Evening's light saw their train climbing through Hagerman Pass, past the Palisades of the Fryingpan River, plunging through the Hagerman Tunnel, swinging across trestles so high up that the tops of tall trees brushed by the cars as they moved past. After arriving in Denver, they quickly boarded another train, perhaps the Union Pacific, or perhaps the

Rock Island, venturing eastward onto the open prairie, where the Front Range of the Rockies devolved into a hazy blue line behind them, a trail of coal smoke betraying their passing. By sunrise on July 4 their train had breached the Kansas prairies, with a flurry of passengers dressing and making themselves up for the day, with momentary displays of bleary eyes, unattached collars, hair down, all of which was overlooked in the common understanding of all people obliged to travel together awkwardly and publicly in small and confined communal spaces. Before long the Missouri River appeared, bracketed by the sharp passing of steel bridge beams, flickering white steamboats, and vast gray water surrounded by grassy banks and a sheer blue sky dotted with the coal smoke of a large, bustling nineteenth-century city: Kansas City, Missouri.

On the surface, it appeared as though the Colorado couple were simply in town to enjoy the patriotic holiday amid the festivities of a large city while visiting Dietrich's sister, Bessie Grannon, whose husband, Joseph, worked as a typesetter for the *Kansas City Journal*. The opportunity to visit distant friends and family was a great pleasure, and Clara's unexpected arrival probably brought great happiness to her sister Bessie.[51] Bessie had married a year before, when she was seventeen, and it appears Dietrich and Chatfield might have stayed to help them celebrate their first wedding anniversary on July 7. Their guests would likely share a single bed as well, but this was a common practice at the time, and nothing would be thought of it. Beneath the surface, however, trouble was brewing. From the moment the news of their elopement was telegraphed to the world, they were effectively fugitives, as well as objects of a bizarre national curiosity. Distance alone offered little protection from news-hungry editors of the nineteenth-century press; only the passage of time could do that, and even this had already fled. "A telegram was sent to this city," the *Kansas City Journal* later reported, adding that the missive was "asking for information regarding the two girls, it being known that a relative of the Detrick girl [sic] was working there. It fell into the hands of Mr. J. H. Grannon, brother-in-law of Miss Detrick [sic], who promptly answered," but he signed his response to the Pitkin County Sheriff's Office only as "Journal," noting simply that the "girls" could be found in Kansas City.[52]

Grannon appears to have concluded that as the "lady lovers" were wanted by the Pitkin County sheriff, the Pitkin County sheriff would have to find them. All he would do was nudge the ball and stand back to watch the rest. The responsibility therefore would not rest on his shoulders, nor would he, he may have imagined, be seen as interfering with his wife's family.

Sheriff White immediately wired the Kansas City chief of police, who responded that the "eagerly sought young ladies" had been found through the aid of a local reporter. The sheriff then made an extended trip to Kansas City, where he met with the city's police chief and "the chief, the sheriff and reporter sallied out after the two girls only to discover that the reporter had located two pretty dressmakers instead of the Colorado couple."[53] The lead had turned out to be false, while the two dressmakers were surprised at finding themselves the object of men's sudden curiosity. But who had sent the telegram? The *Aspen Daily Chronicle* later reported that "a trip to the Journal office failed to discover the person who had sent the message to Sheriff White. No one there knew anything about it."[54] Working deep within the heart of the large newspaper, Joseph Grannon was far from editors and receptionists, who were in turn completely unaware of his actions.

Sheriff John White had taken the risk of going after the two women in order to gain and advance the favor of his community and his political aspirations, and he spent days, miles, and dollars to do so. It wasn't uncommon for him to travel for his duties, but he typically did so within the state.[55] Kansas City was exceptionally distant compared to his other travel destinations, and as his journey stretched over some days it thus required and compelled a successful outcome. Unaware that Clara's sister lived in Kansas City, he had actually been informed that she had family, Andrew and Susan Dietrich, in Leon, Iowa, a small farming town located 125 miles north of Kansas City, just across the Iowa state line in beautiful country near the Thompson River. There, Leon mayor William Albaugh told Sheriff White "to go to the composing room of the Kansas City Journal and he could secure the desired information."[56] A possible lead for the anonymous source buoyed him on the long trip back, and "upon his return to Kansas City the sheriff went to the Journal composing room where he met Joseph Grannon, who was able to tell him the whereabouts of the eagerly sought young ladies."⁵⁷

On the morning of July 17, the sheriff went to the Grannon home on Troost Avenue and "informed Miss Ora Chatfield that he should expect her to accompany him to her home near Aspen this evening. She said she supposed she would have to go, but she did not want to do so," and both women "expressed surprise this morning at the notoriety they had obtained." More significant was the note that "Miss Chatfield laughed about their escapade and said that she and Miss Dietrick [sic] were out for a good time and they had it."⁵⁸ The sheriff told a newspaper reporter upon his return to Aspen that "the girls were happy and contented although they were almost out of money. Their affection had continued, and they had been enjoying themselves riding on the cable cars and in other innocent ways."⁵⁹ "They were somewhat surprised," reported the *Aspen Daily Chronicle*, "to see the tall figure of the sheriff, but Miss Chatfield made no objection when informed that she must come back to Colorado."⁶⁰

Joseph Grannon had enabled Sheriff White to retrieve Ora Chatfield and return her to the enfolding arms of proper family life. It's not known what Bessie Grannon thought of her husband's betrayal of her sister, although she ultimately divorced him several years later. White advised Clara Dietrich that it would be best for her to remain in Kansas City, and he escorted Ora onto that evening's westbound Chicago, Rock Island & Pacific train, where the coaches became a genteel rolling prison with the polite but determined sheriff as her keeper. At Denver they transferred onto a Colorado Midland train, which arrived at Aspen Junction (now known as Basalt) on Friday, July 19, less than three weeks after the elopement. Ora was greeted there by her parents, "overwhelmed with joy at the sight of their child" and greatly relieved to have her back. "The sensational story has come to an end," the *Aspen Daily Chronicle* reported the next day. "Her female adorer is separated by many miles, and the tired sheriff has once more settled down to the routine work of his office. All's well," it summed up, "that ends well."⁶¹

Clara Dietrich did not return to Colorado. Her family immediately compelled her into a "remedial" marriage to Oliver Tyler, a farmer in

Idaho Territory, after a few months' introduction. It's difficult to know just how she reconciled the destruction of her "being's destiny" with this new and enforced reality or whether her brave Amazons ever managed to ride the Car of Enlightenment into Idaho or whether its wheels were simply crushed in Kansas City. It is likely that this process evolved in an unspoken manner embraced and enforced by those surrounding her over the following months and years. The Tylers settled near Caldwell, Idaho, where Clara Dietrich Tyler bore several children before divorcing her husband in about 1909.[62]

Prosperity, ambitions, morality, and electric lighting could not prevent the complete collapse of Aspen's silver mining economy in 1893 or the subsequent loss of its prestige and population. The Chatfields' houses in Aspen, once the symbol of cosmopolitan achievement, became mere provincial residences as Aspen slowly drifted into its "quiet years" as almost a ghost town in a distant valley.[63] Isaac Chatfield's political career faded, and his attention was increasingly focused elsewhere, particularly on Wyoming stock raising. It was not until August 1898 that twenty-five-year-old Ora (practically a maiden lady herself by their standards) was married off; the groom was Charles Shaw, a Wyoming stockman some fifteen years her senior. He took her to Big Horn, Wyoming, where several other Chatfields headed in the following years, and shared a home among their ranch hands and where they had a son. By 1930 they had divorced.[64]

Ora Chatfield and Clara Dietrich discovered that it was nearly impossible to maintain a relationship when the entire community had become their chaperone. And while they reacted by performing the time-honored ritual of elopement, the mechanisms that encouraged their bravery also provided their rout. Iron horses swept them from Aspen to Kansas City in just over forty hours, leaving their societal prison several hundred miles behind. But railroads, combined with newspapers, telegraphs, and an anonymous informant, also allowed the Pitkin County sheriff to find them in a matter of days, after pursuing them across four states at a considerable cost in railroad tickets and hotel bills. Distance alone meant nothing when instantaneous telegraphed news provided details of their elopement to an entire nation.

6

An Anonymous Logger in the Industrial Frontier

As the nineteenth century drew to a close, vast changes were taking place with increasing rapidity across the western landscape. The frontier, it seemed, was finished: the curtains of telegraph lines and railroad iron that descended upon the wilderness had long since carved up the plains into commodified grids, flooded by waves of settlement and combine harvesters. By virtue of population, all of the western states and territories were now declared to be fully settled. The age of expansion had completed its course, people said. The "empire of commerce and industry" had at last arrived.[1]

All across the region, what made the West its own was being rebuilt and transformed into a mirror of the East. The great cities of the West took on an urban aspect. Seattle's business district, rebuilt from a destructive fire in 1889, was as active as that of Pittsburgh or Chicago, presenting a loud tangle of brick walls and switching engines running along its harbor. Large swaths of San Francisco, wiped out by earthquake and fire in 1906, provided opportunity to impose an idealized "City Beautiful" upon the scars of the old city in a gracious, electrically lit, Beaux-Arts culmination of what thinkers of the age considered moral progress, guarded by the genius of technological power.[2] The rubble of the Barbary Coast was hauled away, and the long-buried hulks of the ships that had carried gold rushers to their fate once more saw air before they were buried again, this time under powerful new buildings with electric elevators and steel girders. In the hands of civilization, technology could further moral progress through the *offer* of opportunities as much as through the control of them: the white-enameled sanitary kitchen, the 20-horsepower Ford car, the recorded voices of Enrico Caruso and Adelina Patti in every home.[3] But when necessary, it cast nets of entanglements, snaring and controlling lives with the same unremarkable determination that it used to break up postmistresses and ranchers' daughters.

At the same time, the means of control were changing, in part from near-revolutionary developments in the newly emerging fields of the social and medical sciences. In the course of this development, "sex perversion"—the idea of a sex impulse somehow gone awry—became a common theme among doctors, public speakers, and law enforcement. Much of this discussion referred to homosexuality, although it sometimes included anything outside of a socially acceptable norm, from egotism to an urge to rob banks.[4] These discussions were often accompanied by calls to social activism, such as a 1913 warning given in part by the chancellor of Stanford University against the "evils of sex perversion" before an audience of scientific and civic representatives, noting that "one of the first duties of civilization is stamping out the social plagues."[5] The "social plagues" in the chancellor's list also included the genuine and serious social problems of human trafficking and prostitution, thus linking and tarring gay people by the association. In the 1910s prison sentences for "sex perversion" ranged from three to five years, and police vice raids on places where gay men gathered resembled crusades, with the language of predetermined guilt, high bail, and public humiliation. "The courtroom was suffocating with a morbid crowd of lascivious oglers," reported the *Sacramento Bee* as a group of gay men arrested in San Francisco in 1918 came to trial. "The defendants were abject spectacles of despair, though they tried to steel themselves for the ordeal. A thousand eyes were riveted on their deadened countenances. The wages of their shame were being paid."[6]

There were nonetheless places in the West where the influence of civilization and medical science did not penetrate, at least significantly, and where people could engage each other as they liked with minimal interference. Some of these places drew from a surprisingly unlikely ally: the developing industrial West. The logging engine and air hammer made it practical to operate mines, lumber camps, and other industries in increasingly isolated and previously unworkable parts of the West, where the unexpected liberties of industrialism could flourish far from social prejudice.[7] By moving farther and farther into the "mountain wilds," industrial development placed large groups of men into circumstances that were essentially little different from the brigades of fur trappers a century earlier, in a modern form of frontier culture where male-male relations were embraced within an absolute masculine identity.[8]

The scale of investment could be staggering: in October 1912 the Globe Consolidated mine, high in the Trinity Mountains of Northern California, required no less than three hundred tons of machinery and employed over a hundred men, all for a mine whose entrance was at an elevation of over six thousand feet and snowbound in winter.[9] More than a few lumber operations had their own logging railroads that hauled felled trees from forest to mill, some of those rail routes running up to sixty or even a hundred miles.[10] Even death was modern: a man driving to the mining town of Rhyolite in a new 1913 Regal touring car died of exposure while crossing Death Valley, "the first automobile traveler claimed as a victim by the desert."[11] This modernity and ease of access did not necessarily transform the old way of life among frontiersmen, at least not immediately. The automobile traveler, dying of heat exhaustion just feet from his machine near Stovepipe Wells, simply joined a long line of travelers by wagon who had died before him in the same way. In these industrial frontiers, in the deserts and in the mountains, in fact wherever the realities of survival stripped off the veneer of artificial concerns, people gained or lost stature as they had for generations: by their own works and attitude. The technology itself was inert and neutral—nothing, at least in these environments, to the rise or fall of those within it.

Inside views of these worlds, and the social dynamics within them, occasionally survive, in part from early studies in the field of sociology, an offshoot of medical science. In these studies, newly minted sociologists supplied fact and observation, backed by statistics that quantified the theories of previous generations. Because these developments coincided with the rise of the industrial frontier and its preservation of pragmatic tradition, they fortuitously documented and preserved records of many of the lives that otherwise might have been left unknown. The most notable of these studies would come from Dr. Alfred Kinsey, the now well-known sexologist, from materials gathered and published in the first half of the twentieth century. He concluded that as western outdoorsmen took a necessarily pragmatic view of the world, they were equally forthright in their relations, uncolored and unburdened by arbitrary convictions or the niceties of manner. He also found that in some cases, outdoorsmen in the West engaged each other more frequently than their eastern counterparts.

Many of Kinsey's findings paralleled the work of other professional field researchers, who were already finding that male-male relationships were both common and may have thrived in the environments surrounding the industrial frontier. A specific example of these dynamics in lumber camps was documented in 1914 by a study of itinerant working men in California led by Carleton Parker. As Parker's field agents traveled across the state, from the Sanger Lumber Company camps in the southern Sierra Nevada northward to Redding, they found that male-male relations were relatively common in lumber camps, and a person working there could expect to come across them with reasonable frequency. Most of these men were young, they found, with almost half under thirty, and they came to the work from a variety of backgrounds. Parker added that "investigation reports of a most dependable and technical nature show that in California lumber camps sex perversion [i.e., homosexuality, not egotism or bank robbery] within the entire group is as developed and recognized as the well-known similar practice in prisons and reformatories."[12] Unfamiliar with the biological origins of gay and bisexual men, Parker concluded instead that the large numbers of men thrown together in the distant environment of these lumber and mining camps contributed to the same-sex activity there.[13]

Far more personal accounts occasionally survived in the memories of older gay men, specifically those who lived long enough to record their memories for posterity following the rise of the modern gay civil rights movements. A Colorado man remembered seeing silver miners gambol about with each other during the Rocky Mountain winter of 1914, while a California man recalled his experiences as a young man working in logging and mining camps.[14] "In my youth," he recalled, "I worked in a logging camp for almost seven months and in a gold mining camp for two full years, isolated 75 miles from the nearest town."[15] The identity of this California man remains unknown, but his narratives, together with other anonymous accounts of this type, are often integral artifacts of the era, reflecting a lifetime's familiarity with the risks and dangers of social and legal retribution. Whoever he was, his recollections, first printed in 1973 and expressed in the rather staid language of a man who came of age in a far earlier era, a style shared by many men of his period, straight or gay, working in similar fields, focused on two observations of life among these men that surprised and impressed him. One was the relatively large number of men he saw engaging each other, far more than he had imagined; the other was how their masculinity trampled the clichés of gay men he was taught to expect, to the extent that he wondered whether they were even gay at all. In all probability, some were gay while others were bisexual; none of them identified themselves with the soft and unmanly cliché image of urban homosexuality.

The anonymous man's first experience was at a logging camp in Colorado, most likely in the Rockies, perhaps near Pagosa, Gunnison, Ouray, or Boulder. Logging camps follow the trees, and trees of any size are usually in mountains reached by rudimentary roads, easily closed in winter. Logging is seasonal work, and apart from a few operations where snow was necessary to cushion the felling of particularly large and ancient trees, timber cannot be felled effectively in the snow, nor can lumber be dried on the racks; in addition, log ponds freeze over and flumes must be shut down. With the onset of winter, the majority of men employed at a camp head out to the world below while a small crew remains to take care of the equipment and provide maintenance as necessary.[16] Sawmill machinery has to be kept oiled and free of rust; saw blades polished, oiled, and sharpened; and steam donkey engines protected with grease and their boilers kept dry to prevent ice from damaging the flues. If a camp has horses or draft animals, they must be well supplied with hay and veterinary care; if a camp has a logging railroad, the line of track must be walked to make sure it is in good condition and has not suffered washouts or deadfalls and that it can be put back into operation and profitability with the opening of the spring season. The winter crews stock up with supplies and settle in, expecting to be cut off from the rest of the world for long periods of time. There is no economic incentive to keep a road free of snow in the winter when business is closed, and it's more practical to stock up and sit tight.

While many western logging operations employed a hundred men or more divided into separate camps, this Colorado logging camp was a small one, with only nine men overwintering there.[17] The anonymous memoirist found himself within a masculine and proactive society of men, and as winter approached, he saw the full measure, at least for him, of what this meant. "In the logging camp we were snowed in for a good part of the winter," he recalled. "Nine of us were confined to the camp for weeks of isolation, but not one of us could be considered effeminate, neurotic, or abnormal. Yet all but two engaged in homosexual activities, and those two, who were brothers, could have had their own personal means of relieving themselves."[18] He was both surprised and impressed with what he encountered among these men. He had assumed "that those engaged in homosexual activities were of a specific type," an assumption built over the years through the negative stereotypes he had been taught and conditioned to expect. He found himself instead among regular, no-nonsense men, some of whom were married, who engaged each other as they engaged their work, in an experienced, straightforward way, suggesting an old and established habit, honed and advanced from one generation of outdoorsmen to the next. "There was not great deal of oral sex involved," he recounted, a style of engagement that Kinsey found was closer to urban practice than rural, and one the anonymous man had refused to enact himself. Instead, he remarked that the men preferred to either lend a hand or hit home plate, with little variety in between, and that of the men who engaged him personally, intercourse was "the popular method, preferred by the majority" and that the camp's loggers introduced him to its "discomforts, adjustments and ecstasies."[19]

During his time there, the anonymous man found himself drawn to a burly German man named Al, largely because he was an affectionate "lover-type" who had the ability to "radiate warmth and love" whenever they engaged each other, usually in the camp's barn for protection against the winter cold. These encounters left a lasting impression upon him regarding the value of affection and genuine regard among men, as well as the positive role that male contact had when properly understood and embraced. He also found himself put on by the owner of the logging camp, a big Swedish man who had "no warmth or love" and approached the anonymous man through a series of unwelcome, very uncomfortable engagements he found forceful, careless, and extremely painful. "The pain was almost unbelievable," he recalled. "I almost passed out, and wished I could pass out."[20] These experiences taught him that character mattered more than anything, especially in happiness.

After seven months he decided to move on, leaving the Swede behind. Loggers are famous boomers.[21] The anonymous man had joined this migratory flock of workers and then jumped ship, leaving the logging camp to ramble on, eventually to California, where he worked a large gold mining camp in the mountains for two years followed by work at a small mining outfit in the California desert. Here he found the same social dynamics at play but on a much larger scale: in the mountains, about half of the mining camp's fifty men were engaging each other to some degree, with two pairing up as a committed couple. His description of the camp, the number of men he saw employed there, and the equipment they used suggest a quartz mining operation, with a cable tram and a stamp mill, perhaps in the Plumas district of the Sierra Nevada, or perhaps farther north, toward Redding. He spent an additional seven or so months at the desert mining camp, probably in or near the Mojave along California's eastern border.

The functional elements of quartz mining are much the same across the West. Veins of ore are prospected and located, then reached by digging a series of underground shafts through the rock to gain direct access to the vein. It requires intensive labor to reach, establish, supply, and operate a given mine, and shafts are often several hundred feet deep, with a few extending a thousand feet or more. Until the advent of pneumatic jackhammers and electric lamps, these shafts were dug entirely by hand, using pickaxes, hammers, and stakes combined with blasting powder in rooms lit only by miners' flickering candles. Raw ore was moved out of the shafts by cart, sometimes to a winch-elevator that would lift the ore up out of the mine tunnels, from which it would then be sent for processing through a series of stamp mills and cyanide reduction mills to crush and dissolve the rock and extract the desired metals. Leftover waste rock was then dumped outside in enormous piles known as tailings, still evident today—the near-permanent mark of former mining industries scattered throughout the West. In these mines, men worked for wages, giving them a sense of individual identity separate from the camp. It was a simple but determined way of life. Single men working in either logging or mining camps shared a unique circumstance—that of being among relatively large groups of men living in isolated communities with the benefits of basic amenities and clearly defined off-hours. This meant hard work together with hard play, far from the concerns of a city. "The loggers are generally single men," remarked observers in 1902, "rough by the very nature of the life and surroundings, but withal good hearted and generous."[22] At the Hume-Bennett logging operation on Hume Lake in 1917, the single men's cabins were in effect their own social district, where they could relax and blow off steam as they liked without supervision.[23] Several camps deliberately placed the bachelor quarters far away from the married men's housing, sometimes separated by a "screen" of mess halls and other buildings. Even so, their presence was unmistakable. During the evenings, recalled the wife of an Oregon logger, "I often heard the music of an accordion wafting down the narrow valley" from the bachelor camp above.[24]

The most striking features of this life were the rounds of evening socializing. The anonymous man's mining camp "was located many miles from the nearest settlement," he explained, "and when winter came, and the road out was blocked by snow, a restlessness among the crew was evidenced by a raid on the vaseline [sic] supply in the first aid cabinet, of which I was custodian."[25] As evening drew on, the mining camp became something of a working man's dog run, a place to gambol about and see who was there and what was up. The "brawny, ultra-masculine types," he recalled, "invariably started out increasing their sociabilities, taking booze with them when dropping in on different buddies throughout the camp." At the mining camp, as with the logging camp, the anonymous man was soon pegged as amenable, as he was accommodating. "My own time," he recalled, "was pretty well monopolized in the evenings by first one and then another of those inclined towards homosexuality."[26]

One of these miners was named Chet. "Chet was so handsome, warm and smiling," the anonymous man recalled, "that everyone more or less loved the guy. He was a jackhammer operator, truck driver, or mill hand, depending on where he was needed most."[27] For most of the year Chet joined the carloads of miners heading off to brothels seventy-five miles distant, which specialized in accommodating miners and loggers. "Every Saturday afternoon three or four carloads of the guys," or about fifteen to twenty men, "including Chet," would head out of camp, not returning until the following day. It was not until winter approached and the roads were blocked by snow that Chet's attention drifted over to the anonymous man, where it stayed more or less for the rest of the winter season. "I was speechless with surprise," the anonymous man recalled when Chet first stopped by, slightly drunk on beer, asking, "'Ain't you going to ask me to sit down?'"

"The all-wise psychiatrists would classify Chet as 'straight,' just straying temporarily from the path when he couldn't get to the cat houses," the anonymous man remarked. "They could be right. But when he couldn't get to the cat house he sure got his kicks with the other guys. I wasn't the only one he had." Chet continued to visit occasionally over the warmer months as well, even after he resumed making off for distant brothels. He wasn't necessarily entirely straight, as the anonymous man wondered. He was more likely to have been bisexual, leaning primarily toward heterosexual contacts with a few men thrown in. There were more than a few of them in this mining camp; in fact, he thought that about half or more of the camp's men were "inclined" to a greater or lesser degree.

Crunching the numbers, he thought that of the fifty-five or so men in the camp, "conservatively over half" were "getting relief from one another."[28]

When compared to Kinsey's scale of human orientation and its modern interpretations, these figures suggest that about half of the camp's men were fully heterosexually oriented, with no interest in engaging each other. These men held off, like a 1920s Oregon "bull cook," content to dream of pretty girls while counting "the number of days' work necessary before he will have enough money to go to town."[29] The remaining men, like Chet, were sufficiently bisexually or homosexually oriented to engage each other while in camp, to varying degrees, along lines that appear to have ranged from utility, relief, and pragmatism to companionship, sport, or pleasure. "These are men who have faced the rigors of nature in the wild," Kinsey remarked. "They live on realties and on a minimum of theory. Such a background breeds the attitude that sex is sex, irrespective of the nature with whom the relation is had," resulting in "a minimum of personal disturbance or social conflict over such activity. It is the kind of homosexual experience," Kinsey thought, "which the explorer and pioneer may have had in their histories."[30]

The anonymous man found it difficult to reconcile the images of neurotic gay men he was socially conditioned to expect with the regular, masculine men he encountered in these camps. The blunt reality of outdoor life was miles away from the neurosis, pathologies, and weakness defined by doctors and the popular press. The idea that the stereotypical image was only one part of a far larger and diverse state of life, or that these masculine men might include gay and bisexual men among them, seems to be something he approached without daring to fully embrace. And while he refuted the opinions of men he derided as "experts," the bedrock of his conditioning was so strong that he seems to have hesitated to abandon their opinions completely. He appears to have concluded instead that if the neurotic stereotypes described by the "experts" were the gay ones, the men he was around must be something else. These men thought so too. "Such a group of hard-riding, hard-hitting, assertive males," Kinsey pointed out, "would not tolerate the affectations of some city groups that are involved with the homosexual; but this, as far as they can see, has little to do with the question of having sexual relations with other men."[31]

Researchers sometimes found it difficult to comprehend the depth, importance, and intensity of relationships among these men, or their value as equal to conventional relationships, even when evidence was placed before them. Frederick Mills, one of the field researchers hired by the California Immigration Commission in 1914, readily found that men living a nomadic life often grew lonely and desired companionship, emphasized by an itinerant forty-five-year-old miner in Redding who tried to buy him a meal and "hook up" with him. "It is the constant craving for human company, for friends," Mills wrote afterward, "that is so strong among the floating class." But while Mills recognized the desire for companionship among these men, as well as the organization of these desires by unspoken and common consent among the men along standardized lines, to the extent that he considered it an "institution" he nonetheless appears to have been hesitant to accord much more value to these relationships than a sort of paste imitation of conventional domestic home life. "Denied wives, or families, or circles of sympathetic friends," he wrote, "this feeling, can only be partial[ly] satisfied thru the institution of 'partners.'"[32]

Some of these limitations were present in the encounters experienced by the anonymous man. The Colorado logger Al, for all his affectionate warmth and love, did not partner up with the anonymous man and chose instead to simply engage him through a series of pleasant encounters. Likewise, the California miner Chet took on the man only after snowfall had blocked roads to distant brothels, effectively reproducing his affectionate, down-to-business manner with the brothel's women onto his engagements with the anonymous man, modified by the recognition that the man was less a momentary toy and more of, to some degree, a working community equal. Perhaps more significant was the anonymous man's "mutual love affair" with the foreman of the mining camp's stamp mill. It lasted a year, but by his own account "ended disastrously, I guess by my jealousy," suggesting the foreman did not take him on exclusively and preferred instead to perambulate to some extent through the camp's available options. The anonymous man did not name this man in his recollections, nor did he extend as much detail as he did in describing the other men. It may have been a difficult memory for him.

The anonymous man was seeking the emotional fulfillment of a devoted and monogamous relationship, but he was doing so in the gregarious environment of mining and lumber camps, where the "floating class" and their boomer attitude, at least among the men he encountered, preferred a series of short-term social engagements, weaving these relationships through most of a given camp and forming a network of bonds and experience that paralleled and corresponded to their own ideals and served their own needs, whether intimacy or independence. Their world was a kind of working man's dog run, where the teamwork of working relationships that required trust and skill in handling a saw or mining drill were reinforced by social ones, in a frontier comradeship that served a valuable function in building a repertoire of trust.

Even so, the anonymous man was not alone in dreaming of a devoted partnership. At least two men at his mining camp formed such a connection over his time there; theirs was a strong and devoted pairing that firmly revealed the limitations of Mills's sociological conceptions. There in the camp, recalled the anonymous man, "two of the most masculine of the crew (a tram operator and a jackhammer man) soon started pairing off exclusively," building a relationship based on personal commitment instead of mere relief. The two men had sized each other up, got their own cabin, and proceeded to set up housekeeping, even dressing alike in the habit of devoted couples by "ordering exact duplicates of clothing out of the Montgomery Ward catalog." This relationship went past what men of that environment and era could engage without assuming a homosexual identity and suggests a consciously intimate partnership between men who found themselves fortunate to be together in personal alignment. Their relationship was also well appreciated by several of the men around them: the anonymous man admitted that he, along a few others in that mining camp, looked to them with longing, "the envy of a number of us who had been searching for just such a set up."[33]

Part of their bond may have been a shared work ethic or status within the field of skilled labor as equals. Both men engaged in dangerous work, each critical to a mine's operation and each relentlessly difficult. Jackhammer men used pneumatic drills to bore into rock a series of holes that were then filled with gunpowder and blasted apart to expose a vein of ore. It was among the most dangerous jobs in mining and also the loudest: along with the jackhammer itself, blasts of dynamite continually "echoed and reverberated through the forests and the mountains."[34] In some mines, drillers were responsible for both drilling and blasting. Not all the charges might go off, and a careful man knew to wait before checking.[35] The man's partner worked just as dynamically on the mine's tram, probably a cable tram, used to move buckets of ore from a mine high on a mountain to a processing stamp mill below, using overhead cables, similar to a ski lift.[36] Cable trams were often several miles long, and their complex system of tension and movement effectively made them the largest machines in a mining camp.[37] Tram operators used the force of their whole body while shunting the ore buckets, knew how to splice and repair steel cable, whether the cable was taut or slack, if the machinery was running smoothly, or if the ore bucket grips were firmly fixed to the traveling cable. At each end of the tramway, ore buckets had to be shifted on and off the main cable for loading and unloading, a process producing a perennial clatter and clank as the buckets got up to speed or were braked as they engaged or disengaged from the main cable. Tram operators who fell from the towers or buckets were nearly always killed; a "miraculous escape" for one man included compound fractures. Nearly all these men were in their twenties.[38]

After two years in this mining camp, as well as an additional six months at a mine in the California desert, the anonymous man moved on. When he wrote of his own experiences many years later, he made a point to emphasize how the men in these camps defied the image of urban gay men he had encountered in the outside world and how they lived outside of it themselves—separate, unbothered, and content. At these camps, and at camps like them across the West, he saw the innate human resilience and capacity for authenticity fostered in the western air. The industrial frontier preserved old ways of life that were rapidly vanishing in a civilized and occupied West, and it did so through the most modern of means, placed into the most distant of frontier worlds. The men employed here gathered up and adapted bits of the civilized world to their own use and purpose, much as the trappers had a century earlier, with little bits of the world remade to suit themselves. Nothing was arbitrary in this industrial frontier: everything was there for a reason and existed by virtue of earned practical experience. Living and working dangerously in western lands fostered and preserved a practical way of life in defiance of arbitrary objections, from people who lived in the wild and withstood the "rigors of nature."

Afterword

On a fine evening sometime in the late 1950s, two cowboys stood against the counter of a gay bar in Oklahoma City, having a drink. They were working cowboys, employed on a ranch in Texas, and had driven over a hundred or more miles up from Texas to be there that night.[1] The Mayflower Bar wasn't much—something of a dive, its patrons remembered, with paneled walls stained from cigarette smoke and stale beer and a jukebox alternating viciously between Johnny Horton and Peggy Lee. Its crowd was diverse, from motorcycle men to regular joes to lesbian women, the women having become famous for fighting off and injuring a gang of football players who had come there to harass them one night.[2] People who went there knew they risked harassment from police raids as well, but it was a gay bar in the American West during a deeply prejudiced era, and its reputation had spread by word of mouth across state lines and even onto distant ranches.

One of the two cowboys at the Mayflower Bar remained silent. The other talked a bit, remarking that in Texas, in the ranching country they came from, there were usually from two to three homosexually active cowboys on any given ranch. They recognized each other silently and kept this information among themselves. In the Texas ranching lands where the XIT and the Matador once reigned, the ability to remain quiet and undemonstrative was as much about survival as it was about trust, as it meant laying a foundation for a network of careful support among gay people in the ranching country, in effect paralleling the requirements of survival in the frontier wilderness. They used the language of their working world to shape, express, and protect their personal world: by employing a degree of reticence common among ranchers as a whole, they were able to slowly and, even more important, safely recognize and identify each other while simultaneously gauging each other's ability to keep their counsel, demonstrating that they were cautious, trustworthy, and safe to be around. It was the key to opening the door into a hidden society.

The cattle industry that employed them could trace its roots directly back to the years following the Civil War, when a renewed demand for Texas longhorns brought a price at northern markets ten times that in Texas. At its height, the business was massive: in 1880 nearly 400,000 longhorns were herded north from Texas ranges, with more than 280,000 head sent to Dodge City alone. Cowtowns bristled with spurs, drawls, revolvers, and trade. Cattle trails from Texas to Kansas were several hundred miles long, and drovers spent on average two to three months on the trails with herds of several thousand each and little more than each other to rely upon in times of danger. People who took on this work often started out young, gaining experience and perspectives on life that became lifelong and decisively western. "I was raised on a horse's back," remarked a Texas cowboy, adding that he "never did learn to walk good."[3]

People who take up stock raising adopt very specific sets of requirements necessary for the work, honed by hard-earned, practical, and unforgiving experience. The safety of the herd and their investment was an all-important factor, followed by their own safety and that of their horses. In times of danger, veteran rancher Granville Stuart wrote, "every man would sacrifice his life to protect the herd."[4] Montana cowboy Edward Abbott, who married Stuart's daughter, added that they worked as much if not more for their own reputation as for that of their brand, earning a place among their fellows through their working skill, much as William Stewart had done nearly a century earlier. Everyone had to do their part, and courage was expected at all times; a weak, hesitant, or cowardly man would endanger not only his fellows but the herd itself. The drovers therefore developed a contempt for complaining or quitting; the men had a duty to make the best of things and generally behave in ways that reflected well upon each other. "Living in the open was not bad," recalled one Texas drover, "except when a spell of weather hit on us; then it did call for a home-sweet-home song. The rawhides nesting with the outfit were a jolly bunch of buckaroos who took things as they were and said, 'It could be worse.'"⁵ Lack of sleep while on night guard, alkali dust, hailstorms that dented saddles, or rain that soaked to the skin were all part of the job. "It's hell," wrote Abbott after an eighteen-hour day in 1888, "but it's for Diamond M, and don't you forget it."⁶

This quality of life informed the way the two Texas cowboys at the Mayflower Bar conducted themselves, as both ranchers and as gay men. Just where in Texas they came from is unknown. They might have come from the high and rolling plains in the Texas Panhandle, near Amarillo, more or less following the Canadian River on their way to Oklahoma City. Alternatively, they might have come from the plains and hill country of central Texas that descends to the cities of Fort Worth and Dallas, in effect following the old cattle trails northward and then crossing the Red River on their way toward Oklahoma City. From either one of these locales to the Oklahoma state line, and then from the state line to Oklahoma City, might be two to three hundred miles or more. By the 1950s this distance had been easily tamed by improvements in highways, cars, and trucks, which were equally critical to providing the two men with a measure of safety in the event of trouble in Oklahoma City. In case of a bar raid or something similar, the intervening counties and jurisdictions piled up like sandbags on either side of the state line, itself a kind of moat, effectively insulating them from the chance of any news reaching their home range.

If the lives on these ranches bore any commonalities with the social dynamics of the industrial frontier experienced by the anonymous man among the loggers and miners of California, they also had important differences. Most importantly, the boozy gregariousness of the mining and lumber camp could not exist on the ranch and range, where no one drank on duty. Forests of trees never stampede or run around, but cattle will, and every hand must be absolutely sober at all times, night and day, in case of trouble. A drunken or incapacitated man was a danger to himself and to his outfit. Cowboys and cowmen alike respected the rule. "Everybody knew," remarked an early cowboy, "that drinking and cattle didn't mix, and there was never any trouble."⁷

Another difference may be generational. Writing in the 1940s, Dr. Alfred Kinsey found that the ease of engagement among older generations did not necessarily follow among the younger generations. Older men had come of age before the influence of medical science had recognized and established the "homosexual" as a type, so for them, engaging each other wasn't necessarily considered homosexuality as such and accordingly did not possess a stigma. Younger men, in contrast, appeared to be growing wary of anything that hinted of the unusual, especially as the "homosexual" became an absolute and derogative classification in popular culture, bringing a prejudicial taint with personal risk to any form of bond outside a specific and safe set of norms. As early as 1924, a straight Arizona cowboy recalled being warned about an otherwise ordinary man who was pausing at their camp for the night at the Big Tank in Arizona's Tonto Basin. Although he later questioned this advice, he nonetheless stayed on the opposite side of the campfire, just in case. "I kept my eye out for the cowboy Dell had talked about," he recalled, "and when I was introduced to him I couldn't see he looked much different from anyone else unless maybe he was dressed a little better than most. I still felt uneasy around him and managed to stay on the opposite side of the fire all evening."[8] Dell's gossip had sufficiently planted a seed of doubt and subsequently shaped a stranger's welcome.

Another reason for the change from acceptance to suspicion stemmed from the development of and changes to the ranching environment, drawing those within that environment into tightly supervised boundaries governed by the moral eye of ranching families. Neighbors might still be miles apart, but fences, water rights, and touring cars were merging the independence of old western tradition with the respectability of the reformed, morally pasteurized new West. After railroad networks came into the heart of ranching country, few cattle drives were longer than a week or two; Oklahoma alone was laced with steel rails in every direction by four major railroads, three of which served the ranching country of western Oklahoma and its Panhandle. And despite the absolute supremacy of horsemanship in cattle country, the number of motor cars slowly and steadily rose. By 1922 a brand-new Ford car could be had for as little as $295, and used cars were as cheap as they were plentiful. One Texas puncher used his Ford car to lead a herd of eleven hundred mustangs out of San Angelo on their way to market; another used a Ford to herd cattle.[9] Twenty horses under the little black hood also allowed the off-duty cowpuncher the opportunity to travel farther to Saturday night dances, providing more chances to meet pretty girls. Conversely, a later generation of cars, trucks, and paved highways likewise offered the opportunity to drive across state lines and into Oklahoma City to meet gay people in a safe setting, hundreds of miles from home. The shift and clutch grew as familiar as the pommel and reins.

The final difference was the shift in perception, with the Mayflower Bar itself being emblematic of a series of changes taking place in mid-twentieth-century society: the public recognition of gay people as something one *was*, the rise of corresponding hostility toward this newly directed target, and the ultimate determination of gay people to survive in the face of it established spots like the Mayflower to support and engage this new sense of life. In the 1950s, when felony charges against gay men in Texas and Oklahoma typically brought two years in a penitentiary, most members of the public considered gay people a disfigurement to the social fabric, an opinion shaped in part by popular psychiatrists, often through means beneficial to their own profession.[10] Yet these same psychiatrists noted with bewilderment the numbers of gay people who preferred their own societies despite the consequences. Without realizing it fully, they were describing a nascent self-awareness among gay communities, whether in a city or among the ranges, and with it a corresponding sense of independence.

The Texas cowboys who took a drink at the Mayflower Bar that night were not alone: throughout the ranching world, and in jobs and occupations just like theirs, from oil drilling to lumber working, are men and women, some hidden beyond the landscape, others known among their coworkers and friends, who are gay westerners, all living regular lives on the terms of the West. They were following a well-trod path, initially born of pragmatic reality at a time when the frontier West was new and raw and more than a little dangerous. In doing so, they were also merging traditional life into new worlds, as frontier comrades merging a side of themselves that related to the identity of homosexuality with their side that related to the identity of cowboy. They became cowboys who were also gay men, raising a glass to the music of Bob Wills with the best of them.

Notes

INTRODUCTION

1. Author Gregory D. Smithers's work *Reclaiming Two-Spirits* addresses the history as well as modern aspects and spiritual reclamation of Native identity, while Will Roscoe's works "That Is My Road" and *The Zuni Man-Woman*, on We'wha and Finds Them and Kills Them, describe Two-Spirit and *bote* culture in the Zuni and Crow societies.
2. There are many accounts coming to light that deserve attention. They often engage significant aspects of frontier history, as with Lawrence Murphy, a former military post trader who became active during the Lincoln County Wars of the 1870s; the Denver photographer Charles Hincke and his partner L. E. Hay in the 1880s; or the remarkable career of musician Jesse Shepard and his partner, Waldemar Tonner.
3. "Annexation," *Mississippi Democrat*, September 10, 1845.
4. Migration from what is today Siberia to the Americas took place in several consecutive phases and as early as eighteen thousand years ago, based on stone tools found in southeastern Oregon. The more widespread presence of the "Clovis culture" appeared about thirteen thousand years ago. Traces of human footprints at a New Mexico site may possibly date to twenty-three thousand years ago, but these are not yet fully recognized, and work is ongoing.
5. "Manifest Destiny," *New York Times*, July 7, 1853.
6. "A Returning Gold Hunter," *Sacramento Daily Union*, March 26, 1851. The writer of this article describes an acquaintance who was "one of the many thousands who left the western frontier in the spring of '49," meaning a trip beyond the western borders, or frontier, of civilization to travel westward to California.
7. "In a Sign Language," *Chicago Tribune*, July 13, 1893. Wisconsin history professor Frederick Turner held that "American development has exhibited . . . a return to primitive conditions on a continuously advancing frontier line," something

his contemporaries described as "the outer edge of a wave—the meeting point between savagery and civilization." "Literature," *Weekly Wisconsin*, August 25, 1894.

8. "The London Exhibition," *Sacramento Daily Union*, December 15, 1888. "It may be taken for granted," the *Daily Union* editor continued, "that Buffalo Bill has sufficiently impressed Europeans with the thought that the whole region west of the Missouri is in a semi-barbarous state, where one carries his life in his palm."

9. "The 'Bloomer' in Oregon," *Weekly Oregon Statesman*, September 2, 1851; "Bloomers for Oregon," *Weekly Oregon Statesman*, July 17, 1852.

10. Abbott and Smith, *We Pointed Them North*, 28–29.

11. Alfred Kinsey quoted in Katz, *Gay American History*, 511–12. According to Peter Boag, "Alfred Kinsey reported that the highest frequency of homosexual activity in the United States occurred in the most remote locations, such as logging, mining [and] ranching communities." Boag, *Same-Sex Affairs*, 22. Kinsey also noted that youths in farms and other rural areas in the West tended to engage each other more than their counterparts in the East and that the number of outdoorsmen he found contentedly thus engaged discredited the then-current theory that gay people were the product of urban environments. Kinsey also found that ranchers and other outdoorsmen did not identify themselves as gay or homosexual, nor do they appear to have defined themselves in the same manner as masculine urban men did. Boag, *Same-Sex Affairs*, 21–23.

12. Susan Lee Johnson describes the mid-nineteenth century as "a time when moralists generally considered sex between men a sin or vice, but not necessarily an indicator of an identity or sense of self." S. Johnson, *Roaring Camp*, 173–74.

13. "Social Freedom," *The Freeman*, February 1, 1874. Woodhull suggested that frustration with the formal rules of life led people to seek alternate and less entangled venues for relief.

14. Dugan and Boessenecker, *Grey Fox*, 101–2. Miner had succeeded in robbing an Oregon Railway and Navigation Company express train with the assistance of two accomplices, one an old pal from his time in prison, the other a farm youth.

15. Most behavioral traits are attributed to multiple genes, with only a few, like flavor sensitivity or the ability to roll one's tongue, attributed to a single gene. Eye color is now perceived as resulting from two genes. Human orientation and identity are more complex, with many genetic combinations at work.

16. Stephen Engel cites the work of George Lydston, a contemporary Chicago physician and author of *Diseases of Society and Degeneracy* as an example of physicians who had a preoccupation with societal "degeneracy" and who "considered homosexuality a hereditary trait" that had to be socially managed. Engel, *Fragmented Lives*, 74–75. Lydston correlated skull type with criminal propensity and was fascinated

by bodybuilders and prizefighters. "The Physicians," *Evansville Courier and Press*, September 12, 1889; "Expert Opinion about Fighters," *Philadelphia Inquirer*, January 28, 1894; "Defense of Nordau," *Chicago Tribune*, April 5, 1896; "Uses Skulls to Illustrate Lecture," *Chicago Tribune*, October 19, 1896; "Lessons from Reno Combat," *Burlington Daily News* (Vermont), August 25, 1910.

17. Boag, *Same-Sex Affairs*, 130–33, 142–43. Boag describes the influence (and evolution) of Krafft-Ebing's work, which, while often misdirected and prejudiced, laid the groundwork for modern concepts and academic studies of gay people.

18. "Convict-Labor Garments Sold Extensively, Worn by Whom?," *Organized Labor*, July 18, 1925.

19. Untitled article, *Leadville Daily Herald* (Colorado), April 15, 1882.

20. "A Nasty Mess," *Los Angeles Evening Express*, April 3, 1895.

21. "Curious Cupid Drives His Arrows into the Wrong Place: Mad Infatuation," *Aspen Daily Times*, May 11, 1889 (cited hereafter as "Mad Infatuation"). Only a few years later, another Coloradan was corresponding with a German sociologist, Magnus Hirschfeld, about gay life in Denver. His descriptions were included in Hirschfeld's 1914 work, *Die Homosexualität des Mannes und des Weibes*, published in Berlin. Katz, *Gay American History*, 49–51.

22. "Concert and Festivities at Clinton," *The Comet*, April 17, 1880. A revival of neoclassical culture (or its veneer) among the middle classes led in part to lesbian "ladies' societies," largely made up of respectable young women drawn to literature and music. The extent of their high art can be assumed from an "ice-cream and strawberry social" given by the ladies of the Lesbian Society of Jackson, Mississippi, as a fundraiser for their library in 1880, and a concert given in 1883 by the Lesbian Quartette of Fitchburg, Massachusetts: "May-Time," "Thou Lovely Star," and "Their Sun Shall No More Go Down." "Lesbian Quartette Concert Program," *Fitchburg Sentinel* (Massachusetts), April 23, 1883. More to the point, C. L. James wrote in 1898 that there was "homo-sexual passion among women as well as men (Lesbian love), so-called because [it was] especially prevalent in the societies of actresses and others representing hetaira class, which had their headquarters at [the Greek island of] Lesbos." "Women in Greece," *Lucifer, the Light-Bearer*, December 16, 1898.

23. "Caution—A Base Villain," *The Radical*, April 20, 1844; "The Spread of Sodomy," *Weekly Caucasian*, March 15, 1873; untitled article, *Weekly Kansas State Journal*, September 7, 1876; "A Beast," *Daily Alta California*, May 9, 1879. The song about sodomy with women in brothels, sung to the tune of "The Old Chisholm Trail," was initially collected from what Guy Logsdon describes as "some rodeo cowpokes in Oklahoma" and was one of over one thousand bawdy variants independently made up and sung by cowboys over the nineteenth and early twentieth centuries. Logsdon, "Whorehouse Bells Were Ringing," 64.

24. "The City," *Sacramento Daily Union*, April 18, 1854.
25. "Criminal Code," *Omaha Nebraskian*, October 20, 1858.
26. "Coils Tighten around Vice Club Members," *Sacramento Bee*, March 1, 1918; "$70,000 Bail for Accused in Vice Club Case," *Sacramento Bee*, June 19, 1918. The case involved several gay men who socialized at a private home on Baker Street, one block from the Presidio. The arrested men ranged from businessmen to soldiers, and all received exceptionally harsh bail, while the police officer who patrolled the area of the arrests was directed to retire without a public hearing, avoiding negative publicity for his department.
27. "Correction," *Placer Herald*, February 21, 1874.
28. "Pardoned," *San Francisco Examiner*, September 12, 1873. John Daly was seventeen when convicted of "buggery" in 1872 and sent to San Quentin State Prison for five years. He was pardoned after a year, with the requirement that he leave the state for at least four years. He had returned to California by 1880 and lived in San Francisco for many years, at times employed as a hack driver.
29. "Jottings about Town," *San Francisco Chronicle*, February 16, 1873.
30. "The Legislature," *Galveston Daily News*, February 13, 1874; "Legislative Proceedings," *Weekly New Mexican*, January 11, 1876; untitled article, *Weekly New Mexican*, January 25, 1876; "The News from Austin," *Galveston Daily News*, May 21, 1876; untitled article, *Austin Statesman*, June 20, 1876; "From Austin," *Tri-Weekly Herald* (Marshall TX), July 13, 1876.

1. THE GREAT WEST

1. W. Stewart, *Edward Warren*, 151–52.
2. W. Stewart, *Edward Warren*, 83–84.
3. Porter and Davenport, *Scotsman in Buckskin*, 17–18; Benemann, *Men in Eden*, 24–25; *North British Daily Mail*, December 5, 1872. Stewart's son died in the late 1860s but left a common-law wife of his own, who successfully petitioned for part of Stewart's estate after Stewart died in 1871.
4. W. Stewart, *Altowan*, 26.
5. Hafen, *Trappers of the Far West*, 297–98.
6. Hafen, *Trappers of the Far West*, 300–301. Campbell's letter reflected his frustration with life following a fight between the Gros Ventres and Campbell's party at Pierre's Hole, in the present-day Teton Valley of eastern Idaho.
7. The early eleventh-century Norse settlement at L'Anse aux Meadows offers a factual basis for the trades of pelts with Native Americans, albeit interspersed with conflict and misunderstanding, as described in the eleventh-century *Grœnlendinga saga*.

8. White, *"It's Your Misfortune and None of My Own,"* 46.
9. Hine, *American West*, 64.
10. "American Fur Trade," *Western Flying Post and Yeovil Mercury*, August 27, 1832.
11. "American Fur Trade," *Western Flying Post and Yeovil Mercury*, August 27, 1832.
12. Eulogy of Reverend Eliot, 1838, quoted in Clokey, *William H. Ashley*, 141; White, *"It's Your Misfortune and None of My Own,"* 47. The Reverend William Eliot's description of Ashley's business model was given in St. Louis, Missouri, on June 6, 1838, following Ashley's death. He praised the "regularity in [Ashley's] camp, and order in his marches," standards that William Stewart followed during his own trips west.
13. Clokey, *William H. Ashley*, 170.
14. Hyde, *Empires, Nations, and Families*, 101–2. The shift in acceptability could occur even without moving, given time. Anne Hyde notes that at Fort Vancouver, Indian marriage at the Hudson's Bay post came under fire when American settlers moved into Oregon en masse in the 1840s and 1850s, subjecting John McLoughlin's Métis wife to ridicule by her new American neighbors, while Michigan's territorial governor saw Métis children as having "inherited the vices of both races and none of the virtues" (103, 270).
15. Nells Anderson quoted in Woirol, "Men on the Road," 203.
16. Hyde, *Empires, Nations, and Families*, 100–101. Hyde remarks that "the world of the North American frontier was a complex setting of several generations of mixed race" recognized and appreciated for a certain value and mutual benefit within the fur trade era (101). McLoughlin, born in Quebec with Scottish heritage, married twice, both times to Métis women.
17. Porter and Davenport, *Scotsman in Buckskin*, 51; W. Stewart, *Edward Warren*, 429n48. Most men in the fur trade with an education, such as Campbell, found employment in authoritative positions, rather than as packers.
18. W. Stewart, *Edward Warren*, 428–29n48; Benemann, *Men in Eden*, 80–81. Stewart's later description of this event follows one of Indian women socializing with traders at the rendezvous, leading his readers to assume that his desire for an open bower was for something similar. Who it actually was for is unknown.
19. Hafen, *Trappers of the Far West*, 135; Larpenteur quoted in Benemann, *Men in Eden*, 80–81.
20. Hafen, *Trappers of the Far West*, 135. Larpenteur's source for this account was thirty-two-year-old Lucien Fontenelle, who had extensive experience in the West and was, like Holmes, formally educated.
21. W. Stewart, *Edward Warren*, 428–29n48.
22. Enzler, *Jim Bridger*, 54, 106–7; Porter and Davenport, *Scotsman in Buckskin*, 132, 150–51; Benemann, *Men in Eden*, 199–200; "The Flight of the Antelope," *New York Tribune*, February 23, 1849.

23. Porter and Davenport, *Scotsman in Buckskin*, 143; Benemann, *Men in Eden*, 192.
24. W. Stewart, *Edward Warren*, 87–88. The Whitman quote is from "Among the Multitude" in Whitman, *Leaves of Grass*, 137.
25. W. Stewart, *Altowan*, 45.
26. W. Stewart, *Edward Warren*, 88–91.
27. William Benemann remarks that Sillem was traveling in companionship with Charles Murray, a relative of Stewart who happened to be traveling around the same area. The two men accompanied Stewart to New Orleans and then on to Havana. Once they arrived there, Sillem and Stewart grew close while Murray fell away. Benemann, *Men in Eden*, 160–63.
28. Porter and Davenport, *Scotsman in Buckskin*, 111.
29. "Indian Massacre—Matters at Fort Leavenworth," *New York Daily Herald*, July 22, 1847. The description of Clement comes from a man who encountered him in St. Louis during the summer of 1847, when Clement, along with James Kirker and Thomas Forsyth, were the "lions" of the city and known as "mountaineers and trappers" who had performed well during the Mexican-American War. Clement was born in 1812 and baptized several years later at a French Catholic church outside of St. Louis. He spoke French like his father and was regarded as an expert shot, which gave him a high place within plains society and Stewart's ranking.
30. *Chris and Don: A Love Story*, directed by Tina Mascara and Guido Santi (2008). The comment refers to Isherwood's relationship with a younger German man in the 1920s.
31. W. Stewart, *Edward Warren*, 228.
32. W. Stewart, *Edward Warren*, 88–90, 253, for example.
33. W. Stewart, *Edward Warren*, 123; also quoted in Benemann, *Men in Eden*, 89–90.
34. Untitled article, *Caledonian Mercury*, June 9, 1838.
35. DeVoto, *Across the Wide Missouri*, 360; Porter and Davenport, *Scotsman in Buckskin*, 176. Stewart's letter suggests that Silas was poor company for Sublette because he wasn't a "fairy."
36. Although Stewart would have nothing to do with his late brother's half-completed house, he nonetheless felt free to raid the crates of uninstalled paneling and fittings, installing them in the old Murthly wherever useful or desirable.
37. Miller quoted in Strong, *Sentimental Journey*, 83–84.
38. Quoted in Tyler, *Alfred Jacob Miller*, 42.
39. Alfred Miller, *Sir W. D. S. and Antoine (Canadian Half breed)*, undated, watercolor, gouache, and graphite on paper, Gilcrease Museum, Tulsa, Oklahoma.
40. Alfred Miller, *An Attack by Crows on the Whites on the Big Horn River East of the Rocky Mountains [Crows Trying to Provoke the Whites to and Act of Hostility]*, 1841, oil on canvas, The Anschutz Collection, Denver, Colorado; Nicholas Wiseman

quoted in Strong, *Sentimental Journey*, 69–70. Author Lisa Strong remarks that Wiseman's interpretation of the painting publicly centered on the "command of self" as a virtue, contrasting the perceived primal nature of man. Wiseman visited Stewart at Murthly a decade before his appointment as a cardinal in the Catholic Church, something controversial in Great Britain because of its position on papal authority. See "Cardinal Wiseman," *The Standard*, November 22, 1850; and "Forthcoming Popish Jubilee," *Perthshire Advertiser*, December 5, 1850.

41. "Central Criminal Court," *The Observer*, October 4, 1835; "The Recorder's Report," *Huntington, Bedford and Peterbro' Gazette, and Cambridge and Hertford Independent Press*, November 28, 1835; untitled article, *The Standard*, November 23, 1835; "Weekly Compendium," *Newcastle Journal*, December 5, 1835. Pratt and Smith were among a list of capital offenders, including a number of burglars and an attempted murderer, "to all of whom his Majesty has extended the royal mercy, except John Smith and Henry Pratt, who are left for execution on Friday next." Untitled article, *The Standard*, November 23, 1835. A third man associated with Smith and Pratt was more fortunate and was exiled to Australia instead.

42. Documentary filmmaker Stewart Marshall to the author, 1986.

43. "A Character," *Hull Packet and East Riding Times*, October 28, 1842. The "rakish, cool [and] fierce" *Great Western* was the first purpose-built transatlantic steamer, a wooden side-wheel ship with sail-assist completed in 1838 for the Great Western Railway as a marine extension of their railway services, under the supervision of civil engineer Isambard Brunel. "Triumph of Steam," *New York Daily Herald*, April 24, 1838.

44. Rolle, *John Charles Frémont*, 50–55; White, *"It's Your Misfortune and None of My Own,"* 72. Frémont's report was officially titled *Report of the Exploring Expedition to the Rocky Mountains in the Year 1842 and to Oregon and North California in the Years 1843–44*. Rolle remarks that while on the expedition, Frémont's manners were lacking. For example, he took the prime parts of a turkey offered him by some passing hunters, contrary to western etiquette, which expected that anyone offered parts of an animal would take lesser parts, leaving the best parts for the hunter as a courtesy.

45. "News from the Mountains," *New-York Tribune*, July 17, 1843. The *New-York Tribune* article states that the Oregon Company had a total of 990 persons, but the figures cited total to exactly 1,000 persons.

46. "News from the Mountains," *New-York Tribune*, July 17, 1843.

47. "The Rocky Mountain Party," *Buffalo Daily Gazette*, July 29, 1843; Benemann, *Men in Eden*, 250–51, 255–57.

48. "The Rocky Mountain Party," *Buffalo Daily Gazette*, July 29, 1843.

49. "Sir William Drummond Stewart," *Brooklyn Eagle*, August 16, 1843; Benemann, *Men in Eden*, 257–58.
50. Porter and Davenport, *Scotsman in Buckskin*, 233–35, 238–40.
51. Matthew Field, "Prairie and Mountain Sketches," *New Orleans Picayune*, reprinted in *Pittsburgh Daily Post*, December 12, 1843; Porter and Davenport, *Scotsman in Buckskin*, 237; Benemann, *Men in Eden*, 263–64.
52. Benemann, *Men in Eden*, 281–82.
53. "The Battle of Sacramento," *Courier-Journal* (Louisville KY), May 3, 1847; "Indian Massacre—Matters at Fort Leavenworth," *New York Daily Herald*, July 22, 1847 (quote).

2. THE GOLD RUSH SCENE

1. *Providence Directory* (1836), 88, accessed at the Rhode Island Historical Society, Providence.
2. "Knew Charley Parkhurst," *Santa Cruz Morning Sentinel*, January 31, 1903.
3. "The Female Stage-Driver," *Providence Journal*, reported in the *San Francisco Call*, January 25, 1880.
4. "The Female Stage-Driver," *Providence Journal*, reported in the *San Francisco Call*, January 25, 1880.
5. "Good Appointment," *San Luis Obispo Tribune*, April 9, 1870; "Duplicity of the Independents," *San Francisco Examiner*, August 27, 1870. Abolitionists employed the term to describe the hypocrisy of people who "attempt to unite a love of slavery and of liberty. Like all hermaphrodites, they are merely monsters." "A Perverted Sympathy," *The Liberator*, September 5, 1856. In California the term figured in an 1856 murder, when a man who refused to sit with a "hermaphrodite" was stabbed in response. "The Indian Murder—Coroner's Inquest," *Sacramento Daily Union*, May 21, 1856.
6. "The Female Stage-Driver," *Providence Journal*, reported in the *San Francisco Call*, January 25, 1880.
7. Stage superintendent William Buckley's recollection of Parkhurst was positive and impressive: "He is as brave as Julius Caesar; he never drinks nor smokes, nor uses profane language; he is always social, but never convivial; a pleasant, but not a jovial companion." "Famous Whips of the Past," *Los Angeles Times*, January 7, 1912.
8. "The Female Stage-Driver," *Providence Journal*, reported in the *San Francisco Call*, January 25, 1880. He claimed New Hampshire as his birthplace when he registered to vote in California in 1867.

9. "The Late Female Husband at Kennington," *Bell's New Weekly Messenger*, reprinted in *Bristol Mercury and Daily Post, Western Countries and South Wales Advertiser*, December 27, 1834; Brodell, *Butch Heroes*, 36–37. News of Wright's death in December 1834 would have reached the United States after a month or more, given the necessity of a transatlantic crossing by sail.
10. Manion, *Female Husbands*, 120–26; "From the Manchester Guardian of April 14," *The Tennessean*, June 5, 1838; untitled article, *Leeds Mercury*, April 21, 1838. News of the bricklayer's divorce, which afforded "much gossip," spread rapidly through Britain in April 1838 and reached newspapers in the United States two months later. Jen Manion remarks that "a female husband was always more vulnerable than a female wife [because the wives had] the power of truth—and could hold it against [their husbands] if they wanted to." Manion, *Female Husbands*, 123.
11. Rhode Island stable owner William Tennant advertised in 1836 that he "keeps to let in his stable at Green-street, horses and carriages of all descriptions" and that "Persons desirous of enjoying the pleasures of a ride in the country, can at all times be furnished with saddle-horses, horse and chaises, open wagons, barouches and close carriages. . . . Horses kept for any length of time, terms liberal." Advertisement, *Rhode Island Republican*, March 2, 1836.
12. "Sonoma," *Daily Alta California*, February 12, 1869, describes how another hostler sustained work-related injuries as well: that man, Mike Driskle, was "kicked by a vicious horse, breaking his left leg between the ankle and the knee."
13. "The Wealth of Providence," *Pittsburgh Gazette*, October 10, 1854.
14. "The Female Stage-Driver," *Providence Journal*, reported in the *San Francisco Call*, January 25, 1880. The matched set of gray horses mentioned in the article may have been the pair owned by Charles Childs and valued at $500 but lost to a stable fire in June 1852. *Providence Journal*, reprinted in "Destructive Fire," *Albany Evening Journal*, June 17, 1852; "Destructive Fire," *Herald of the Times*, June 17, 1852.
15. "The Female Stage-Driver," *Providence Journal*, reported in the *San Francisco Call*, January 25, 1880.
16. "The Female Stage-Driver," *Providence Journal*, reported in the *San Francisco Call*, January 25, 1880. Pawtucket is about five or six miles northeast of Providence. Parkhurst's route between Providence and Pawtucket might have been along Main Street, now known as Route 1. Liberty Childs had a rough life, was once accidentally shot at, and died of exhaustion in January 1885.
17. "The Female Stage-Driver," *Providence Journal*, reported in the *San Francisco Call*, January 25, 1880. The *Providence Journal* reported that Parkhurst went to California in 1851, although his listings in the Providence city directory indicate that he was

not absent from Providence until 1853, the same year that Birch bought back his old California stage lines. The discrepancy may be attributed to old memories.

18. "Mr. James E. Birch," *New York Herald*, September 23, 1857; "Biographical Sketch of James E. Birch," *Daily Alta California*, November 5, 1857. Birch died when the steamer *Central America* sank in 1857.

19. Ralph Waldo Emerson, "The Conduct," quoted in Kowalewski, *Gold Rush*, 299.

20. Birch's reputation for staging was so solid that by the spring of 1850 the *Daily Alta California* was reporting that "no stage line in the States is conducted with more undivided attention to the comfort of passengers, or one where drivers are more gentlemanly and careful." "From the Mines," *Daily Alta California*, May 29, 1850.

21. "Stage Fare, &c.," *Sacramento Daily Union*, January 19, 1854.

22. Craig MacDonald describes Parkhurst using a steamer named the *R. B. Forbes* to reach California via the Panamanian Isthmus, with no citation. Only two vessels had that name in the 1850s: an iron steam tug based in Boston and a clipper that was in the Indian Ocean en route to India at the time Birch returned to California in March 1853. There is no record of an ocean-going steamer so named, much less one on the Panama run. MacDonald, *Cockeyed Charley Parkhurst*, 22; "Home Ports—Boston," *New York Herald*, November 14, 1853; "The Great Republic," *Detroit Free Press*, December 1, 1853; "Ships," *The Polynesian*, February 12, 1853.

23. "Stages," *Weekly Placer Herald*, July 2, 1853; "New Stage Proprietorship," *Nevada Journal*, April 1, 1853.

24. Bartholomew Moore's account of Parkhurst in Sacramento in 1853 is supported by the absence of an entry for Parkhurst in the 1853 Providence city directory and subsequent return in time for the 1854 editions. Moore was a Rhode Island native who sometime between 1850 and 1853 had moved to California, where he sold furniture in Sacramento with his brother Daniel. In February 1854 Moore traveled to New York, where he married his waiting fiancée on February 27 before returning with his wife to California on the steamer *North Star*. By 1862 the Moores had moved to San Francisco, where Moore worked for the furniture showrooms of Jonas G. Clark & Company and then Snelling, Marx & Company before becoming a director of the California Furniture Company by 1875. The Moores were socially popular and appear to have had a stable and contented life. On Moore's retirement, they moved to Ben Lomond, a small town in the mountains just north of Santa Cruz, above Felton and Boulder Creek. Moore took up writing, and his recollections of Charley Parkhurst were published in the *Santa Cruz Sentinel* on January 31, 1903. "Knew Charley Parkhurst," *Santa Cruz Sentinel*, January 31, 1903; advertisement, *Sacramento Daily Union*, October 4, 1853; "Departures," *New York Daily Herald*, April 7, 1854; advertisement, *Daily Alta California*, July 13, 1862; "Inside Matters," *San Francisco Examiner*, October 23, 1875.

25. "Stage Fare, &c.," *Sacramento Daily Union*, January 19, 1854.
26. "California Stage Co.," *Placer Herald*, January 14, 1854; "Combination Again," *California Farmer and Journal of Useful Sciences*, January 18, 1854.
27. "Travel Up the Sacramento," *Daily Alta California*, November 2, 1859.
28. The Concord, New Hampshire, coach-building firm of Lewis Downing & Sons later merged with its Concord rivals, J. S. and E. A. Abbott, to form Abbott, Downing & Company, later known as Abbott-Downing, well known for their stagecoaches. Parkhurst may have driven a surviving California Stage Company coach, preserved at the Autry Museum of the American West in Los Angeles. It was built in about 1853 by Lewis Downing & Sons and was numbered sixty-five of the hundred or so coaches used by the California Stage Company during its first year of operation in 1854.
29. "California Stage Company," *California Farmer and Journal of Useful Sciences*, August 17, 1855. Two of these impressive Concord coaches each carried fifty-six passengers, while a six-horse coach carried thirty-one passengers and a four-horse coach carried twenty-five passengers. Big Jake, the driver of a particularly large coach delivered in the fall of 1853 for service between Sacramento and Marysville, didn't think thirty passengers any "great shakes for them kind of machines." "A Magnificent Coach," *Sacramento Daily Union*, September 2, 1853.
30. "Stage Consolidation," *Daily Alta California*, December 11, 1854.
31. Untitled article, *California Farmer and Journal of Useful Sciences*, April 12, 1861.
32. "Knew Charley Parkhurst," *Santa Cruz Sentinel*, January 31, 1903.
33. "Arrival of the Northern Light," *Washington Sentinel*, February 25, 1854. The *Cortes* was a wooden side-wheel steamer of eleven hundred tons, built in 1852 for service between San Francisco and the Isthmus. It had a capacity for one hundred cabin and some six hundred steerage class passengers and was acquired by Vanderbilt in the summer of 1853 for the Nicaragua route. It was lost to fire in 1865. The steamer *Brother Jonathan* of 1851 was in its prime when Parkhurst saw it, but over a decade later rough seas brought it against rocks off the Northern California coast with a substantial loss of life. The Vanderbilt steamer *Sierra Nevada*, which Parkhurst saw steaming past Baja California, was a twelve-hundred-ton vessel built in 1852, employed on the San Francisco–to–Nicaragua run in line with the *Cortes*.
34. "Knew Charley Parkhurst," *Santa Cruz Sentinel*, January 31, 1903.
35. The *Northern Light* was completed in 1852 for Vanderbilt service between New York and Nicaragua. It was a wooden side-wheel steamer of 1,700 tons, over 250 feet long, with a 38-foot beam, and room for 250 passengers in first cabin, 150 in second cabin, and over 400 in steerage. It was a fast steamer and long in service, not being scrapped until 1875, long after its type had become obsolete.
36. "Passengers Arrived," *New York Times*, February 24, 1854, lists both Birch and Moore among the *Northern Light*'s 152 first cabin passengers as it arrived in New

York. Parkhurst is not listed among them and was presumably among the 248 passengers in the second and third cabins whose names were considered unimportant and rarely included in newspaper passenger lists. Status was apparent even in the first cabin list: the *Times* reported the passengers by social rank, with the prominent Birch relatively near the head of the list while Moore, a respectable but young furniture salesman, was toward the end.

37. Moore's account of the sea voyage is supported by several contemporary sources, including the details of a departure on the first day of February, an especially fast trip despite heavy weather on the Atlantic side, and the *Northern Light*'s crew rescuing the crew from the sinking coal schooner *Teren*, although Moore did not know which vessel it was. "Latest Intelligence," *Washington Sentinel*, February 25, 1854. The schooner *Teren* of Cape May was loaded with coal and bound for New York. Its captain complained that before the *Northern Light* arrived to rescue them, they were refused assistance by the captain of a passing Parker Vein steamer, a rival coal shipping firm, contrary to maritime tradition.

38. Parkhurst is missing from the 1853 Providence city directory, only to reappear in time for the directory's 1854–55 edition at the same 30 Dorrance Street address recorded in 1852. He was again listed as a coachman. "The Female Stage-Driver," *Providence Journal*, reported in the *San Francisco Call*, January 25, 1880.

39. The Bella Union was an influential social establishment on Portsmouth Square in 1850s San Francisco that set the tone for the sociopolitical environment that Parkhurst would have encountered in California.

40. Delgado, *Gold Rush Port*, 89; advertisements, *San Francisco Daily Herald*, November 13, 1852.

41. "Steamers," *Daily Alta California*, February 5, 1855. The Sacramento Valley Railroad completed its twenty-two-mile line from Sacramento to Folsom in 1856, scheduling its trains to accommodate daylight hours as its locomotives were not equipped with headlights. Its New Jersey–built locomotive, the *L. L. Robinson*, assembled in 1855 by the New Jersey Locomotive & Machine Works, was named for Lester Robinson, who may have had a relationship with François Pioche, a gold rush era entrepreneur and namesake of Pioche, Nevada. Conversation with Wendell Huffman, curator, Nevada State Railroad Museum, December 2017.

42. "Hangtown or Placerville," *Sacramento Transcript*, October 11, 1850.

43. Issel and Cherny, *San Francisco 1865–1932*, 18–22. Richard White remarks that the San Francisco vigilance committees of 1851 and 1856 were "not so much interested in suppressing crime as in taking political control of the city against the dominant faction of Irish Catholic Democrats" in favor of American-born Protestants. Membership in the Committee of Vigilance of San Francisco in 1856 was recorded on elegant documents with illustrations by the notable San Francisco

artist Charles Nahl depicting allegories of commerce, industry, and the sciences along with Hercules and a book labeled "Moral Power." White, *"It's Your Misfortune and None of My Own,"* 333–34.

44. "Route to the Yosemite Valley," *California Farmer and Journal of Useful Sciences*, April 29, 1859; "Travel Up the Sacramento," *Daily Alta California*, November 2, 1859.

45. "New Overland Mail Route," *California Farmer and Journal of Useful Sciences*, July 30, 1858. Another report describes "four Sharp's [sic] rifles, and cartridges in abundance" along with seats designed to fold down so passengers could sleep. "Particulars of the Overland Mail Route," *Sacramento Daily Union*, August 13, 1858.

46. While watching Greeley's "bare head bobbing, sometimes on the back and then on the front seat, sometimes in the coach and then out," Monk shouted the famous punch line: "Keep your seat! I told you I would get you there by five o'clock, and by God I'll do it, if the axles hold!" The story had entered national circulation by 1865, along with a catchier punch line—"Keep your seat, Horace!"—making Monk a national figure. Monk's statement as reported in the *Golden Era*, April 15, 1860, quoted in Pitter, *Hank Monk*, 3; "Horace Greeley's Ride to Placerville," *Spirit of Democracy*, December 20, 1865; "Horace Greeley's Ride to Placerville," *Wisconsin State Register*, February 10, 1866.

47. "Charley Parkhurst," *San Francisco Call*, January 1, 1880.

48. "Notes of a Trip through Southern Counties," *Daily Alta California*, August 1, 1860.

49. "Game on the Southern Mountains," *Sacramento Daily Union*, October 16, 1858.

50. "Reported Homicides in Mariposa," *Daily Alta California*, May 17, 1858.

51. "Murder on the Merced River," *Sacramento Daily Union*, December 10, 1857; "Horrible Murder," *Mariposa Democrat*, December 19, 1857; "Horrible Tragedy at Snelling's—Three Men Killed," *San Joaquin Republican*, January 26, 1858; "Desperate Affray," *Mariposa Democrat*, January 28, 1858; "The Late Murder at Snelling's," *Sacramento Daily Union*, January 30, 1858. While Edwards was on the run, friends of both the murderer and the murdered violently shot it out inside the local sheriff's office, leaving three dead and several wounded. Snelling's murderer, a man named Edwards, was later found and hanged in the Carson Valley.

52. "Scenes in the Valleys and Mountains of California," *Hutching's California Magazine*, May 1859, reprinted in Olmstead, *Scenes of Wonder & Curiosity*, 158.

53. About 150 persons, primarily Maidu and Yana men, women, and children, were killed by Frémont's men on the Sacramento River, among others. Hyde, *Empires, Nations, and Families*, 400–401; Rolle, *John Charles Frémont*, 90–102.

54. Rolle, *John Charles Frémont*, 141, 164–75; "Col. Fremont," *Detroit Free Press*, May 28, 1854; "The Mariposa Land Case: Fremont's Claim Confirmed," *Daily Alta California*, March 29, 1855; "The Miners and Settlers of Mariposa in Resistance to

the Fremont Claim," *Sacramento Daily Union*, July 25, 1855. Frémont's standing in Mariposa County was reflected by the election returns of 28 precincts, with 156 going for Frémont, 738 for Millard Fillmore, and 1,002 for James Buchanan. "The Election," *Sacramento Daily Union*, November 8, 1856.

55. "California Stage Company," *Sacramento Daily Union*, June 17, 1854; advertisement, "McLaughlin's (Late California Stage Company's) United States Mail," *California Farmer and Journal of Useful Sciences*, July 25, 1856; "U.S. Mail Stages," *Daily Alta California*, December 5, 1858; "Staging," *Sonoma Democrat*, May 30, 1858.

56. "Famous Whips of the Past," *Los Angeles Times*, January 7, 1912. William Buckley was famously employed as superintendent of the Coast Route stages from San Juan to Santa Barbara and Los Angeles beginning in 1860. He was as thorough as he was engaged in the staging business and known as "Genial Buck" to his drivers but died in poverty in San Jose in 1901. Hoag, *Stagecoaching on the California Coast*, 14–17; "By Telegraph to the Nevada Democrat," *Nevada Democrat*, February 16, 1861; "Letters from Fides," *San Francisco Examiner*, May 10, 1869; "William Buckley," *Los Angeles Times*, March 9, 1901.

57. Although McLaughlin was not hit by her shots, Sophia Bishop was convicted of assault with intent to kill and ordered to leave the state. She claimed a complex relationship with McLaughlin and was described in newspaper reports as weighing three hundred pounds. Untitled article, *Sacramento Daily Union*, February 24, 1857; "An Amazon," *Red Bluff Beacon*, January 27, 1858; untitled article, *Sacramento Daily Union*, April 27, 1858; untitled article, *Sacramento Daily Union*, June 5, 1858.

58. "Grand Celebration of the Opening of the San Jose Railroad," *Daily Alta California*, January 17, 1864.

59. Captain Robert Howe Fletcher, commenting for the *San Francisco Argonaut*, September 9, 1889, quoted in Banning and Banning, *Six Horses*, 374–75.

60. Banning and Banning, *Six Horses*, 360.

61. "Stage Accident," *Daily Alta California*, July 8, 1857. The projecting lumber "struck the leaders of the stage, frightened them and rendered them unmanageable," explained the *Daily Alta California*. "They sheered and plunged to one side of the road into the gulch, and upset the stage."

62. In this, Parkhurst was like another veteran driver, Charley O'Connell, whose "beautifully handled" reins made for "some splendid driving" between Tehama and Oroville. "Charley is a brick," O'Connell's passengers remarked, "and has been connected with the California Stage Company since its inception." "A Good Jehu," *Red Bluff Beacon*, October 23, 1862.

63. "The Stage Driver," *Connecticut Western News*, February 4, 1880. The report of Parkhurst's attempted runaway sounds possible, and incidents like it did occur elsewhere, but it should be read with a critical eye, as it joins other accounts,

some true and others doubtful, that surfaced immediately following Parkhurst's death.

64. "A Runaway," *Sacramento Daily Union*, April 25, 1854; "Stage Accident," *National Daily Democrat*, December 24, 1859; "An Orderly Runaway," *Daily National Democrat*, June 29, 1861. Examples of runaway stages include the Bidwell coach at Marysville, where the horses ran wild and smashed into buildings, and the 1859 Alameda stage upset, when an unbroken colt sent the coach into San Antonio Creek, injuring two women. More unusual and equally impressive, horses drawing a coach on the Carson City run calmly and dutifully trotted on for three miles after their driver was accidentally knocked off the stage by a sudden jolt. The coach was stopped only by some passing horsemen, who discovered a passenger inside, completely unaware of what had just happened.

65. "The Salinas and Carmelo Valley," *Sacramento Daily Union*, October 26, 1855.

66. "A Trip to Santa Cruz," *Sacramento Daily Union*, September 1, 1854; "Brief Mention," *Santa Cruz Weekly Sentinel*, August 22, 1862. A statewide shift in attention from the mining counties to the "cow counties" began to occur around 1854, as the mining boom settled down, farming began in earnest, and the region steadily grew more populated.

67. Ignacio Villegas, "Boyhood Days," reprinted in Kowalewski, *Gold Rush*, 221.

68. Hyde, *From Nations to Nation*, 392–93; letter of José Castro in "California," *Vermont Phoenix*, September 17, 1846.

69. Hyde, *From Nations to Nation*, 352; White, *"It's Your Misfortune and None of My Own,"* 207.

70. Bryant, *What I Saw in California*, 260–65; "Donner Monument," *Salinas Daily Index*, September 16, 1903; "Last of the Donners," *Woodland Daily Democrat*, April 6, 1935.

71. "Notes on the Pajaro Valley," *Daily Alta California*, October 16, 1864. This second roadway, the Pajaro Turnpike, was excavated over the course of 1860 and opened for traffic late in the year. Many years later, Watsonville resident Ed Ferguson thought he remembered seeing Parkhurst driving this road, but in fact Parkhurst had already retired from staging around the time Ferguson was born. He saw another stager and in his old age imagined it was the legendary Parkhurst. Ferguson's mistaken memory underscores the social lore surrounding Parkhurst's story following his death. Unpublished manuscript, Watsonville Historical Society, Watsonville, California.

72. Account book, 55, Pajaro Valley Historical Association, Watsonville, California, also cited in a letter from Mrs. Albert Snyder to Mr. McArthur, March 7, 1972, Pajaro Valley Historical Association. Also on August 6, 1859, and on the same page of entries, the dry goods store recorded business from Charles Moss, the namesake

of Moss Landing on Monterey Bay, and from representatives of Lee, Watson & Company, who named their town Watsonville and were putting finishing touches on a large flour mill.

73. The application process for land grants in Mexican-era California is described in Robinson, *Land in California*, 93–95.
74. Coal mining was largely a fad in the Monterey region, stimulated by the discovery of genuine coal deposits on distant Mount Diablo, east of Oakland. A few attempts had been made locally to develop coal mines, but they were nearly all ambitious, exploratory, and unsuccessful. The principal fuel of the region was wood.
75. Frederick Hihn Papers, Santa Cruz Museum of Art & History, Santa Cruz, California.
76. Mariano Guadalupe Vallejo, *Recuerdos históricos y personales tocante a la Alta California*, quoted in Kowalewski, *Gold Rush*, 166.
77. Legal filing against Parkhurst, Hihn Papers.
78. McChristian, *U.S. Army in the West*, 72, 151; Rickey, *Forty Miles a Day on Beans and Hay*, 124–25.
79. "A Strange History," *Petaluma Weekly Argus*, January 23, 1880.
80. "Famous Whips of the Past," *Los Angeles Times*, January 7, 1912.
81. "False Sights," *Morning Appeal*, January 6, 1880; "Finis," *Morning Appeal*, October 6, 1877; untitled article, *Vancouver Independent*, February 12, 1880; "Hank Monk on 'Saratoga,'" *Daily Alta California*, July 18, 1874.
82. "A Strange History," *Petaluma Weekly Argus*, January 23, 1880. His storied count of attackers repelled increased over time. "He was never held up successfully," remarked Benjamin Truman, "but in one year he had shot two highwaymen dead." "Famous Whips of the Past," *Los Angeles Times*, January 7, 1912.
83. "The Freshet in Auburn," *Sacramento Daily Union*, December 13, 1861.
84. "Stage Lost," *Sacramento Daily Union*, March 26, 1859; "Rivers and Rain," *Daily Alta California*, October 19, 1857.
85. "Narrow Escape," *Marysville Daily Appeal*, October 14, 1864; untitled article, *Daily Alta California*, October 13, 1864.
86. "The Marysville Robbery," *Sacramento Daily Union*, August 14, 1856; "Attempted Highway Robbery," *California Farmer and Journal of Useful Sciences*, August 15, 1856; "Terrible Affair," *Weekly Butte Record*, August 30, 1856. On the Camptonville stage "an indiscriminate fire commenced between the robbers and the passengers. The robbers finding themselves strenuously opposed, retreated, leaving the passengers masters of the field." While the Camptonville affair introduced the armed stage robbery to California, an Adams & Company express box had quietly been pilfered off the back of a Sonora stage three years earlier—a successful but not sensational act of theft. "Daring and Heavy Robbery," *Daily Alta California*, September 7, 1853.

87. Dutch Kate, who "generally wears man's apparel, plays cards, drinks whisky, and all that sort of thing," was largely unhappy, at least in 1858: she was robbed of $400 at Marysville that June and lost $2,000 at cards a month later, followed by a suicide attempt using poison. Peter Boag cites several similarly dressed and accessorized women engaged as prostitutes in 1862 Canada. Whether this applies to Dutch Kate is uncertain. "The Robbery Near Forest City," *Sacramento Daily Union*, September 9, 1858; "Robbery in Marysville," *Sacramento Daily Union*, June 12, 1858; "Marysville," *Sacramento Daily Union*, July 9, 1858; "Divorce Suit," *Sacramento Bee*, August 3, 1866; "A Destructive Fire," *San Francisco Examiner*, January 7, 1869; Boag, *Re-dressing America's Frontier Past*, 35.

88. Wiswell was rewarded with a "heavy gold watch chain" from the express firm of Wells, Fargo & Company, which had a shipment of $10,000 on board the coach. "A Robber Probably Done For," *Sacramento Daily Union*, October 16, 1858; "A Present," *Daily Alta California*, November 4, 1858.

89. A "Sugarfoot, bandit" entry in the *Encyclopedia of Frontier Biography* cites Craig MacDonald's 1973 book *Cockeyed Charley Parkhurst*, which in turn cites, uncritically, the imaginary tall tales attributed to Parkhurst. There was no bandit named "Sugarfoot" in reality.

90. "Fatal Shooting Affray," *Gold Hill Daily News*, October 26, 1863; "A Relic," *Gold Hill Daily News*, February 19, 1864; advertisement, *San Francisco Chronicle*, February 27, 1866; "The Stockton Fair," *Santa Cruz Weekly Sentinel*, November 4, 1871; "Still Alive," *Daily Evening Herald*, June 1, 1875; "A Pioneer Gone," *The Mail*, October 26, 1880. Another "Sugarfoot" was Mike Dunn, a brutal alcoholic in Sacramento. "Peace Disturbances," *Sacramento Daily Union*, August 15, 1872.

91. "Stock for Sale," *Santa Cruz Weekly Sentinel*, March 30, 1872; "Stock for Sale," *Santa Cruz Weekly Sentinel*, April 27, 1872.

92. "Charley Parkhurst," *San Francisco Call*, January 1, 1880.

93. The description of his shriveled limbs might also suggest poliomyelitis, an infectious disease that withers and atrophies muscles and can lead to paralysis.

94. "Charley Parkhurst," *San Francisco Call*, January 1, 1880.

95. "A Strange History," *Petaluma Weekly Argus*, January 23, 1880; Curtis, *Coachman Was a Lady*, 14; author's visit to the gravesite, 2018. The burial plot was provided by Watsonville businessman Otto Stroesser and is only a few dozen yards from the old stage road, marked by a stone monument placed by the Pajaro Valley Historical Association in 1955.

96. Claims that the discovery of Parkhurst's female anatomy was a surprise are countered by an abundance of remarks dating back to the 1840s, when he was widely considered a hermaphrodite by his associates and targeted in drinking games to see if anything would slip—a kind of nineteenth-century version of *That's Pat*.

Nor did Parkhurst live "back East" as a woman before dressing as a man to travel in the West. "The Female Stage-Driver," *Providence Journal*, reported in the *San Francisco Call*, January 25, 1880; Boag, *Re-dressing America's Frontier Past*, 106, 116.

97. "In Disguise," *Castroville Argus*, reported in the *Petaluma Weekly Argus*, January 9, 1880.

98. "Here, There & Everywhere," *Santa Cruz Weekly Sentinel*, January 10, 1880. The construct of cross-dressing as a necessary disguise in order to get ahead has been described by historian Peter Boag as the "progress narrative," meaning a social assumption held by straight society to explain cross-dressing in a heterosexual way, mainly that one takes on the guise of the opposite sex not from personal identification but rather when compelled by necessity in order to advance, or progress, from one place to another within the limitations or boundaries of a given society, which "normalizes the cross-dresser by maintaining that 'she' changed her clothing for some purpose related to securing personal advancement in a world with a deck that was otherwise stacked against her." Descriptions that centered on disguise sometimes took on Parkhurst's life as one of suffrage and gumption, something one *did*, and that was compelled by some unknown burden, rather than something one *was*, as identity. Part of this process, Boag remarks, heterosexualizes Parkhurst and others like him through the means of narrative as "part and parcel of western myth. In fact," he concludes, "it *is* western myth." Boag, *Re-dressing America's Frontier Past*, 19, 129.

99. "Too Strange Not to Be True," *Daily Alta California*, January 1, 1880; "A Most Wonderful Case," *Sacramento Daily Record-Union*, January 1, 1880.

100. "A Strange History," *Petaluma Weekly Argus*, January 23, 1880.

101. "Charley Parkhurst a Woman," *Santa Cruz Weekly Sentinel*, January 3, 1880.

102. "Hank Monk Astonished," *Carson City Morning Appeal*, January 4, 1880.

103. This Curly Bill was unrelated to an Arizona bandit of the same name described in a later chapter. "Sketch of Hank Monk, the Noted Stage Driver," *Morning Union*, March 3, 1883; "False Sights," *Carson City Morning Appeal*, January 6, 1880. In 1857 Monk moved to the Overland Stage route between Placerville and Genoa and to a local summer route between Carson City and the resort of Glenbrook on Lake Tahoe around 1872. Monk died on February 28, 1883.

104. "Knew Charley Parkhurst," *Santa Cruz Evening Sentinel*, January 31, 1903.

105. "Chevalier D'Eon," *United States Gazette*, July 26, 1810.

106. The *Sacramento Daily Union*'s editor probably became aware of D'Eon through references following the 1863 publication of the anonymous and intriguingly written *Heroes, Philosophers, and Courtiers of the Time of Louis XIV.* by the popular London publishers Hurst and Blackett. An account of D'Eon was published by the *St. Louis Daily Globe-Democrat* as late as January 1879, a year before Parkhurst's

death. Anonymous, *Heroes, Philosophers, and Courtiers of the Time of Louis XIV*; "The Chevalier D'Eon," *St. Louis Daily Globe-Democrat*, January 2, 1879; Alexandre-August Robineau, *Assaut d'armes Carlton House 9 avril 1787 d'Eon de Beaumont contre Saint George*, 1787–89, Royal Collection.

107. "The Reported Man-Woman Case," *Sacramento Daily Union*, January 3, 1880.

3. THE SEVENTH CAVALRY

1. General Edward S. Godfrey, "General Sully's Expedition against the Southern Plains Indians, 1868," 5–6, Bates Collection, Museum Collection, Little Bighorn Battlefield National Monument, Crow Agency, Montana.
2. E. Custer, *"Boots and Saddles,"* 204.
3. Utley, *Life in Custer's Cavalry*, 177; Godfrey, "General Sully's Expedition against the Southern Plains Indians, 1868," 5–6.
4. The words "Laundress" with a capital *L* and Teamster with a capital *T* both refer to Mrs. Noonan, who adopted that name at the time of her third marriage.
5. Utley, *Life in Custer's Cavalry*, 262.
6. White, *"It's Your Misfortune and None of My Own,"* 44–46; Hine and Faragher, *Frontiers*, 66.
7. "The Santa Fe Trade," *Missouri Intelligencer*, May 8, 1824; "The Latest News from New Mexico," *Olive Branch and Danville Advertiser*, August 11, 1825; "Santa Fe Trade," *Missouri Intelligencer and Boon's Lick Advertiser*, May 1, 1829; Connor and Skaggs, *Broadcloth and Britches*, 69–72.
8. "That Fleet," *Leavenworth Bulletin*, August 14, 1863.
9. "Another Mexican Train," *Leavenworth Bulletin*, August 19, 1863; untitled article, *Leavenworth Times*, November 25, 1865; "240,000 Bushels of Corn Wanted," *Leavenworth Times*, March 21, 1865.
10. McChristian, *Regular Army O!*, 368. This story was told by Seventh Cavalry member John Ryan, who had heard it from soldiers at Fort Hays, Kansas.
11. "The Mystery of Mrs. Noonan," *St. Louis Globe-Democrat*, November 5, 1878.
12. Research by Peter Boag notes that the November 16, 1878, *Davenport Daily Gazette* claimed that the teamster-turned-laundress was thought to be a man named Carlos Marrillo, although the source of its information is not clear and Boag remarks that it was "written from afar and [is] unique in its claims." The more ordinary terms "the Teamster" and "the Laundress" used here describe him before and after he transitioned to the identity of a woman and testifies to a persistent anonymity, even after she took up the names of soldier-husbands during her time with the cavalry. *Davenport Daily Gazette*, November 16, 1878, reported in Boag, *Re-dressing America's Frontier Past*, 139.

13. Godfrey, "General Sully's Expedition against the Southern Plains Indians, 1868," 5–6.
14. Utley, *Life in Custer's Cavalry*, 262; Heitman, *Historical Register and Dictionary of the United States Army*, 494.
15. "The Great West," *New York Times*, May 25, 1857.
16. "The Great West," *New York Times*, May 25, 1857.
17. "Hunting Them Down," *Sacramento Daily Union*, December 19, 1874.
18. Frazer, *Forts of the West*, 183; Utley, *Cavalier in Buckskin*, 50–51; "From New York," *Alton Telegraph* (Illinois), July 12, 1867; "The Indian War," *Chicago Tribune*, July 15, 1867; "From the Plains," *Daily Davenport Democrat*, August 17, 1867; Hoig, *Battle of the Washita*, 11–12.
19. Utley, *Life in Custer's Cavalry*, 107–16 (Barnitz quotes, 115).
20. Quoted in Utley, *Life in Custer's Cavalry*, 137–38.
21. Godfrey, "General Sully's Expedition against the Southern Plains Indians, 1868," 5–6.
22. McChristian, *Regular Army O!*, 368.
23. There were other examples, of which he would have had at best limited, if any, knowledge, of the seventeenth- and eighteenth-century men-transitioning-into-women François De Choisy, Philip of Orleans, and most notably the Chevalier D'Eon. Gilbert, *Men in Women's Guise*.
24. "News of the Day," *Charleston Daily News* (South Carolina), June 10, 1871. The *Sioux City Journal*, March 28, 1873, reported sixty laundresses for the Seventh Cavalry specifically.
25. Utley, *Life in Custer's Cavalry*, 143.
26. Quoted in Utley, *Life in Custer's Cavalry*, 148–49, 151.
27. Frazer, *Forts of the West*, 186.
28. The Kansas Pacific Railway was officially named the "Union Pacific Railway, Eastern Division," but confusion with its rival, the unrelated Union Pacific Railroad, led onlookers to informally call it the Kansas Pacific as early as August 1866. Untitled article, *Carson Daily Appeal*, August 23, 1866.
29. White, *"It's Your Misfortune and None of My Own,"* 222; "The Indian Troubles," *New York Herald*, June 25, 1867.
30. Greene, *Washita*, 112.
31. G. Custer, *My Life on the Plains*, 88–89.
32. Quoted in Hutton, *Custer Reader*, 167.
33. Greene, *Washita*, 117.
34. Quoted in Hutton, *Custer Reader*, 363.
35. White, *"It's Your Misfortune and None of My Own,"* 97–98; Greene, *Washita*, 129–30.
36. Quoted in Greene, *Washita*, 130; Hoig, *Battle of the Washita*, 130–31.

37. Quoted in Hoig, *Battle of the Washita*, 204, 132, respectively.
38. Greene, *Washita*, 137–38; Hoig, *Battle of the Washita*, 200–202, 131, 203–7. Two additional soldiers died in the days following the battle.
39. Quoted in Hutton, *Custer Reader*, 177.
40. Greene, *Washita*, 135.
41. "The Mystery of Mrs. Noonan," *St. Paul Daily Globe*, November 6, 1878.
42. Stallard, *Glittering Misery*, 11–13.
43. Rickey, *Forty Miles a Day on Beans and Hay*, 182; "Company C Gave a Ball," *Bismarck Tribune*, August 13, 1873.
44. Quoted in Stallard, *Glittering Misery*, 63.
45. E. Custer, *"Boots and Saddles,"* 133.
46. Rickey, *Forty Miles a Day on Beans and Hay*, 135; Frazer, *Forts of the West*, 183.
47. "The Mystery of Mrs. Noonan," *St. Paul Daily Globe*, November 6, 1878.
48. McChristian, *U.S. Army in the West*, 72, 151; Rickey, *Forty Miles a Day on Beans and Hay*, 124–25.
49. E. Custer, *"Boots and Saddles,"* 204.
50. McChristian, *U.S. Army in the West*, 67–68, 160–61. Cotton flannel shirts were not issued by the army until the 1880s.
51. "The Seventh Cavalry Man-Woman," *Sioux City Journal*, November 6, 1878.
52. Connor and Skaggs, *Broadcloth and Britches*, 149–50.
53. "A Complicated Case," *Bismarck Tribune*, November 4, 1878.
54. Matt Lagerberg, "Transcript of an interview of Mrs. Fred Klawitter by Matt Lagerberg concerning life at Fort Abraham Lincoln in 1876 and the Battle of the Little Big Horn. Wife of soldier stationed at Fort Abraham Lincoln," manuscript 1935, B18, State Historical Society of North Dakota, Bismarck.
55. For a further discussion of prejudice and the Laundress, see Boag, *Re-dressing America's Frontier Past*, 139–44. The quotations attributed to the Laundress in Katherine Gibson Fougera's "smoothly and entertainingly written" 1940 work *With Custer's Cavalry* cannot be taken reliably and are best viewed as a romanticized construction influenced by contemporary stereotypes. Fougera, *With Custer's Cavalry*, 190–92; Redford H. Dibble, "Custer's Cavalry Is Subject of New Book—Lead Man Recalls 1876," *Rapid City Daily Journal*, September 12, 1941.
56. "A Complicated Case," *Bismarck Tribune*, November 4, 1878.
57. Malcolm [pseud.], "The Man Wife," *Sioux City Journal*, December 28, 1878.
58. Malcolm [pseud.], "The Man Wife," *Sioux City Journal*, December 28, 1878. Peter Boag describes robberies under similar circumstances by male prostitutes in Washington State who stole from their customers, knowing they could not raise alarm without being implicated themselves. Boag, *Same-Sex Affairs*, 78. Most contemporary sources for the Laundress's husbands date to immediately after her death, in

November 1878. They all agree that the Laundress married three times and that the first two husbands deserted her, taking her savings with them. The deserters didn't waste time—the correspondent "Malcolm" from Fort Lincoln remarked in December 1878 that both men absconded after only a few days. One of the men is generally identified as James Nash and the other as either Clifton or Clifford. "Malcolm" recalled in December 1878 that the nickname "Old Jennie Nash" was "known throughout the 'Seventh'" and was later echoed by Elizabeth Custer as "Old Nash." E. Custer, *Boots and Saddles*, 204. Charles W. Clifford, a private with Company F, deserted the Seventh Cavalry while on furlough in June 1869. Two men named Clifton were assigned to the Laundress's Company A: Frank Clifton deserted just two months after Captain Hamilton's death, while Sergeant Harry O. Clifton deserted on June 12, 1871, two months before his term of enlistment was up. "Malcolm" identified Harry Clifton as the Laundress's husband. "The Man Wife," *Sioux City Journal*, December 28, 1878, described both Clifton and Nash as taking advantage of the Laundress by marriage to steal her savings before deserting. Harry O. Clifton was a native of St. Louis, Missouri, stood five foot six and one half inches in height, had brown eyes, and enlisted in the cavalry just as it was forming in August 1866 at Philadelphia, Pennsylvania. Correspondence with Doug McChristian, chief historian, Little Bighorn Battlefield National Monument, October 4, 1991. A quartermaster sergeant named Clifton is also described in John Burkman's army recollections; see Wagner, *Old Neutriment*, 113. Seventh Cavalry member John Burkman's recollections of army life were recorded by I. D. O'Donnell shortly before Burkman's death and later handed to Glendolin Wagner, a Billings, Montana, writer. Her heavily romanticized 1934 work on Burkman followed the embellished style of popular western writers such as Walter Noble Burns and Stuart Lake and should be taken cautiously. Wagner was no stranger to crafting fiction: she won a prize in June 1932 for writing part of a radio mystery called "The House of Retrogression" and was teaching fiction writing classes by 1949. "Mrs. Wagner Wins Radio Story Prize," *Billings Gazette*, June 28, 1932; advertisement, *Billings Gazette*, October 31, 1949; "Local Writer Received No Pay for Long Sought-After Custer Item," *Billings Gazette*, July 7, 1957; correspondence with Doug McChristian, July 1991; Boag, *Re-dressing America's Frontier Past*, 228.

59. Schneider, *Enigma Named Noonan*, 3; "Crumbs," *Charleston Daily News*, March 11, 1871.
60. Charles Braden was injured in August 1873 and retired from active duty in 1878 after prolonged medical leave. As a graduate of West Point, Braden later retired to Highland Falls, New York, just walking distance from West Point, saw his daughter marry a West Point officer in 1908, and died there in January 1919.
61. Quoted in Utley, *Cavalier in Buckskin*, 168.

62. "Serious Accident," *Daily Phoenix*, October 19, 1872. Despite his injuries, Weston was soon on his feet and went to Louisville for new recruits and subsequently to New Orleans that December.
63. "Echoes from the Stump," *Charleston Daily Courier*, September 14, 1872.
64. HVR, "The Ku-Klux Campaign in South Carolina," *Weekly Panola Star*, December 2, 1871.
65. "The Situation," *New Orleans Times-Picayune*, January 6, 1873; Stiles, *Custer's Trials*, 354–58, 397.
66. Untitled article, *Sioux City Journal*, April 11, 1873. The cavalry companies arrived on trains chartered from the Illinois Central Railroad.
67. Quoted in Hutton, *Custer Reader*, 183–84.
68. "Mere Mentions," *Sioux City Journal*, April 22, 1873; "River Items," *Sioux City Journal*, April 22, 1873. The steamboat contractor was possibly Walter Burleigh, who also arranged for the contracted wagons. "River Intelligence," *Cincinnati Enquirer*, April 2, 1872; "Dr. Burleigh and the Government," *Sioux City Journal*, June 26, 1873. Burleigh had previously served as an Indian agent and later entered politics and lent his name to Burleigh County, Dakota Territory. His tenure as Indian agent, the *Bismarck Tribune* noted a century later, was marked by "graft, corruption and nepotism." "Walter Burleigh: A Political Boss," *Bismarck Tribune*, July 11, 1973.
69. "River Business," *Sioux City Journal*, October 18, 1871; Petsche, *Steamboat "Bertrand,"* 5–7; "River Items," *Sioux City Journal*, June 7, 1873.
70. Quoted in Hutton, *Custer Reader*, 188.
71. "River Items," *Sioux City Journal*, June 7, 1873; Frazer, *Forts of the West*, 113; Larned quote from Hutton, *Custer Reader*, 188. Larned was impressed by a pair of "English lords" who for fun brought their own wagon team to accompany them along the Yellowstone River.
72. By 1873 the Northern Pacific's eastern section had built out from Duluth, Minnesota, as far as the Missouri River at a point just north of Fort Rice, while the western section had built more or less eastward a hundred or so miles out from its Pacific terminus at Tacoma, Washington Territory.
73. "Sioux Warriors Indignant," *New York Daily Herald*, February 1, 1873; Utley, *Cavalier in Buckskin*, 112.
74. Utley, *Cavalier in Buckskin*, 117–19. Conflict between Custer and Stanley was persistent and well known throughout the expedition.
75. Quoted in Hutton, *Custer Reader*, 190.
76. Hutton, *Custer Reader*, 206–7.
77. Hutton, *Custer Reader*, 269–71.
78. "General Custer's Official Report of the Indian Fight on the Yellowstone," *Bozeman Avant Courier*, September 12, 1873.

79. "An Indian Fight," *Springville Journal* (New York State), September 27, 1873.
80. The U.S. Post Office officially recognized the new name in early August 1873. "News and Notes," *Bismarck Tribune*, August 6, 1873.
81. "The Bismarck Sabbath-School," *Bismarck Tribune*, July 16, 1873.
82. E. Custer, *"Boots and Saddles,"* 102.
83. E. Custer, *"Boots and Saddles,"* 205.
84. McChristian, *U.S. Army in the West*, 52–55, 58–64, 158–59.
85. "The Black Hills," *Chicago Inter-Ocean*, August 17, 1874.
86. Scout [pseud.], "Dark Suspicions," *Black Hills Central*, December 28, 1878.
87. Quoted in Hutton, *Custer Reader*, 185.
88. Jackson, *Custer's Gold*, 43.
89. Quoted in Rickey, *Forty Miles a Day on Beans and Hay*, 68, 70, 347–48.
90. E. Custer, *"Boots and Saddles,"* 205.
91. "Camped in Dakota," *Chicago Inter-Ocean*, July 9, 1874.
92. "More of the Seventh Cavalry," *Sioux City Journal*, April 11, 1873.
93. "Army Life at Fort Lincoln," interview with Emma Klawitter, a laundress with Company B, 9–11, manuscript 1935, B18, North Dakota Historical Society Library.
94. Anonymous, "The Seventh Cavalry Man-Woman," *Sioux City Journal*, November 6, 1878. The letters written between the Noonans were scattered following their deaths and are now lost. Both descriptions of their letters come from an anonymous correspondent from Bismarck to the *St. Paul Pioneer-Press*, reprinted in the *Sioux City Journal*. This correspondent evidently had access to the letters through associates at the fort and was not part of the Bismarck press, which did not mention them. The timing of the two reports of letters suggests that Noonan's letters to his wife were found immediately after her death, as people went through her possessions, while her letters to Noonan were found later, after Noonan committed suicide and his trunk was opened posthumously. The Bismarck correspondent thought that Mrs. Noonan could not write and had the letters to her husband dictated by a third person, and in turn his letters to her read out to her, although the basis for this impression is not clear apart from a possible assumption of prejudice on the writer's part that she was beyond literacy because she was from Mexico and of a lower class of society. Anonymous, "The Man Wife," *Sioux City Journal*, January 10, 1879.
95. "Army Life at Fort Lincoln," interview with Emma Klawitter, 9–11.
96. "Mystery of Mrs. Noonan," *St. Paul Daily Globe*, November 6, 1878.
97. E. Custer, *"Boots and Saddles,"* 205.
98. Mulford, *Fighting Indians in the 7th United States Cavalry*, 52.
99. Untitled article, *Bismarck Tribune*, February 9, 1878.
100. Untitled article, *Bismarck Weekly Tribune*, January 26, 1876.

101. "Company L's Ball," *Bismarck Tribune*, February 21, 1878.
102. E. Custer, *"Boots and Saddles,"* 109–11.
103. "Mystery of Mrs. Noonan," *Pittsburgh Post*, November 7, 1878.
104. "The Mystery of Mrs. Noonan," *Bismarck Tribune*, November 11, 1878; Rickey, *Forty Miles a Day on Beans and Hay*, 198–99. Military balls in Fort Leavenworth were held every two weeks in 1867, according to Jennie Barnitz. Utley, *Life in Custer's Cavalry*, 130.
105. E. Custer, *"Boots and Saddles,"* 203–4.
106. Elizabeth Custer does not mention which of Annie Yates's three children was delivered with Mrs. Noonan's help. It was presumably Bessie Yates, as Annie Yates's oldest son, George, named after his father, was born in December 1872 while the cavalry was stationed in Louisville, Kentucky, and her youngest son, Milnor, named after his grandfather, was born at Fort Lincoln in early November 1875, when Elizabeth Custer was in New York City with her husband. Heavy snows shutting down railroad service were common during the winter of 1874–75, with some such blockades lasting as much as two weeks. Untitled article, *Bismarck Tribune*, March 24, 1875; "A Train Two Weeks Blockaded," *Mower County Transcript* (Minnesota), February 25, 1875; untitled article, *Grange Advance* (Red Wing MN), February 9, 1875.
107. E. Custer, *"Boots and Saddles,"* 206.
108. E. Custer, *"Boots and Saddles,"* 203, 206.
109. E. Custer, *"Boots and Saddles,"* 35.
110. Jackson, *Custer's Gold*, 3.
111. Limerick, *Legacy of Conquest*, 334; Jackson, *Custer's Gold*, 3–7.
112. Utley, *Cavalier in Buckskin*, 133.
113. Jackson, *Custer's Gold*, 47–49, 59–60; "Prof. Winchell's Report," *Bismarck Tribune*, September 23, 1874; Jackson, *Custer's Gold*, 108–9.
114. Jackson, *Custer's Gold*, 81–83; "Prof. Winchell's Report," *Bismarck Tribune*, September 23, 1874; "Custer," *Bismarck Tribune*, June 24, 1874.
115. "Custer," *Bismarck Tribune*, June 24, 1874.
116. "The Black Hills," *Chicago Inter-Ocean*, August 17, 1874.
117. Jackson, *Custer's Gold*, 63–65.
118. "Custar's Expedition," *Weekly Democratic Statesman* (Austin TX), July 23, 1874; "Custer," *Bismarck Tribune*, June 24, 1874; Jackson, *Custer's Gold*, 33–34, 142–43. Lieutenant Chance likely knew John Noonan from the Black Hills Expedition as well as the 1876 campaign.
119. Jackson, *Custer's Gold*, 84, 76.
120. "The Black Hills," *Chicago Inter-Ocean*, August 17, 1874.
121. Jackson, *Custer's Gold*, 39.

122. Quoted in Utley, *Cavalier in Buckskin*, 137; Jackson, *Custer's Gold*, 97.
123. Quoted in Jackson, *Custer's Gold*, 87–88.
124. "Gold!," *Bismarck Tribune*, August 12, 1874. The *Tribune*'s reporter was Nathan Knappen, whose byline carried only his initials, NHK.
125. Jackson, *Custer's Gold*, 102.
126. "John Nunan apptd. Corpl to date Mar. 24, '76 per SA No 22, HQ 7th, Ft A Lincoln 4/8/76," from Doug McChristian notes on muster roll for Company L, Seventh Cavalry, April 30, 1876.
127. Utley, *Cavalier in Buckskin*, 144–47.
128. Utley, *Cavalier in Buckskin*, 161–63. Custer nearly didn't make it, held back by the Grant administration as punishment for criticizing it on other matters. He was allowed to join the expedition only after the request of Terry and his own personal, last-minute plea to Grant.
129. Mark Kellogg, corresponding from the Powder River on June 12, 1876, printed in "Big Horn Expedition," *Bismarck Tribune*, June 21, 1876.
130. Utley, *Cavalier in Buckskin*, 172–77.
131. "The Chronicles of the Yellowstone," *Bozeman Weekly Chronicle*, September 19, 1883.
132. Utley, *Cavalier in Buckskin*, 188–93.
133. "Custer's Fate," *Sioux City Journal*, July 8, 1876; "Army Life at Fort Lincoln," interview with Emma Klawitter. Her husband survived, having been assigned to the supply depot alongside Noonan and others and thus away from the battle.
134. *Bismarck Weekly Tribune*, August 2, 1876. The Northern Pacific Railroad set aside a special car for Elizabeth Custer, her sister-in-law Margaret Calhoun, and Annie Yates as a token of gratitude for all Custer had done to advance the railroad's work. They left Bismarck for the East on July 31. "A Sad Reunion," *Perrysburg Journal* (Ohio), August 11, 1876.
135. Mrs. Noonan's statement recalled in "Army Life at Fort Lincoln," interview with Emma Klawitter.
136. White, *"It's Your Misfortune and None of My Own,"* 107–8.
137. White, *"It's Your Misfortune and None of My Own,"* 107–8; "Joseph's Banquet," *Bismarck Tribune*, November 23, 1877. George Sweet, an early Bismarck promoter, later became a marginal figure in Noonan's story through *Bismarck Tribune* editor Stanley Huntley.
138. Correspondence with Doug McChristian, chief historian, Little Bighorn Battlefield National Monument, August 1991.
139. "Army Life at Fort Lincoln," interview with Emma Klawitter, also cited in Hammer, *Men with Custer*, 261.

140. The Reverend P. John Chrysostom Foffa, OSB, was commonly called "Father Chrysostom" among his peers. He was a Swiss-born man in his late forties when he arrived in Bismarck in late 1877 and began working to expand St. Mary's Parish in 1878. The bell at the church was consecrated and first rung during Sunday afternoon services on November 17, 1878. "St. Mary's Parish Has Colorful History—Growth Has Been Steady since First Priest Came in 1877," *Bismarck Tribune*, November 17, 1927; "St Mary's Bell," *Jamestown Alert* (North Dakota), November 14, 1878; "The Seventh Cavalry Man-Woman," *Sioux City Journal*, November 5, 1878; Hammer, *Men with Custer*, 261.
141. "The Mystery of Mrs. Noonan," *St. Louis Globe-Democrat*, November 5, 1878.
142. Godfrey, "General Sully's Expedition against the Southern Plains Indians, 1868," 5–6.
143. "The Mystery of Mrs. Noonan," *St. Louis Globe-Democrat*, November 5, 1878.
144. "A Complicated Case," *Bismarck Tribune*, November 4, 1878.
145. Report of post surgeon W. D. Wolverton, Fort Abraham Lincoln DT, October 31, 1878, photocopy of original document courtesy of John Langellier, PhD. Wolverton reported "a laundress of Co. L, 7th Cav., known as 'Mrs. Noonan' and wife of Srgt Noonan died at this post at 4.30 A.M. on the 30th of October of Pleurisy and Pneumonia. The woman who dressed the deceased for burial reported that the supposed woman and wife was 'a man.' This morning I examined the deceased in question assisted by A.A. Surgeon C. C. Miller U.S.A. and found the body that of a fully developed male in all that makes the difference in sex, without any abnormal condition that could cause doubt on the subject."
146. "A Complicated Case," *Bismarck Tribune*, November 4, 1878.
147. Correspondence and notes of Doug McChristian, Little Bighorn Battlefield National Historic Site, 1991.
148. First Lieutenant John W. Wilkenson, "Application for Discharge of Corporal John Nunan 'L' Company 7th Cavalry," Fort Lincoln DT, November 22, 1878, photocopy of original document courtesy of John Langellier, PhD.
149. Scout, "Dark Suspicions," *Black Hills Central*, December 28, 1878.
150. Wagner, *Old Neutriment*, 114.
151. Stallard, *Glittering Misery*, 110–11; untitled article, *The Head-Light*, January 17, 1879. Stallard notes that while the court recommended Noonan be dismissed from the service, French was ultimately suspended from command for a year at half pay, a considerably lighter punishment than what was awaiting Noonan.
152. Reno was exonerated, but questions remained, and for this and other circumstances his military career was finished. Historian Robert Utley has remarked that Custer's battle plan in 1876 "might have worked had Reno not lost his nerve. To continue his charge into the [Indian] village with 112 men required a fortitude and

blind loyalty to Custer that Reno . . . did not possess." Utley, *Cavalier in Buckskin*, 7, 200–201.

153. Wilkenson request for dishonorable discharge, November 22, 1878, photocopy of original document courtesy of John Langellier, PhD.
154. Second Endorsement, Headquarters Department of Dakota, November 26, 1878, photocopy of original document courtesy of John Langellier, PhD.
155. "On the River," *Bismarck Tribune*, October 30, 1878; "The Pay of Pilots," *Bismarck Tribune*, October 9, 1878; "Westward, Ho!" *Jamestown Alert*, November 21, 1878.
156. The *Bismarck Tribune*'s account of Noonan's suicide within the fort's stables is contemporary and presents the most likely location. Glendolin Wagner's heavily romanticized 1933 account of John Burkman portrays it in a crowded blacksmith shop, a narrative device that reflects her training as a fiction writer. Two of the people Wagner described in the scene, a blacksmith named Edson Archer and Private Nathan Brown, had died a year earlier at Canyon Creek, Montana Territory, in September 1877. Wagner, *Old Neutriment*, 114–16.
157. Outlook [pseud.], "Bismarck," *Chicago Tribune*, January 7, 1879. The focus of "Outlook" on Bismarck, Fort Lincoln, and the advance of civilization brought a prejudicial yet revealing view of Mrs. Noonan.
158. "The Seventh Cavalry Man-Woman," *Sioux City Journal*, November 6, 1878.
159. "The Spoopendyke Papers," *Streator Daily Press* (Illinois), April 23, 1890.
160. "Personal," *Daily Globe* (St. Paul MN), September 27, 1878.
161. *Bismarck Tribune*, December 2, 1878. Huntley incorrectly referred to Noonan as sergeant despite the newspaper having reported on the death of Mrs. Noonan and then of Corporal Noonan, just days earlier.
162. *Bismarck Tribune*, December 2, 1878.
163. "From Out of the Depths of Hell," *Bismarck Tribune*, December 30, 1878.
164. "Strange Skipping Spirits," *Bismarck Tribune*, January 27, 1879.
165. "Sweet and Cary," *Bismarck Tribune*, April 4, 1878.
166. Sweet's own life was something of a gig economy, of dabbling in Bismarck real estate and Northern Pacific lands beyond Fort Benton before later retiring to Minnesota with his wife. He was later credited for locating Bismarck's townsite in May 1872 under its initial name of Edwinton, after a Northern Pacific Railroad director. "Early Days of Bismarck," *Bismarck Tribune*, June 8, 1883.
167. Untitled article, *Jamestown Weekly Alert*, February 6, 1879.
168. "Tribune Moving into New Home in Same Block Where It Came into Being 'Way Back in 1873," *Bismarck Tribune*, December 15, 1919; "North Dakota's Oldest Still Kicking After 107," *Bismarck Tribune*, October 9, 1980.
169. "Struggles and Triumphs," *Bismarck Tribune*, June 8, 1883.
170. E. Custer, "*Boots and Saddles*," 203.

171. E. Custer, *"Boots and Saddles,"* 205.
172. E. Custer, *"Boots and Saddles,"* 205.
173. The theme of American Progress was most directly illustrated by the painting of the same name that appeared on the cover of a transcontinental railroad timetable. John Gast, *American Progress*, 1872, oil on canvas, 11½ × 15¾ inches, collections of the Autry Museum of the American West, Los Angeles.

4. THE HUMAN BORDERLANDS

1. Seymour, *Reminiscence of the Union Pacific Railroad*, 16–17. Seymour served as consulting engineer for the Union Pacific Railroad.
2. Seymour, *Reminiscence of the Union Pacific Railroad*, 18.
3. Seymour, *Reminiscence of the Union Pacific Railroad*, 18.
4. Quoted in J. Taylor, *Fast Life*, 145, 147–49. Breakenridge also worked passenger trains for a while, largely through the interest of a conductor who took a shine to him.
5. Breakenridge, *Helldorado*, 6–12.
6. Breakenridge, *Helldorado*, 15.
7. "Denver City and a Daily Paper," *Daily Herald and Rocky Mountain Advertiser*, May 1, 1860.
8. "Denver City and a Daily Paper," *Daily Herald and Rocky Mountain Advertiser*, May 1, 1860.
9. A log house of business built in Denver in either 1859 or 1860 survives. It was built of logs along the sides and back and was fitted with a more expensive sawn lumber front for show. *Plank House*, 76.156.1, History Colorado Collection, Colorado History Museum, Denver.
10. Breakenridge, *Helldorado*, 28; "Telegraph Meeting," *Rocky Mountain News*, March 31, 1863; "The Telegraph Coming," *Rocky Mountain News*, October 5, 1863.
11. Ray Colton remarks that "John M. Chivington, the presiding elder of the Methodist church in Denver, refused the offer of chaplain, preferring a strictly fighting position." Colton, *Civil War in the Western Territories*, 43.
12. "The Battle of Apache Canyon, or Pigeon's Ranch," *Rocky Mountain Sun*, May 10, 1862.
13. White, *"It's Your Misfortune and None of My Own,"* 96–97; Ostler, *Surviving Genocide*, 178; "Chivington's Brutality," *Kansas State Journal*, February 2, 1865. "Enraged by the unprovoked massacre," Pekka Hämäläinen writes, "Cheyenne and Arapahoes approached their Lakota allies and declared war on the United States [attacking] wagon trains, stage stations, military posts, and ranches across the Platte River valley." Hämäläinen, *Comanche Empire*, 321.

14. "Home Again," *Atchison Weekly Patriot*, August 28, 1875.
15. Breakenridge, *Helldorado*, 49.
16. Breakenridge, *Helldorado*, 56–57. After sending the scalps to his sister, he received a "good dressing down" from his mother "for sending such horrid things" to the family home. Breakenridge describes his own hair as cut short to "prevent being scalped," although shorter hair than was usually fashionable at the time was generally sported by men in mountain life for the ease of care.
17. The younger Vanderbilt was "amongst those who are at present visiting Colorado Springs," remarked *Out West*. The *Denver Times* noted two weeks later that Vanderbilt and Terry had "left for Idaho [Springs] this morning, where they will sojourn for a week or two." "News of the Week," *Out West*, June 20, 1872; untitled article, *Denver Daily Times*, July 9, 1872. Breakenridge recalled having driven them there: "I took them in a democrat wagon [a type of light spring wagon] with a good team through the south and middle park, and wound up at Idaho Springs, where they bade me good bye." Breakenridge, *Helldorado*, 109.
18. "Personal," *Chicago Tribune*, April 1, 1872. Young Vanderbilt's wife, Ellen, died of pneumonia at the Vanderbilt home in West Hartford, Connecticut. George Terry, widely understood as the "companion" of Vanderbilt, ran the United States Hotel, a venerable New York institution at the corner of Water and Fulton Streets, two blocks from the old New York waterfront, for twenty years. He was reported to have lost a lease of the Hoffman House, a newer and more fashionable hotel in midtown Manhattan, as a result of his relationship with Vanderbilt. Terry died of heart failure in Atlantic City at the age of sixty-one in June 1899. He never married. "Mr. C. J. Vanderbilt's Trip," *New York Times*, September 5, 1880; "Vanderbilt as an Explorer," *Charlotte Observer*, September 11, 1880; "Suicide of C. J. Vanderbilt," *New York Times*, April 3, 1882; "Old Hotel Man Dead," *Sunday Leader* (Wilkes-Barre PA), June 4, 1899; "Col. George N. Terry Dead," *Evening Times* (Washington DC), June 5, 1899; "Old-Time Hotel Man Dead," *Muscatine Semi-Weekly News* (Iowa) June 6, 1899.
19. Breakenridge, *Helldorado*, 107. Breakenridge described the mountain that Vanderbilt climbed as opposite the hotel and covered with loose shale, making for a challenging ascent and descent. By the summer and fall of 1873, E. Nye, the man Vanderbilt boasted to have beaten in climbing, was running the Rustic House in Manitou. Untitled article, *Rocky Mountain News*, August 20, 1873; advertisement, *Rocky Mountain News*, September 12, 1873.
20. Breakenridge, *Helldorado*, 109. *Out West* reported that Vanderbilt, who had "been spending some weeks at Colorado Springs and Manitou, is now visiting the northern parts of the Territory." "Personal," *Out West*, July 4, 1872. The *Denver Daily*

Times added that Vanderbilt visited Golden on July 5. "Personal," *Denver Daily Times*, July 6, 1872.
21. Breakenridge, *Helldorado*, 109.
22. "The Narrow Gauge," *Rocky Mountain News*, June 29, 1873. The editors noted that James and William Orman had previously worked on the Denver Pacific, Colorado Central, and Kansas Pacific railroads in addition to the first leg of the Denver & Rio Grande.
23. "Pueblo," *Colorado Weekly Chieftain*, October 3, 1872.
24. Breakenridge, *Helldorado*, 113–14; "Mules Strayed," *Colorado Daily Chieftain*, May 6, 1873. James Orman offered a $300 reward to anyone who could recover the mules, but Breakenridge does not say whether he received that or not.
25. "The Atchison, Topeka & Santa Fe Railroad," *Atchison Champion*, May 9, 1875; "The New Line," *Western Home Journal*, September 2, 1875.
26. Untitled article, *Chase County Leader*, August 28, 1874; "Railroad Situation," *Las Animas Leader*, May 28, 1875. The Atchison, Topeka & Santa Fe used a paper company to charter and advance construction work between its main line and Pueblo. Called the Pueblo & Salt Lake Railroad, it was later absorbed into the main system.
27. Breakenridge, *Helldorado*, 110–13; untitled article, *Oskaloosa Independent* (Kansas), July 3, 1875; untitled article, *Las Animas Leader* (Colorado), July 5, 1875; "Railroad Matters," *Atchison Daily Patriot*, July 16, 1875; "Our Letter from the New Mines," *Kansas Tribune*, November 4, 1875. Breakenridge mistakenly recalled the contest as between the Santa Fe and the Denver & Rio Grande, despite the latter railroad never grading east of Pueblo. Serious railroad wars between the Rio Grande and the Santa Fe would occur between 1877 and 1880 over rights-of-way, and it appears that Breakenridge, who had moved to Arizona by that time, may have conflated the earlier incident with the latter in his later recollections. He could not have alerted the Rio Grande railroad president, as he later claimed in *Helldorado*.
28. Breakenridge, *Helldorado*, 117; "The Second Arizona Party," *Boston Globe*, May 15, 1876. Breakenridge's detailed discussion of how he set up the stock, paired up the animals, configured the wagons, and rigged up the jerk lines between leaders and wheelers demonstrates and reveals his experience and pride in this work, gained and earned through many years of freighting.
29. "A Letter from the Camp," *Boston Globe*, June 3, 1876. Hunt referred to Breakenridge as the "train-master" of their wagons.
30. "School Committee," *Boston Globe*, August 16, 1873; "Choice Concert," *Boston Globe*, January 22, 1875; "The Spelling Match," *Boston Globe*, April 2, 1875; "Spelling Match," *Boston Globe*, April 14, 1875; "Letter from Phoenix," *Weekly Arizona Miner*,

January 19, 1877; "Library and Literary Association," *Weekly Arizona Miner*, April 20, 1877; "Death of a Former School Teacher," *Boston Globe*, July 14, 1877. Hunt served as principal of the Prospect Hill Grammar School in 1873 and the Luther V. Bell Grammar School in 1874, the latter named after an early researcher in the field of mental health. Hunt's Arizona work as a theater and concert director continued previous efforts from when he lived in the Boston suburb of Somerville, such as a concert and two spelling bees, including a particularly difficult one for adults that wiped out its contestants within an hour. Hunt was reported to have rented the farm from Charles Tweed, a Massachusetts native who came west to serve as judge in Arizona Territory. Tweed died in July 1887, and the press recalled him as a "pronounced anti-slavery man and a champion of women's rights." "Funeral of Judge Tweed," *San Francisco Chronicle*, July 25, 1887.

31. Breakenridge, *Helldorado*, 130; "Death of a Former School Teacher," *Boston Globe*, July 14, 1877. Hunt was "seriously ill from a disease of the lungs" and presumably died of tuberculosis, an infectious disease Breakenridge did not contract, suggesting that his relationship with Hunt prudently avoided intimacy. Hunt was buried in Attleboro, Massachusetts.

32. "Town and Country," *Weekly Republican* [*Salt River Herald*], January 4, 1879; "Court Proceedings," *Weekly Republican* [*Phoenix Herald*], April 19, 1879; "Sheriff's Sale," *Weekly Republican*, May 17, 1879; "Death of a Pioneer," *Arizona Daily Star*, August 1, 1893. Breakenridge regularly advertised himself as "Wm. M. Breckenridge, Civil Engineer and County Surveyor, Phoenix, A.T. Office with Linville & Wiley, one door east of Express office. All orders promptly attended to." Advertisements, *Weekly Republican* (Phoenix), February 22, 1879, May 21, 1879, June 7, 1879.

33. A third man, jailed for slashing at a crowd while drunk, was shot in his cell after attacking an undersheriff with a wooden board, apparently pried up from the cell floor. Jesus Romero was known as the "sabre slasher," although Breakenridge did not recall his name. "Carnival of Crime," *Weekly Republican*, August 23, 1879.

34. Breakenridge, *Helldorado*, 131–34; "Carnival of Crime," *Weekly Republican*, August 23, 1879. Breakenridge claimed credit for arresting LeBarr's murderer, a "rough character by the name of McCloskey," while the newspaper stated only that "the assailant was promptly arrested" without naming who made the arrest. According to the *Weekly Republican*, someone named McCloskey and another man, arrested for killing a rancher over a grudge, were hanged on Friday, August 22, 1879.

35. "Tombstone Letter," *Arizona Weekly Citizen*, February 1, 1879.

36. "Tombstone, by an Outsider," *Tucson Citizen*, January 8, 1880.

37. The *Arizona Daily Star* reported that "Frank Cox, G. W. Merald [and] W. M. Breckenridge" of Phoenix were among those checking into Tucson's Palace Hotel. Oth-

er guests came from Denver, San Francisco, Calabasas, and Tombstone. "Hotel Arrivals," *Arizona Daily Star*, January 10, 1880.
38. "Tombstone, by an Outsider," *Tucson Citizen*, January 8, 1880.
39. "Characteristics of Tombstone Mines," *Colorado Miner*, December 25, 1880.
40. "Another Quartz Mill," *Arizona Weekly Citizen*, April 18, 1879; "Meaning in Names of Ships," *Sacramento Bee*, August 7, 1909. The Guion line's *Arizona*, launched into the Clyde River at Fairfield on March 10, 1879, was an elegant sail-assist liner with compound steam engines rated at fifty-five hundred tons, making it the second-largest steamship in the world at the time.
41. "Bloodshed in Arizona," *Sacramento Daily Union*, March 30, 1882; "Another Bloody Affray near Tombstone," *Los Angeles Herald*, March 30, 1882; "A Desperate Fight with the Cowboys," *Arizona Weekly Citizen*, April 2, 1882; "Desperate Fight," *Tombstone Weekly Epitaph*, April 3, 1882; untitled article, *Arizona Weekly Citizen*, April 9, 1882. "Zwing" Hunt's subsequent escape from custody and eventual fate remains a topic of romance among enthusiasts of the Wild West.
42. "Doc Holliday Gunfighter and Allround Thug," *Arizona Daily Star*, August 3, 1910. The observer was Christopher Selman, well known in his later life for his mineral collections. Selman supported the Earps and considered them necessary to rid the country of outlaws. He thought Wyatt Earp to be "a very quiet man, but a terror in action, either with his fists or a gun."
43. "The Stillwell Assassination," *Tombstone Weekly Epitaph*, March 27, 1882; "The Stillwell Inquest," *Arizona Weekly Citizen*, April 2, 1882. The Southern Pacific passenger train was taking the body of Morgan Earp to Colton, California, for burial, and it was accompanied by the injured Virgil Earp and, as far as Tucson, by his brothers, along with John Holliday and others, all of whom were heavily armed. When the train paused at Tucson for meals to be had, the group encountered the rustler Frank Stilwell, who had previously claimed credit for killing Morgan Earp, and shot him in a heavy volley. "Tombstone," *Anaheim Gazette*, March 25, 1882; "Assassinated," *Los Angeles Daily Times*, March 22, 1882.
44. Rosa, *The Gunfighter*, 133–40. Joseph Rosa remarks that, following the Stilwell shooting, "from then on the Earps were finished in Arizona. Opinions differ about the fight at the OK Corral, but it seems certain that pride and basic ambition were the basic causes" (140).
45. "Desperate Fight," *Tombstone Weekly Epitaph*, April 3, 1882.
46. Breckenridge, *Helldorado*, 238–41. Eliphalet Butler Gage, known almost universally as "E. B. Gage," was general superintendent of the Grand Central mine, not the Contention mine as Breakenridge recalled. He was engaged in Arizona mining for many years and was considered "the real leading man in the Tombstone District," according to Fred Dodge, who asserted that "a finer Gentleman never lived." "The

Grand Central," *Arizona Weekly Citizen*, December 11, 1880; "Personal Mention," *Tucson Weekly Citizen*, September 18, 1881; "Tombstone Mines Will Be Reopened," *San Francisco Chronicle*, April 12, 1901; "Death, Long Expected, Overtakes E. B. Gage," *Oakland Tribune*, March 13, 1913; Dodge, *Under Cover for Wells Fargo*, 105.

47. Breakenridge, *Helldorado*, 240; "Virgil W. Earp," *San Francisco Examiner*, May 27, 1882. Ike Clanton and Frank McLaury, who tipped off and retrieved the horse for Breakenridge, were both involved in the OK Corral fight in Tombstone, which resulted in the death of McLaury while leaving the unarmed and retreating Clanton uninjured. Sherman McMasters, who stole the horse in the first place, later joined the Earp party in gunning down Frank Stilwell in Tucson.

48. Breakenridge, *Helldorado*, 241.

49. "Curly Bill," *Arizona Weekly Star*, May 26, 1881.

50. Breakenridge, *Helldorado*, 225–28.

51. Breakenridge, *Helldorado*, 227–28.

52. "Shooting at Tombstone," *Tucson Citizen*, October 29, 1880; "The White Tragedy," *Arizona Daily Star*, December 28, 1880.

53. "An Episode," *Eureka Daily Sentinel*, March 5, 1882; "An Episode," *Silver State*, March 7, 1882. The *Eureka Daily Sentinel* remarks that the fandango incident occurred not long after December 1880, when Brocius was acquitted of the murder of Frederick White.

54. "Tragical Tales," *Watertown News*, May 25, 1881.

55. Chauncy, *Gay New York*, 103–8; Boag, *Same-Sex Affairs*, 105–7. The pressures of conformity that Breakenridge may have faced in the 1880s would evolve and increase over the following decades, when, as Chauncy and Boag note, the progressive reform movement placed increasing pressure upon both middle-class gay men and their working-class counterparts.

56. Ramon Adams describes the term "thicker 'n spatter" as referencing strong or devoted partnerships: "Of a certain spurred and chapped Damon and Pythias it was said that they were 'thicker 'n spatter.'" Other "objects or persons being thick" were "as thick as hoss-flies in May" or "as thick as seven men on a cot." R. Adams, *Cowboy Lingo*, 215.

57. "Row between Cow Boys—Curly Bill Mortally Wounded," *Los Angeles Herald*, May 21, 1881; "Curly Bill," *Arizona Weekly Star*, May 26, 1881; Breakenridge, *Helldorado*, 278–85.

58. "Curly Bill," *Arizona Weekly Star*, May 26, 1881.

59. Breakenridge, *Helldorado*, 278–81. Breakenridge's recollection of Wallace suggests a man whose bold front fell apart when faced with having upset his partner, a situation made worse after their fight and Brocius's injury. Wallace asking about

Brocius suggests the broken-hearted realization of having completely messed up in life, both professionally and personally.

60. Breakenridge, *Helldorado*, 294–97; "Telegraphic Items," *Silver State*, March 27, 1882.

61. "Phenix Clips," *Arizona Daily Star*, June 29, 1886; "Tucson and Vicinity," *Arizona Daily Star*, September 19, 1886; "Tonto Basin Reservoir Site," *Weekly Journal-Miner* (Prescott AZ), August 28, 1889; "A Change of Base," *Arizona Daily Star*, November 3, 1889; "Roscoe Robbers," *Los Angeles Herald*, February 17, 1894; "His Name Is Rogers," *Los Angeles Herald*, October 8, 1894; "Dies to Escape Arrest," *San Francisco Call and Post*, April 19, 1895; "Nogales Bank Robbers," *Arizona Daily Star*, August 29, 1896; untitled article, *Arizona Sentinel*, October 24, 1896. Grant Wheeler, who robbed a Southern Pacific train in January 1895, was cornered by Breakenridge and killed himself to avoid capture.

62. Untitled article, *Los Angeles Herald*, August 2, 1900; "At the Hotels," *Los Angeles Herald*, August 29, 1900; "Personals," *Los Angeles Herald*, December 22, 1906. The August 2, 1900, *Herald* article described Breakenridge as a special officer for the Southern Pacific Company (the holding company for the Southern Pacific Railroad and its interests) who over time had "killed three outlaws in the discharge of his duty." Six years later, the *Herald* merely remarked that "Major W. M. Breakenridge . . . is in the government service."

63. Fred Dodge to John Clum, December 16, 1930, James Fred Dodge Papers, Huntington Library, San Marino, California. Clum "heartily" agreed with Dodge's opinion. "Poor Billy is now 84 years of age," Clum wrote, "and has only a little time left in which to enjoy his imaginary glory." John Clum to Fred Dodge, December 26, 1930, James Fred Dodge Papers.

5. THE "LADY LOVERS"

1. Malcolm J. Rohrbaugh's *Aspen: The History of a Silver Mining Town, 1879–1893* gives an overview of Aspen's growth and socio-political development during its peak years as a silver mining camp and town.

2. Rohrbaugh, *Aspen*, 34, 39.

3. News of the "Whitechapel Fiend," or "Jack the Ripper," was regularly reported in newspapers in Aspen over the course of 1889, providing an example of Coloradans staying abreast of events in the rest of the world.

4. "A New Movement," *Rocky Mountain Sun*, March 12, 1887. The newspaper went on to report that this movement "will do a great deal to enhance the value of real estate and aid in the development of the mines."

5. *Rocky Mountain Sun*, October 29, 1887, quoted in Rohrbaugh, *Aspen*, 154. The nickname "Baby Railroad" for the Denver & Rio Grande comes from its choice of narrow-gauge tracks, three feet across, which could support only small locomotives and train cars.
6. McFarland, *Midland Route*, 17. The Colorado Midland was built with standard-gauge track (four feet, eight and a half inches across), compatible with all mainline American railroads. Heavy, full-size locomotives and cars made the "Midland" a comfortable way to travel to Denver, and it did so over four hours faster than the Rio Grande.
7. "Among the Ranchers," *Rocky Mountain Sun*, October 17, 1885.
8. "Etchings from Emma," *Aspen Daily Chronicle*, February 19, 1889. The correspondent also visited the ranch of Isaac Chatfield, "which convinced her that nothing was wanting in the line of agriculture. Fine stock, abundance of hay and necessary machinery and farming implements. Elmer Chatfield [Isaac's son] feels proud of his charge."
9. Katz, *Gay/Lesbian Almanac*, 209–12. Excerpts of a May 11, 1889, *Aspen Times* article describing the "mad infatuation" between Ora Chatfield and Clara Dietrich in Katz's *Gay/Lesbian Almanac* served as the initial introduction to the account and a springboard for the research included here.
10. Isaac Chatfield was nearly always referred to as I. W. Chatfield in the press, while his brother Clark was likewise known to nearly everyone as C. S. Chatfield.
11. "Personal," *Aspen Daily Chronicle*, October 8, 1888. The Chatfields' Denver home was on Eighteenth Street, east of the Denver business district; it no longer stands. Mrs. Chatfield was not alone in preferring the more lively social environment of a larger city than Aspen. Harriet Wheeler likewise refused to live in Aspen or the brick home her husband, Jerome, had built, preferring their home in Manitou Springs. The Wheeler home, now known as the Wheeler/Stallard house, is presently occupied by the Aspen Historical Society.
12. Information regarding the extended Chatfield family is drawn from several sources. The *Aspen City Directory*, 1889–90, vol. 2 (Aspen CO: Sayer & Goza, October 1889), lists "Chatfield, I. W., mining and stock raising, r. Lake Ave.," while the *Aspen City Directory* (Aspen CO: D. J. Sayer, March 1892) lists "Chatfield, I. W., mining and cattle, r. 706 Third, corner Gillespie." (This lot was purchased by C. S. Chatfield on June 1, 1889; the house, still standing today, was constructed during the fall of that year.) The *Aspen City Directory* (Aspen CO: Garraham & Vinton, March 1893), lists "Chatfield, I. W., mining and cattle, r. 706 N. Third." The *Grand Junction District Telephone Book* for 1910 lists C. S. Chatfield's son Arthur at the Emma ranch under the telephone number "Carbon 51-31." Further information

is available in *Colorado Genealogical Etcetera*, vol. 11; Pitkin County Marriages for 1882–1930, vol. 7; 1910 Census, vol. 1.
13. Isaac and Clark Chatfield served in the Twenty-Seventh Illinois Infantry and Second Illinois Cavalry, respectively, during the Civil War. By 1869 they were engaging in farmland pursuits in Colorado, and in 1880 I. W. Chatfield was operating a grocery business in Leadville under the business name of Chatfield & Wing. The brothers later moved to Aspen, where I. W. Chatfield briefly operated a grocery and invested in mines and ranching.
14. Quoted in Rohrbaugh, *Aspen*, 136.
15. Rohrbaugh, *Aspen*, 122–28.
16. "At Christ Church," *Aspen Times*, August 17, 1889; Rohrbaugh, *Aspen*, 138. Aspen's churches also served Congregationalists, Methodists, Protestants, and Roman Catholics, while its schools had room for more than four hundred students in 1889.
17. *Aspen Daily Times*, May 19, 1889. An Aspen school report does not list Ora Chatfield in Aspen schools; she may have been schooled locally in Emma.
18. "Married," *Aspen Daily Chronicle*, June 11, 1891. Jacqueline Chatfield married Fred Adams, a bank teller with the Jerome B. Wheeler bank, at a small ceremony in her parents' Aspen home on Lake Avenue.
19. *Denver & Rio Grande Aspen Branch Timetable No. 9*, May 19, 1889, Colorado Railroad Museum Library and Archives, Golden, Colorado. The two Denver & Rio Grande passenger trains serving Aspen daily were No. 235, the Aspen Mixed, and No. 203, the Leadville & Aspen Mail and Express.
20. Emma File, State Department of Highways, Aspen Historical Society.
21. "The great moral wave," as described in an article with that title in the *Aspen Daily Chronicle* of May 9, 1889, referred to efforts to force prostitutes and saloon keepers out of town, following similar movements in Denver and Leadville. A "Mother Hubbard" was a type of loose housedress, usually made of calico, flannel, or light wool, suitable for morning chores. While comfortable and popular, wearing one outside the house or on the street was akin to wearing pajamas in public and considered disrespectful to society and a sign of loose morals or degraded ethics.
22. John Snellinghausen's memories of Emma Garrison and the Roaring Fork in the 1880s are preserved through a letter he wrote to the *Aspen Times* in 1934, in which he specifically stated that he had helped rename the place "Emma" after Garrison. "Interesting Letter from Subscriber of Half-Century," *Aspen Times*, February 15, 1934. Emma Garrison should not be confused with Emma Shehi, who also lived in the Roaring Fork Valley and was buried in Basalt in 1927. Shehi was associated with the death of two of the Chatfield children while practicing Christian Science,

a charge she denied. "Faith Cure Was Not Employed," *Aspen Daily Times*, February 21, 1909; "Deny Responsibility," *Eagle County Blade*, March 4, 1909; "Basalt News," *Eagle Valley Enterprise*, May 27, 1927; "The Funeral of Mrs. Shehi," *Aspen Times*, May 27, 1927.

23. "The Masquerade," *Aspen Times*, January 27, 1883. Other attendees appeared as Night, a Snow Storm, and Mother Goose. Men appeared as George Washington, Henry VIII, and the "Girl of the Period," a contemporary stock character. "And what a smashing girl she was too," remarked the *Times* reporter.

24. "Personal Mention," *Aspen Times*, October 6, 1883; "Aspen Echoes," *Aspen Times*, December 1, 1889. Emma Garrison appears to have been actively involved in business and society along the entire length of the Roaring Fork Valley in the 1880s.

25. "Mad Infatuation," *Aspen Daily Times*, May 11, 1889.

26. "Mad Infatuation," *Aspen Daily Times*, May 11, 1889.

27. Untitled article, *Morning News*, July 10, 1889. The *Morning News* was published in Savannah, Georgia, demonstrating just how far news of the women's elopement had traveled within a single week. Its editors added that "one woman very rarely elopes with another."

28. "Lovelorn Girls," *Denver Times*, July 6, 1889.

29. Untitled article, *Morning News* (Savannah GA), July 10, 1889.

30. "Mad Infatuation," *Aspen Daily Times*, May 11, 1889.

31. "Mad Infatuation," *Aspen Daily Times*, May 11, 1889; "Lovelorn Girls," *Denver Times*, July 6, 1889.

32. Quoted in "Mad Infatuation," *Aspen Daily Times*, May 11, 1889.

33. "The Disappearance," *Rocky Mountain Sun*, June 12, 1886; "General News," *Meeker Herald* (Colorado), June 12, 1886; untitled article, *Rocky Mountain Sun*, June 12, 1886; "Ida Chatfield's Body Found," *Aspen Times*, August 7, 1886; "The Late Miss Chatfield," *Aspen Times*, August 14, 1886. The circumstances of Ida Chatfield's death were not easily confirmed, and her body was found fully dressed, with shoes and jewelry intact and no signs of assault. She was thought to have become distraught and apparently suicidal.

34. "Sheriff John W. White," *Aspen Daily Times*, June 5, 1889; "Sheriff John W. White," *Aspen Weekly Times*, June 8, 1889. White was a native of Pennsylvania who arrived in Colorado in 1878 and engaged in freighting, farming, and contracting before running for Pitkin County sheriff. Popular and successful in this work, he was praised as "an exceptionally good officer" and reelected to the office in November 1889. He was a bachelor until the age of forty-nine, when he married thirty-nine-year-old Sarah Holtz, whom he previously had met on a train, in 1896. They settled on a ranch on Capitol Creek, off the Roaring Fork Valley, and by 1920 the couple

had moved to Basalt, where he died. They had no children. White's own ranching partner, William Barom, worked as a chemist and sold groceries in Buena Vista before moving with White to the Roaring Fork, where he became a lifelong rancher, and later to Delta County. Like White, he married late, in 1898, and had no children. "Ranch Notes," *Aspen Daily Times*, October 3, 1885; untitled article, *Aspen Times*, October 26, 1889; "The Juries," *Aspen Daily Chronicle*, November 8, 1889.

35. "All Love Affairs Outdone," *Aspen Daily Chronicle*, July 7, 1889.
36. "Mad Infatuation," *Aspen Daily Times*, May 11, 1889.
37. "Mad Infatuation," *Aspen Daily Times*, May 11, 1889.
38. "Mad Infatuation," *Aspen Daily Times*, May 11, 1889.
39. *Aspen Daily Times*, May 15, 1889.
40. *Aspen Daily Times*, May 16, 1889.
41. *Aspen Daily Chronicle*, May 6, 1889; advertisement, *Aspen Daily Chronicle*, June 23, 1889.
42. *Aspen Daily Times*, May 5, 1889, May 12, 1889; "Aspen vs. Denver," *Aspen Daily Times*, May 14, 1889, May 29, 1889. Aspen's baseball team was particularly good, knocking Colorado Springs 14–4, reported on the same *Aspen Daily Times* page as the first printed mention of the "lady lovers." Five days earlier, it had declared victory over Leadville.
43. "Presentation Ball," *Aspen Daily Times*, May 12, 1889. The ball's raffle prizes included a copy of Thomas Moran's 1875 painting *Mount of the Holy Cross* and an embroidery work of flowers on white satin.
44. "Niblo's Garden," *New York Times*, March 9, 1886; "Powers in the 'Ivy Leaf,'" *Denver Times*, May 11, 1889; "The Grand Bill at the Grand," *Salt Lake Herald*, July 7, 1889; "W. H. Powers' 'Ivy Leaf' at the Grand," *Los Angeles Herald*, June 18, 1889. *Ten Nights in a Bar Room*, a teetotaling warhorse drama of the 1840s, probably found favor with Aspen's Temperance Union. "The G.A.R. Hop," *Aspen Daily Times*, May 16, 1889.
45. The brick buildings that stand today along the Emma road and former Denver & Rio Grande right-of-way were built following Mather's acquisition of the property in 1889. They replaced the wooden structures that Dietrich worked in before she sold the business and eloped with Ora Chatfield.
46. *Aspen Daily Times*, June 28, 1889; *Aspen Daily Chronicle*, June 29, 1889.
47. "Lovelorn Girls," *Denver Times*, July 6, 1889.
48. "Lovelorn Girls," *Denver Times*, July 6, 1889.
49. Advertisement, *Aspen Daily Chronicle*, June 18, 1889; "Railway Time Table, Denver Time, Colorado Midland Railway," *Aspen Daily Times*, July 4, 1889; McFarland, *Midland Route*, 214–19; *Denver & Rio Grande Railroad Employees' Time-Table No. 10*, August 4, 1889, Colorado Railroad Museum Library and Archives.

50. "Railway Time Table, Colorado Midland Railway," *Aspen Daily Times*, July 4, 1889. The Colorado Midland's night trains from Aspen to Denver were equipped with Pullman Palace sleeping cars, available at no extra charge. The locomotive that took their train out of Aspen was probably Colorado Midland No. 21 or its sister locomotive, No. 22, both engines built in 1887 by the Schenectady Locomotive Works of New York and regularly used on the Colorado Midland's Aspen service.
51. The 1900 U.S. Federal Census lists Joseph Henry Grannon as a printer and Linotype operator. He and Bessie Dietrich were married on July 7, 1888, and divorced sometime between 1900 and 1920.
52. "Traced to Kansas City," *Kansas City Journal*, July 18, 1889.
53. "Brought Home," *Aspen Daily Chronicle*, July 20, 1889.
54. "Brought Home," *Aspen Daily Chronicle*, July 20, 1889.
55. Sheriff White regularly collaborated with other sheriffs via telegraph and railroad to apprehend targets across their respective jurisdictions, collecting prisoners from Ouray and Grand Junction and once advising another sheriff of a suspect available in Pitkin County. A man arrested at Grand Junction had stolen horses from the Chatfield ranch at Emma and was chased for some distance by Elmer Chatfield before escaping briefly to Utah. People judged to be insane were likewise "taken to Pueblo . . . by Sheriff White and placed in the asylum." "Bagged at Ouray," *Aspen Daily Chronicle*, July 16, 1888; "Local Miscellaney," *Rocky Mountain Sun*, December 14, 1889; untitled article, *Aspen Weekly Chronicle*, December 23, 1889; "Adjudged Insane," *Aspen Weekly Chronicle*, March 18, 1889; "The Insane Woman," *Aspen Daily Chronicle*, October 4, 1890.
56. William Albaugh lived in Leon for most of his life, working as a teacher before practicing as an attorney. He died there in September 1938.
57. "Brought Home," *Aspen Daily Chronicle*, July 20, 1889.
58. "Quite an Escapade," *Wichita Star*, July 18, 1889. The newspaper also pointed out the possible connection between Ora Chatfield's disappearance and that of her older sister a few years earlier.
59. Before the introduction of electric streetcars in the 1890s, several cable car lines provided Kansas City (built on a series of bluffs along the Missouri River) with an efficient system of public transportation; their presence was a sign of Kansas City's status as a metropolitan community. Hilton, *Cable Car in America*, 255–87.
60. "Brought Home," *Aspen Daily Chronicle*, July 20, 1889.
61. "Brought Home," *Aspen Daily Chronicle*, July 20, 1889.
62. Clara Dietrich married Oliver Tyler on February 26, 1890, in Wiser, Idaho Territory, shortly before Idaho achieved statehood. After divorcing in about 1909, Dietrich eventually followed her older daughter's family to Washington State and lived in the greater Seattle region. Remarkably, Oliver Tyler reapproached Dietrich after

the death of his second wife, and the two were remarried in Seattle in August 1932, an event that made a considerable stir among the newspapers. Oliver Tyler died in 1942 and Clara Dietrich Tyler moved to California a decade later, where she died in Porterville, on the western Sierra slopes, on October 23, 1955. She was buried in Visalia. "Elderly Idaho Couple Remarry," *Post-Register* (Idaho Falls), August 26, 1932; "Aged Divorced Pair to Rewed," *Spokesman Review* (Spokane), August 27, 1932.
63. Rohrbaugh, *Aspen*, 208–21.
64. After her divorce Ora Chatfield was living in downtown Los Angeles, where she worked as a clerk in a gift shop while living at the Finkle Arms Apartments on Figueroa Street. She died on July 24, 1936, just a few days after her sixty-third birthday, and was buried at Forest Lawn Memorial Cemetery in Glendale, California. Her son Charles Jr. married a woman fifteen years his senior, which brought him a fifteen-year-old stepson when he was only thirty-one.

6. AN ANONYMOUS LOGGER

1. "The Great West," *New York Times*, May 25, 1857. William Gilpin's 1857 remarks regarding the West's industrial and commercial potential are presented in chapter 3, on Mrs. Noonan.
2. The "City Beautiful" movement in San Francisco sought architect Daniel Burnham to design a city that would be commercially and progressively uplifting. Richard White notes that while Burnham's plan was not fully implemented, "the city continued to move incrementally towards greater planning and municipal control." White, *"It's Your Misfortune and None of My Own,"* 415. William Issel and Robert Cherny remark that although San Francisco mayor James Rolph personally considered purity crusaders "well-meaning hysterics" who would "not be satisfied until they destroyed all the amusement and entertainment that have given San Francisco life and character," he still felt politically obliged to accommodate them publicly, leading to a morals squad, raids, and an underground economy in response. Issel and Cherny, *San Francisco, 1865–1932*, 106–9.
3. The Ford Model T varied between 20 and 22 horsepower. This book uses the 20-horsepower figure, as stated in the 1916 Ford catalog, *Ford, The Universal Car*.
4. "Convict-Labor Garments Sold Extensively, Worn by Whom?," *Organized Labor*, July 18, 1925; "Look at This Face," *San Francisco Chronicle*, August 31, 1919; "Believes Kirk Victim of Mistake," *Calexico Chronicle*, July 28, 1925; "Danger of Egotism," *San Bernardino Sun*, April 13, 1929.
5. "Contribution of School Hygiene to Human Conservation," *San Jose Mercury News*, July 26, 1913. The paper, written by the Stanford chancellor, Dr. David Jordan, and

Professor Lewis Terman, was presented at the Fourth International Congress of School Hygiene, held at Buffalo, New York.

6. "Salesman Named Upright Is 14th Vice Ring Victim," *Sacramento Bee*, March 5, 1918; "Death His Means of Escaping Disgrace," *Oakland Tribune*, March 10, 1918; "70,000 Bail for Accused in Vice Club Case," *Sacramento Bee*, June 19, 1918. The men were arrested during a raid upon a private home on Baker Street between Vallejo and Green, one block from the Presidio. Some of the men were soldiers, others ranged from salesmen to professionals. One of the men, an insurance broker in his thirties, fled to his ranch in Hollister before attempting to commit suicide as officers started to break down the door. Bail for these men ranged from $20,000 to $50,000, an amount of money few could hope to scrape up at that time. Remarkably, while most of the courtroom crowd were against the men, a few spoke up in their defense. Other raids from this period are described by Boag as occurring in Portland, Oregon, and Long Beach, California. Boag, *Same-Sex Affairs*, 152–53.

7. These industrial outliers also included infrastructure projects, whose construction camps for workers building dams, power plants, irrigation projects, and highways became in effect miniature frontiers in distant territories building the very mechanisms that would enable civilization to shut them down.

8. "Pack Trailing in the High Sierras into and out of the Tehipite Gorge," *Fresno Morning Republican*, September 27, 1914; Deutsch, *Making a Modern U.S. West*, 20–21. Sarah Deutsch describes the means and context by which commercial enterprises acquired large tracts of ranching, timber, and coal lands across the West, part of a larger trend at the turn of the twentieth century that generally favored large enterprises.

9. "Mine Tunnel Pierces Globe Mountain," *Sacramento Bee*, October 15, 1912.

10. K. Adams, *Logging Railroads of the West*, 146–57; Replinger, *Schafer Brothers*, 223–29. The Pickering, Bloedel-Donovan, and Schafer logging companies each operated over one hundred miles of track.

11. "Dies in Desert as Help Arrives," *San Francisco Examiner*, July 12, 1913; "Roy Shaw near Death on the Desert," *San Bernardino County Sun*, July 13, 1913.

12. Parker, quoted in Woirol, "Men on the Road," 203; and in Boag, *Same-Sex Affairs*, 22. For clarity, Gregory Woirol substituted "homosexuality" for Parker's term "sex perversion."

13. Woirol explains that the 1914 California Immigration Commission study headed by Carleton Parker reflected growing concerns about itinerant labor, following a riot in Wheatland, California, where several thousand men had arrived to pick fruit on the Durst ranch, only to find "that the jobs advertised were not really available, and [that the] housing conditions were disgraceful." The study was

intended to comprehend and effectively manage state populations, mitigating further problems such as at Wheatland. Woirol, "Men on the Road."

14. "Memoirs: Logging Camp Lovers," *Straight to Hell: The American Journal of Revenge Therapy*, no. 7 (1974): 6–7; Leyland, *Flesh*, 14. (The "Memoirs" were subsequently reprinted, in part, in Leyland, *Flesh*.) The anonymous man's account is included in a letter sent to and published in STH magazine in 1974; the titles "Logging Camp Lovers" and "Mining Camp Lovers" were added by the editors of the magazine. If the anonymous man's original letter is found and his identity established, it may be possible to determine at which two mining camps he worked, and possibly which lumber camp, along with the people, circumstances, and environment that surrounded his recollections.

15. "Memoirs: Logging Camp Lovers," 6–7; Leyland, *Flesh*, 14.

16. "Logging Season Is about Closed," *Fresno Morning Republican*, September 10, 1914; "Close Logging Camp," *San Francisco Chronicle*, November 15, 1914.

17. A large company might have as many as twenty-one individual camps, like the Schafer Logging Company of Washington State, each camp its own miniature town, with its own complement of men and support staff.

18. Quoted in Leyland, *Flesh*, 14.

19. Quoted in Leyland, *Flesh*, 14. Boag remarks that according to Kinsey's research, "oral eroticism" was "associated with the [gay male] upper and middle classes" and spread in practice with the development of middle-class gay male subcultures from 1900 on; it was so modern as to be known as the "twentieth-century way." Boag, *Same-Sex Affairs*, 118, 119. Kinsey's research indicated that while upper- and lower-middle-class men averaged 75 percent, among working-class men just under 60 percent engaged in oral sex. About 20 percent of working-class men "never or rarely" engaged in oral sex, twice the rate of middle-class men (table 3, 120).

20. "Memoirs: Logging Camp Lovers," 11.

21. In this context, "boomer" means someone who "boomed" from town to town in search of opportunity, not someone born during the postwar "baby boom."

22. "Among the Timber Men," *North Platte Telegraph* (Nebraska), January 11, 1902. The description referred to loggers in the Pacific Coast region. It also described them as free with their earnings, to the point that some of these men were well up in years with no savings to support them, only labor.

23. The camp's married men's homes were a quarter mile farther off, farthest from the noise of the mill and blocked from the bachelor cacophony by a screen of utility buildings. Johnston, *They Felled the Redwoods*, 109, 115.

24. Mrs. Ben [Lavina] Hartsuck's reminiscences of life in the lumber mill towns of Washington and Oregon in the 1910s and 1920s, written sometime in the

late 1950s, 28, Pacific Northwest Documents, University Libraries, University of Washington, Seattle.
25. "Memoirs: Logging Camp Lovers," 6–7. The anonymous man's position as custodian of the first aid cabinet suggests a support job within the camp itself, perhaps in an office or cookhouse rather than the mineshafts or mills, a situation that would explain his unfamiliarity with the conditions he found in the camps and the corresponding impression they left upon him.
26. "Memoirs: Logging Camp Lovers," 6–7.
27. "Memoirs: Mining Camp Lovers," *Straight to Hell: The American Journal of Revenge Therapy*, no. 8 (1974): 22–23.
28. "Memoirs: Mining Camp Lovers," *Straight to Hell: The American Journal of Revenge Therapy*, no. 6 (1974): 7; no. 8 (1974): 22–23.
29. See Stewart Hollbrook, "The Bull-Cook," *Century Magazine*, July 1926, 289–94.
30. Quoted in Katz, *Gay American History*, 511–12. Jonathan Ned Katz reprints from the January 4, 1948, *New York Times Book Review* a write-up by Dr. Howard Rusk on Kinsey's book *Sexual Behavior in the Human Male*. In it he writes of Kinsey's "courage to fight taboos and prejudices" to describe male sexuality through "scientific objectivity" and "without moralizing." Rusk remarks that "Dr. Kinsey points out that homosexual experience is much more common than previously thought" and that people will often have "a mixture of both homo- and heterosexual experience." Quoted in Katz, *Gay/Lesbian Almanac*, 630–33.
31. Quoted in Katz, *Gay American History*, 511–12.
32. Quoted in Woirol, "Men on the Road."
33. "Memoirs: Logging Camp Lovers," 11.
34. "Water Run-Off from Big Area Now Conserved," *Hanford Morning Journal* (California), May 15, 1921. The term "jackhammer man" was used in the California press from 1918 through the 1920s in the context of mining and tunneling. By the 1930s, however, its use in the popular press had shifted to descriptions of men engaged in outdoor construction work. The anonymous memoirist's description of the mining camp's jackhammer man might therefore suggest a date of the 1920s or slightly later.
35. "How to Cut Toll of Failed Shots," *Miami News-Record* (Oklahoma), August 23, 1925. According to this article, one safety engineer was attempting to reduce the percentage of explosive accidents in zinc and lead mining, where 13.5 percent of fatal accidents were caused by premature explosions and "picking into failed shots."
36. In mining, the term "tram" can refer to several things, from hand-pushed ore cars that ran on light tracks laid through the mine tunnels to utilitarian plant railways that moved heavy ore cars using specially designed mining locomotives. The anonymous man's description suggests a cable tramway, used to move ore

from a mine to processing mill via overhead cables. Cable trams were also used for coal mining, salt mining, and construction projects. "Pardee Dam Work Is Being Pushed," *Sacramento Bee*, December 3, 1927.

37. "Daily Gossip along Finance Row," *Los Angeles Herald*, July 25, 1912; "Nevada—Tonopah's Wonderful Showing," *San Francisco Call*, January 12, 1913; Polkinghorn, *Pino Grande*, 49–59.

38. "Alamedan Falls with Tram Bucket," *Evening Times-Star and Alameda Daily Argus* (California), July 16, 1912; "Line Tender Hurled Forty Feet from Tram Bucket," *Weekly Searchlight* (Redding CA), December 25, 1925; "Tram Lineman Falls 87 Feet to His Death at Hornet Mine," *Searchlight* (Redding CA), April 13, 1927; "Walker Mine Tram Rider Has Miraculous Escape," *Plumas Independent* (Quincy CA), March 28, 1929. Newspaper accounts of these accidents indicate that the linemen and tram operators were young, between nineteen and twenty-eight years old.

AFTERWORD

1. Keith Rutledge to the author, 1990 and 1994. Rutledge (1930–1997) was in his late twenties when he ran into the two Texas cowboys at the Mayflower Bar. He first told this story to the author during a visit to Oklahoma City and again when the author visited him at his home in Norman, Oklahoma.
2. "Books in Review," *Gayly Oklahoman*, March 15, 1994. In this review column, the reviewer recalled "a conversation in the old Mayflower Bar, on 23rd near Classen, one Saturday night [about] the excitement the previous evening. It seems a group of 'football players came to beat up on the queers,' but were ejected after the football players allegedly received injuries at the hands of the lesbians."
3. Quoted in Lanning and Lanning, *Texas Cowboys*, 93.
4. Quoted in Dary, *Cowboy Culture*, 278.
5. Quoted in Lanning and Lanning, *Texas Cowboys*, 62.
6. Abbott, *We Pointed Them North*, 202n1. "I rode 5 horses down to a whisper," Edward Abbott wrote in his diary, "got into the saddle at 3 A.M. and quit her at 9:15 P.M. to bed slept until 2 o'clock then I went out on night guard till breakfast" (202n1).
7. Abbott, *We Pointed Them North*, 97.
8. Quoted in Hughes, *Hashknife Cowboy*, 24, 26–27. Who this visitor was is hard to say. He was called a "'maphrodite" which could mean a transgender man or alternatively just someone pausing at the camp for the night on his way somewhere, in some way different enough to become an unknowing target of suspicion.
9. Brook Campbell led the herd of eleven hundred mustangs in his Ford while the other men "rode horses and drove [the herd]." He later recalled that his herd was "stretched out down Chadbourne Street about half a mile. All traffic was stopped,

several pictures were made, and the local paper gave us a big write up." They created just as big a scene in El Paso. Lanning and Lanning, *Texas Cowboys*, 131.

10. "Sodomy Charges Denied by Pair," *Shawnee News-Star* (Oklahoma), January 25, 1950; "Pair Given Two Years on Charge of Sodomy," *Shawnee News-Star*, January 27, 1950; "Two Are Facing Sodomy Charges," *Odessa American* (Texas), March 20, 1950; "Attitudes of Sex Are Conditioned, Not 'Born,'" *Shawnee News-Star*, August 4, 1955; "Felony Charges of Sodomy," *Lubbock Evening Journal*, May 26, 1958; "2 Men Charged with Sodomy," *Abilene Reporter-News* (Texas), July 2, 1958; "Male 99th Court Jury Gives Man Two Years for Sodomy," *Lubbock Morning Avalanche*, August 1, 1958.

Bibliography

Abbott, E. C. "Teddy Blue," and Helena Huntington Smith. *We Pointed Them North: Recollections of a Cowpuncher*. 1939. Norman: University of Oklahoma Press, 1989.

Adams, Andy. *The Log of a Cowboy: A Narrative of the Old Trail Days*. Lincoln: University of Nebraska Press, 1964.

Adams, Kramer A. *Logging Railroads of the West*. Seattle: Superior, 1961.

Adams, Ramon F. *Cowboy Lingo*. Boston: Houghton Mifflin, 1936.

Andrews, Ralph W. *Timber: Toil and Trouble in the Big Woods*. Atglen PA: Schiffer, 1984.

Anonymous. *Heroes, Philosophers, and Courtiers of the Time of Louis XIV, by the Author of "The Secret History of the Court of France under Louis XV."* London: Hurst and Blackett, 1863.

Banning, William, and George Hugh Banning. *Six Horses*. New York: Century, 1930.

Benemann, William. *Men in Eden: William Drummond Stewart and Same-Sex Desire in the Rocky Mountain Fur Trade*. Lincoln: University of Nebraska Press, 2012.

Boag, Peter. *Re-dressing America's Frontier Past*. Berkeley: University of California Press, 2011.

——— . *Same-Sex Affairs: Constructing and Controlling Homosexuality in the Pacific Northwest*. Berkeley: University of California Press, 2003.

Breakenridge, William M. *Helldorado: Bringing Law to the Mesquite*. Boston: Houghton Mifflin, 1928.

Brewer, William. *Up and Down California in 1860–1864: The Journal of William H. Brewer*. Berkeley: University of California Press, 2003.

Brodell, Ria. *Butch Heroes*. Cambridge MA: MIT Press, 2018.

Bryant, Edwin. *What I Saw in California*. Lincoln: University of Nebraska Press, 1985.

Burns, Walter Noble. *The Saga of Billy the Kid*. Garden City NY: Garden City Publishing, 1925.

Carranco, Lynn. *Redwood Lumber Industry*. San Marino CA: Golden West, 1982.

Carroll, John M. *A Bit of Seventh Cavalry History with All Its Warts*. Bryan TX: John M. Carroll, 1987.

Chauncy, George. *Gay New York: Gender, Urban Culture, and the Making of the Gay Male World, 1890–1940*. New York: Basic Books, 1994.

Clark, Carol. *Charles Deas and 1840s America*. Norman: University of Oklahoma Press, 2009.

Clokey, Richard M. *William H. Ashley: Enterprise and Politics in the Trans-Mississippi West*. Norman: University of Oklahoma Press, 1980.

Collins, Robert. *Kansas Pacific*. David City NB: South Platte Press, 1998.

Colton, Ray C. *The Civil War in the Western Territories: Arizona, Colorado, New Mexico, and Utah*. Norman: University of Oklahoma Press, 1959.

Connor, Seymour V., and Jimmy M. Skaggs. *Broadcloth and Britches: The Santa Fe Trade*. College Station: Texas A&M University Press, 1977.

Conrads, Margaret C., ed. *Alfred Jacob Miller: Romancing the West in the Bank of America Collection*. Kansas City MO: Nelson-Atkins Museum of Art, 2010.

Cross, Coy F., II. *Go West Young Man! Horace Greeley's Vision for America*. Albuquerque: University of New Mexico Press, 1995.

Curtis, Mabel Rowe. *The Coachman Was a Lady: The Story of the Life of Charley Parkhurst*. Watsonville CA: Pajaro Valley Historical Association, 1959.

Custer, Elizabeth. *"Boots and Saddles," or, Life in Dakota with General Custer*. 1885. N.p.: Cirignani Enterprises, 2015.

Custer, George. *My Life on the Plains, Or, Personal Experiences with the Indians*. Mount Pleasant SC: Arcadia, 2009.

Dary, David. *Cowboy Culture: A Saga of Five Centuries*. 1981. Lawrence: University Press of Kansas, 1989.

Delgado, James. *Gold Rush Port: The Maritime Archeology of San Francisco's Waterfront*. Berkeley: University of California Press, 2009.

Deutsch, Sarah. *Making a Modern U.S. West: The Contested Terrain of a Region and Its Borders, 1898–1940*. Lincoln: University of Nebraska Press, 2022.

DeVoto, Bernard. *Across the Wide Missouri*. Boston: Houghton Mifflin, 1947.

Dodge, Fred. *Under Cover for Wells Fargo: The Unvarnished Recollections of Fred Dodge*. 1969. Norman: University of Oklahoma Press, 1998.

Dugan, Mark, and John Boessenecker. *The Grey Fox: The True Story of Bill Miner, Last of the Old-Time Bandits*. Norman: University of Oklahoma Press, 1992.

Engel, Stephen M. *Fragmented Citizens: The Changing Landscape of Gay and Lesbian Lives*. New York: New York University Press, 2016.

Enzler, Jerry. *Jim Bridger: Trailblazer of the American West*. Norman: University of Oklahoma Press, 2021.

Fone, Byrne R. S. *Masculine Landscapes: Walt Whitman and the Homoerotic Text*. Carbondale: Southern Illinois University Press, 1992.

Fougera, Katherine Gibson. *With Custer's Cavalry: From the Memoirs of the Late Katherine Gibson, Widow of Captain Francis Gibson of the Seventh Cavalry, U.S.A. (Retired)*. 1940. Caldwell ID: Caxton Printers, 1942.

Frazer, Robert W. *Forts of the West: Military Forts and Presidios, and Posts Commonly Called Forts, West of the Mississippi River to 1898*. Norman: University of Oklahoma Press, 1965.

Gilbert, O. P. *Men in Women's Guise: Some Instances of Female Impersonation*. Translated from the French by Robert B. Douglas. London: John Lane/Bodley Head, 1926.

Greene, Jerome A. *Washita: The U.S. Army and the Southern Cheyennes, 1867–1869*. Norman: University of Oklahoma Press, 2004.

Hafen, LeRoy R., ed. *Trappers of the Far West: Sixteen Biographical Sketches*. Selected and with an introduction by Harvey L. Carter. 1965. Lincoln: University of Nebraska Press, 1983.

Hämäläinen, Pekka. *The Comanche Empire*. New Haven: Yale University Press, 2008.

———. *Lakota America: A New History of Indigenous Power*. New Haven: Yale University Press, 2019.

Hammer, Kenneth. *Men with Custer: Biographies of the 7th Cavalry, June 25, 1876*. Hardin MT: Custer Battlefield Historical & Museum Association, 1995.

Heitman, Francis. *Historical Register and Dictionary of the United States Army, from Its Organization, September 29, 1789, to March 2, 1903*. Washington DC: Government Printing Office, 1903.

Hilton, George W. *The Cable Car in America*. San Diego CA: Howell-North Books, 1982.

Hine, Robert. *The American West: An Interpretive History*. Boston: Little, Brown, 1973.

Hine, Robert V., and John Mack Faragher. *Frontiers: A Short History of the American West*. New Haven: Yale University Press, 2007.

Hoag, Maury. *Stagecoaching on the California Coast: The Coast Line Stage from Los Angeles to San Juan*. Santa Barbara CA: Fithian Press, 2001.

Hoig, Stan. *The Battle of the Washita: The Sheridan-Custer Indian Campaign of 1867–69*. Lincoln: University of Nebraska Press, 1979.

Holliday, J. S. *Rush for Riches: Gold Fever and the Making of California*. Berkeley: University of California Press with the Oakland Museum of California, 1999.

Hughes, Stella. *Hashknife Cowboy: Recollections of Máck Hughes*. Tucson: University of Arizona Press, 1984.

Hutton, Paul Andrew, ed. *The Custer Reader*. Norman: University of Oklahoma Press, 2004.

Hyde, Anne F. *Empires, Nations, and Families: A History of the North American West, 1800–1860*. Lincoln: University of Nebraska Press, 2011.

Issel, William, and Robert W. Cherny. *San Francisco, 1865–1932: Politics, Power, and Urban Development*. Berkeley: University of California Press, 1986.

Jackson, Donald. *Custer's Gold: The United States Cavalry Expedition of 1874*. 1966. Lincoln: University of Nebraska Press, 1972.

Johnson, Colin R. *Just Queer Folks: Gender and Sexuality in Rural America*. Philadelphia: Temple University Press, 2013.

Johnson, Susan Lee. *Roaring Camp: The Social World of the California Gold Rush*. New York: Norton, 2000.

Johnston, Hank. *They Felled the Redwoods*. 1966. Fish Camp CA: Stauffer, 2007.

———. *The Whistles Blow No More: Railroad Logging in the Sierra Nevada, 1874–1942*. Glendale CA: Trans-Anglo Books, 1984.

Jones, Karen R. *Calamity: The Many Lives of Calamity Jane*. New Haven: Yale University Press, 2020.

Katz, Jonathan Ned. *Gay American History: Lesbians and Gay Men in the U.S.A.* N.p.: Meridian, 1992.

———. *Gay/Lesbian Almanac: A New Documentary*. New York: Harper & Row, 1983.

King, Clarence. *Mountaineering in the Sierra Nevada*. Lincoln: University of Nebraska Press, 1970.

Kirby, Georgiana Bruce. *Georgiana, Feminist Reformer of the West: The Journal of Georgiana Bruce Kirby, 1852–1860*. Santa Cruz CA: Santa Cruz County Historical Trust, 1987.

Kowalewski, Michael, ed. *Gold Rush: A Literary Exploration*. Berkeley CA: Heyday Books, 1997.

Kraft, Louis. *Ned Wynkoop and the Lonely Road from Sand Creek*. Norman: University of Oklahoma Press, 2011.

Kreck, Dick. *Hell on Wheels: Wicked Towns along the Union Pacific Railroad*. Golden CO: Fulcrum, 2013.

Lake, Stuart N. *Wyatt Earp: Frontier Marshal*. Boston: Houghton Mifflin, 1931.

Lanning, Jim, and Judy Lanning, eds. *Texas Cowboys: Memories of the Early Days*. College Station: Texas A&M University Press, 1984.

Leyland, Winston, ed. *Flesh: True Homosexual Experiences from S.T.H., Volume 2*. San Francisco: Gay Sunshine Press, 1982.

Limerick, Patricia. *The Legacy of Conquest: The Unbroken Past of the American West*. 1987. New York: Norton, 2007.

Logsdon, Guy. *"The Whorehouse Bells Were Ringing" and Other Songs Cowboys Sing*. Urbana: University of Illinois Press, 1989.

Lord, Eliot. *Comstock Mining and Miners*. Washington DC: Government Printing Office, 1883.

MacDonald, Craig. *Cockeyed Charley Parkhurst: The West's Most Unusual Stagewhip*. Palmer Lake CO: Filter Press, 1873.

Mangan, Terry William. *Colorado on Glass: Colorado's First Half Century as Seen by the Camera*. Denver: Sundance, 1975.

Manion, Jen. *Female Husbands: A Trans History*. Cambridge: Cambridge University Press, 2020.

McChristian, Douglas. *Regular Army O! Soldiering on the Western Frontier, 1865–1891*. Norman: University of Oklahoma Press, 2017.

———. *The U.S. Army in the West, 1870–1880: Uniforms, Weapons, and Equipment.* Norman: University of Oklahoma Press, 1995.

McFarland, Edward M. "Mel." *The Midland Route: A Colorado Midland Guide and Data Book.* Golden: Colorado Railroad Museum, 1980.

Meldahl, Keith Heyer. *Rough-Hewn Land: A Geologic Journey from California to the Rocky Mountains.* Berkeley: University of California Press, 2011.

Moon, Michael. *Disseminating Whitman: Revision and Corporeality in "Leaves of Grass."* Cambridge MA: Harvard University Press, 1991.

Mulford, Ami Frank. *Fighting Indians in the 7th United States Cavalry, Custer's Favorite Regiment.* Bellevue NB: Old Army Press, 1970.

Myrick, David F. *Railroads of Nevada and Eastern California: Volume I, the Northern Roads.* Reno: University of Nevada Press, 1990.

———. *Railroads of Nevada and Eastern California: Volume II, the Southern Roads.* Reno: University of Nevada Press, 1990.

———. *Railroads of Nevada and Eastern California: Volume III, More on the Northern Roads.* Reno: University of Nevada Press, 2007.

Nolan, Frederick. *The West of Billy the Kid.* Norman: University of Oklahoma Press, 1998.

Olmstead, Roger R., ed. *Scenes of Wonder and Curiosity from "Hutching's California Magazine," 1856–1861.* Berkeley CA: Howell-North Books, 1962.

Ostler, Jeffrey. *Surviving Genocide: Native Nations and the United States from the American Revolution to Bleeding Kansas.* New Haven: Yale University Press, 2019.

Petsche, Jerome E. *The Steamboat "Bertrand": History, Excavation, and Architecture.* Washington DC: National Park Service, 1974.

Pitter, Rich. *Hank Monk: He'll Get You There on Time.* South Lake Tahoe CA: Lake Tahoe Historical Society, 1995.

Polkinghorn, R. S. *Pino Grande: Logging Railroads of the Michigan-California Lumber Company.* Berkeley CA: Howell-North Books, 1966.

Pomeroy, Earl. *The Pacific Slope: A History of California, Oregon, Washington, Idaho, Utah & Nevada.* New York: Knopf, 1965.

Porter, Mae Reed, and Odessa Davenport. *Scotsman in Buckskin: Sir William Drummond Stewart and the Rocky Mountain Fur Trade.* New York: Hastings House, 1963.

Quinn, D. Michael. *Same-Sex Dynamics among Nineteenth-Century Americans: A Mormon Example.* Urbana: University of Illinois Press, 1996.

Replinger, Peter J. *The Schafer Brothers: Pioneer Loggers of the Satsop Valley.* Shelton WA: P. J. R. Publications, 2018.

Rickey, Don. *Forty Miles a Day on Beans and Hay: The Enlisted Soldier Fighting the Indian Wars.* Norman: University of Oklahoma Press, 1989.

Robinson, W. W. *Land in California: The Story of Mission Lands, Ranchos, Squatters, Mining Claims, Railroad Grants, Land Scrip, Homesteads.* Berkeley: University of California Press, 1948.

Rohrbaugh, Malcolm J. *Aspen: The History of a Silver Mining Town, 1879–1893.* New York: Oxford University Press, 1986.

Rolle, Andrew. *John Charles Frémont: Character as Destiny.* Norman: University of Oklahoma Press, 1991.

Rosa, Joseph G. *The Gunfighter: Man or Myth?* Norman: University of Oklahoma Press, 1969.

Roscoe, Will. "That Is My Road: The Life and Times of a Crow Berdache." *Montana: The Magazine of Western History,* Winter 1990, 46–55.

———. *The Zuni Man-Woman.* Albuquerque: University of New Mexico Press, 1991.

Schneider, James V. *An Enigma Named Noonan.* N.p., 1988.

Schumacher, Genny. *Deepest Valley: Guide to California's Owens Valley and Its Mountain Lakes, Roadsides and Trails.* 1969. Berkeley CA: Wilderness Press, 1972.

Sears, Clare. *Arresting Dress: Cross-Dressing, Law, and Fascination in Nineteenth-Century San Francisco.* Durham NC: Duke University Press, 2015.

Seymour, Silas. *A Reminiscence of the Union Pacific Railroad, Containing Some Account of the Discovery of the Eastern Base of the Rocky Mountains; and of the Great Indian Battle of July 11, 1867.* Quebec: A. Cotli & Co., 1873.

Sleeper-Smith, Susan, ed. *Rethinking the Fur Trade: Cultures of Exchange in an Atlantic World.* Lincoln: University of Nebraska Press, 2009.

Smith, Henry Nash. *Virgin Land: The American West in Symbol and Myth.* 1950. New York: Vintage Books, 1961.

Smithers, Gregory D. *Reclaiming Two-Spirits: Sexuality, Spiritual Renewal, and Sovereignty in Native America.* Boston: Beacon Press, 2022.

Sprague, Marguerite. *Bodie's Gold: Tall Tales and True History from a California Mining Town.* Reno: University of Nevada Press, 2003.

Stallard, Patricia. *Glittering Misery: Dependents of the Indian-Fighting Army.* Norman: University of Oklahoma Press, 1992.

Starr, Kevin, and Orsi, Richard J., ed. *Rooted in Barbarous Soil: People, Culture and Community in Gold Rush California.* Berkeley: University of California Press, 2000.

Stewart, Edgar I. *Custer's Luck.* Norman: University of Oklahoma Press, 1955.

Stewart, Sir William Drummond. *Altowan; or, Incidents of Life and Adventure in the Rocky Mountains.* New York: Harper & Brothers, 1846.

———. *Edward Warren.* Missoula MT: Mountain Press, 1986.

Stiles, T. J. *Custer's Trials: A Life on the Frontier of a New America.* New York: Vintage Books, 2015.

Stoker, Patty Haden. "The Burden of Charley Parkhurst." Manuscript, Watsonville Historical Society, Watsonville CA.

Strong, Lisa. *Sentimental Journey: The Art of Alfred Jacob Miller*. Fort Worth TX: Amon Carter Museum, 2008.

Taylor, Bayard. *Eldorado: Adventures in the Path of Empire*. Santa Clara CA: Heyday Books, Santa Clara University, 2000.

Taylor, Joseph. *A Fast Life on the Modern Highway; Being a Glance into the Railroad World from a New Point of View*. New York: Harper & Brothers, 1874.

Tyler, Ron, ed. *Alfred Jacob Miller: Artist on the Oregon Trail*. With a catalogue raisonée by Karen Dewees Reynolds and William R. Johnston. Fort Worth TX: Amon Carter Museum, 1982.

Utley, Robert M. *Cavalier in Buckskin: George Armstrong Custer and the Western Military Frontier*. Norman: University of Oklahoma Press, 1988.

———. *High Noon in Lincoln: Violence on the Western Frontier*. Albuquerque: University of New Mexico Press, 1987.

———, ed. *Life in Custer's Cavalry: Diaries and Letters of Albert and Jennie Barnitz, 1867–1868*. Lincoln: University of Nebraska Press, 1987.

Vestal, Stanley. *Queen of Cowtowns: Dodge City*. Lincoln: University of Nebraska Press, 1972.

Wagner, Glendolin Damon. *Old Neutriment*. New York: Sol Lewis, 1973.

Walker, Franklin. *San Francisco's Literary Frontier*. New York: Knopf, 1939.

Walters, Jordan Biro. *Wide-Open Desert: A Queer History of New Mexico*. Seattle: University of Washington Press, 2023.

White, Richard. *"It's Your Misfortune and None of My Own": A History of the American West*. Norman: University of Oklahoma Press, 1991.

———. *The Republic for Which It Stands: The United States during Reconstruction and the Gilded Age, 1865–1896*. New York: Oxford University Press, 2017.

Whitman, Walter. *"Leaves of Grass" by Walt Whitman, Including a Fac-Simile autobiography variorum readings of the poems and a department of Gathered Leaves*. Philadelphia: David McKay, 1900.

Wishart, David J. *The Fur Trade of the American West, 1807–1840*. 1979. Lincoln: University of Nebraska Press, 1992.

Woirol, Gregory R. "Men on the Road: Early Twentieth-Century Surveys of Itinerant Labor in California." *California History* 70, no. 2 (Summer 1991): 192–205.

Young, James A., and Abbott B. Sparks. *Cattle in the Cold Desert*. Reno: University of Nevada Press, 2002.

Index

Abbott, Downing & Company, 223n28
Abbott, E. A., 223n28
Abbott, Edward, 7, 208–9, 257n6
Abbott, J. S., 223n28
Adams, Fred, 249n18
Adams, Ramon, 246n56
Adams & Company, 50–51, 61, 228n86
Al (logger), 199, 203
Albaugh, William, 190, 252n56
Alden, Mr., 64–65
Altowan (Stewart), 40–41
American Fur Company, 22
American Progress (Gast), 241n173; theme of, 140, 241n173
American Psychiatric Association, 14
Americans: and American Progress, 140; expansionism of, 4–6, 59–60, 76; and Indians, 79–80, 86–87, 148–49; new experiences for, 2; speech habits of, 68; in trapping business, 22
American West. *See* West
anonymous correspondent, 236n94
anonymous logger, 197–98, 225n14; observations of, 198–99, 201–2, 205–6; partners of, 199, 203–4; work of, 200–201, 256n25
Arapaho Indians, 148–49, 241n13
Arizona, 160, 162

Arizona (steamer), 160, 245n40
Arizona Colonization Company, 156–57
Arizona Daily Star, 244n37
Arizona Weekly Star, 167
Army Act (1866), 78–79
Ashley, William, 22–23, 217n12
Aspen CO, 173–75, 176–77, 186, 187, 192, 249n16
Aspen Daily Chronicle, 187, 190, 191, 249n21
Aspen Daily Times, 183–85, 186, 251n42
Aspen Historical Society, 248n11
Aspen Mountain, 174
Aspen Times, 178, 248n9, 249n22
Astor, John, 22
Atchison, Topeka & Santa Fe Railroad, 154–55, 243nn26–27
Atchison Champion, 154
An Attack by Crows on the Whites on the Big Horn River East of the Rocky Mountains (Miller), 35, 218n40
Autry Museum of the American West, 223n28

Banning, William, 57–58
Barnitz, Albert, 81–82, 84–85
Barnitz, Jennie, 82, 237n104
Barom, William, 250n34

baseball, 186, 251n42
Battle of the Little Bighorn (1876), 119–24, 129, 238n128, 238n133, 239n152
bears, 117–18
beavers, 21, 22–23
Becker, Charles, 116
Bella Union, 53, 224n39
Benemann, William, 218n27
Benteen, Frederick, 121
Benton, Thomas, 19
Bighead, Kate, 87–88
Big Jake, 223n29
Birch, James, 48–52, 222n18, 222n20, 223n36
bisexual (word), 11
bisexuality, 201–2, 204
Bishop, Sophia, 56, 226n57
Bismarck, Otto von, 101–2
Bismarck ND, 101–2, 130–31, 136–37, 236n80, 240n166
Bismarck Tribune: distribution of, 134; on John Noonan, 240n156; management of, 137; on military balls, 109; on military expedition, 120; on mining expedition, 116, 118; on Mrs. Noonan, 92–93, 126–27, 132–33; on Walter Burleigh, 235n68
Black Americans, 95
Black Hills, 115, 125
Black Hills Expedition (1874), 115–19
Black Kettle (Cheyenne man), 87, 88, 148
Bloedel-Donovan logging company, 254n10
Bloody Knife (Indian man), 117–18
Boag, Peter, 214n11, 215n17, 229n87, 230n98, 231n12, 233n58, 246n55, 255n19
"boomers," 199, 255n21

"Boots and Saddles" (Custer), 137
bower incident, 25, 217n18
Braden, Charles, 94, 234n60
brakes and brakemen, 145
Breakenridge, George, 147
Breakenridge, William, 145–46; acquaintances of, 150–53, 242n17, 244n31; adaptability of, 153; character of, 162–64; companions of, 164–68, 169; *Helldorado*, 170, 243n27; incidents involved in, 154–55, 160, 167–68, 243n24, 243n27; and Indians, 149, 242n16; reflections of, 169–70, 170–71, 247n63; taken advantage of, 155–57; work of, 147–48, 150, 153–55, 157–61, 243nn28–29, 244n32, 244n34, 247nn61–62
Breen family, 59–60
bricklayer (transgender man), 46
bridge incidents, 64–65
Bridger, Jim, 26–27, 155
British, in America, 21–22, 30
Brocius, William "Curly Bill," 164–68, 246n53, 246n59
Brother Jonathan (steamer), 51, 223n33
Brown, Nathan, 240n156
Buckley, William, 46, 56, 220n7, 226n56
buffalo, 15, 16–17, 34, 38, 41, 85, 117
Buffalo Bill, 6, 214n8
Burkman, John, 129, 233n58, 240n156
Burleigh, Walter, 235n68
Burnham, Daniel, 253n2
business model, in fur trade, 22–23, 217n12

cable cars, 191, 252n59
cable trams, 205, 256n36
Caledonian Mercury, 32
Calhoun, James, 121

Calhoun, Margaret, 238n134
California Immigration Commission study (1914), 254n13
California Stage Company, 50–51, 53, 56, 223n28
Campbell, Brook, 257n9
Campbell, Hugh, 19
Campbell, Robert, 19–21, 216n6
Camptonville stage robbery, 65, 228n86
cancer, 67–68
caravans, 19–21, 23, 76
cars, 193–94, 195, 210–11, 253n3, 257n9
Castro, José, 59–60
Castroville Argus, 67–68
Catholic Church, 125, 140, 218n29, 218n40
cattle, 85, 120–21, 208–9, 210–11
Central Pacific Railroad, 85
Chance, Josiah, 116, 121, 237n118
Chatfield, Clark, 176, 182–83, 248n10, 249n13
Chatfield, Della, 177
Chatfield, Eliza, 176, 182
Chatfield, Elmer, 176–77, 248n8, 252n55
Chatfield, Ida, 182–83, 250n33, 252n58
Chatfield, Isaac, 175–76, 182–83, 186, 192, 248n8, 248n10, 249n13
Chatfield, Jacqueline (married to Fred Adams), 176–77, 249n18
Chatfield, Mary, 176, 182
Chatfield, Ora: daily life of, 186–87, 253n64; death of, 253n64; education of, 249n17; elopement of, 187–91, 192, 250n27; expectations for, 177, 180; family of, 175, 252n58; marriage of, 192; newspapers on, 184–85, 248n9; response to sexuality of, 183
Chatfield family, 175–76, 192, 248n11, 249n22
Chauncy, George, 246n55
Cherny, Robert, 253n2
Chet (miner), 201, 203
Cheyenne Indians, 81–82, 87–88, 99, 119, 121, 124–25, 148–49, 241n13
Chicago, Rock Island & Pacific Railroad, 191
Chicago Inter-Ocean, 116
Chicago Telegraph, 132
Chicago Times, 132
Chicago Tribune, 132
Chief Joseph, 124
Childs, Charles, 44, 47, 48, 221n14
Childs, Liberty, 48, 221n16
Chivington, John, 148–49, 241n11
Choisy, François De, 232n23
Christ Episcopal Church, 176
Christian Science, 249n22
churches, 125, 140, 166, 176, 218n29, 241n11, 249n16
"City Beautiful" movement, 193, 253n2
civilization: and frontier, 5–7, 14, 41–42, 146, 213n7, 254n7; and military, 127–28, 137, 140; and railroad, 143–46; symbols of, 138–39; technology advancing, 194–95; West changed by, 2–3, 155
Civil War, 75–76, 78, 95–96, 249n13
Clanton, Ike, 163, 246n47
Clark, William, 19, 26
Clement, Antoine, 27–32, 33, 35–41, 218n29
Clement, François, 38, 39–40
Clifton (quartermaster sergeant), 233n58
Clifton, Frank, 233n58
Clifton, Harry O., 93, 233n58
clothing, military, 91–92, 103–4, 118
clothing, women's, 90–91, 108–9, 110–11, 249n21

Clum, John, 169, 170, 247n63
Coast Line (stagecoaches), 60–61
Cockeyed Charley Parkhurst (MacDonald), 229n89
Colorado, as tourist destination, 150
Colorado Midland Railway, 174, 188, 191, 248n6, 252n50
Colorado Miner, 159–160
Colorado Volunteers, 148
Colton, Ray, 241n11
Committee of Vigilance of San Francisco, 224n43
Company A, 79, 83, 89, 93
Company F, 109
Company L, 101, 109, 121, 122, 128
Concord coaches, 50, 54, 57–58, 223n29
Constitution, 95
Cook, Jay, 101
Corbie (Scottish man), 39
Cortes (steamer), 51, 223n33
cowboys, 163, 168, 170, 207–10, 211–12
Cox, Frank, 159, 244n37
Crook, George, 119–20
cross-dressers and cross-dressing, 65, 229n87, 230n98
Crow Indians, 35, 100
Curly Bill (stagecoach driver), 69, 230n103
Curtis, William, 106, 116
Custer, Elizabeth: "Boots and Saddles," 137; and husband's return, 119; and John Noonan, 103, 106; on laundresses, 89, 102; and Mrs. Noonan as midwife, 112–14, 237n106; on Mrs. Noonan's appearance, 110; and Mrs. Noonan's character, 137–38; on Mrs. Noonan's home, 108, 111; on Mrs. Noonan's laundry skills, 90–91; on Mrs. Noonan's life, 74; on Mrs.

Noonan's marriages, 93, 103, 233n58; as widow, 122–23, 238n134; writing skills of, 139–40
Custer, George: about, 79; in Battle of the Little Bighorn, 120–21, 239n152; and Black Hills expedition, 115–16, 118–19; in cavalry relocation, 97; clothing of, 90; death of, 121; disciplining of, 238n128; and fellow soldiers, 105–6, 235n74; as hunter, 117–18; and John Noonan, 106, 112; and Mrs. Noonan, 123; and railroad, 99–101, 238n134; in skirmishes, 81, 87–88, 100–101
Custer, Thomas, 88, 106

Daily Alta California, 68, 222n20
Daly, John, 216n28
Davenport Daily Gazette, 231n12
Declaration of Independence (western version), 143–45
Dell (gossiper), 210
Denver & Rio Grande Railroad, 150, 153, 174, 177, 179, 187–88, 243n27, 248n5, 249n19
Denver CO, 147–48, 149–50
Denver Pacific Railway, 149–50
Denver Times, 180, 187, 242n17
D'Eon, Chevalier, 70, 230n106, 232n23
Department of the South, 93, 95–96
Deutsch, Sarah, 254n8
Die Homosexualität des Mannes und des Weibes (Hirschfeld), 215n21
Dietrich, Andrew, 190
Dietrich, Clara (married to Oliver Tyler): circumstances surrounding, 175, 179; elopement of, 187–91, 250n27; marriage of, 191–92, 252n62; newspapers on, 184–86, 187, 248n9; response

to sexuality of, 180, 183–84; self-awareness of, 181–82; work of, 179
Dietrich, Susan, 180, 190
Diseases of Society and Degeneracy (Lydston), 214n16
Dodge, Fred, 169, 170–71, 245n46
Dodge, Grenville, 143
Donner Party, 60
Driskle, Mike, 221n12
drivers, of horses, 47, 56–59, 61, 64–65, 226n62
Dunn, Mike "Sugarfoot," 229n90
Dutch Kate, 65, 229n87

Earp, Morgan, 161–62, 245n43
Earp, Virgil, 245n43
Earp, Wyatt, 169, 170, 245n42
Earp brothers, 161–62, 165, 168, 169, 170, 245n42, 245n44, 246n47
Edwards (killer), 55, 225n51
Edward Warren (Stewart), 40–41
elections, 225n54
Eliot, William, 217n12
Elliott, Joel, 84
Emma CO, 174–75, 177–78, 249n22
Emma Road, 177, 251n45
Emma Store, 177, 179
English, and fur trade, 21
Eureka Daily Sentinel, 246n53
executions. *See* hangings

fandango incident, 165, 246n53
farming, 61, 63, 157, 227n66, 248n8
Far West (steamer), 97–98, 120–21, 122, 123
Ferguson, Ed, 227n71
Field, Matthew, 40
Fifteenth Amendment, 95
Fillmore, Millard, 225n54

Foffa, John, 125, 136, 239n140
Fontenelle, Lucien, 26, 217n20
football players, 207, 257n2
Ford cars, 170, 210–11, 253n3, 257n9. *See also* cars
foreman of mining camp, 203–4
Forsyth, Thomas, 218n29
Forsythe, George, 89
Fort Abraham Lincoln. *See* Fort Lincoln
Fort Laramie Treaty (1868), 115, 119
Fort Leavenworth, 82
Fort Lincoln, 96, 98, 99, 102–3, 126–27
Fort Lyon, 76
Fort Rice, 98
Fort Riley, 79
Fort Vancouver, 25, 217n14
Fourteenth Amendment, 95
freight wagons, 76–77, 125, 147
Frémont, Jessie, 56
Frémont, John C., 38, 55–56, 59–60, 219n44, 225nn53–54; *Report of the Exploring Expedition to the Rocky Mountains*, 219n44
French, and fur trade, 21
French, Thomas, 129, 239n151
frontier: and civilization, 5–7, 14, 41–42, 146, 213n7, 254n7; concept of, 213n6; early, 2; in humanity, 138–39; industrial, 195–96, 205–6, 209; negative views of, 178; personal accounts of, 213n2
furniture business, 222n24
fur trade, 19–23, 76, 216n7, 217n17
F. Y. Batchelor (steamer), 131

Gage, Eliphalet, 162–63, 245n46
Gall (Hunkpapa man), 100–101
Gambert, Felix, 61, 62–63
Garrison, Emma, 178, 249n22, 250n24

Index · 271

"Garry Owen," 87, 119
gay men: accounts of, 196–97, 255n14; challenges for, 166–67, 246n55; commitment levels of, 204–5; in legal proceedings, 194, 211, 216n26, 254n6; masculine appearance in, 195, 197, 201, 202; sexual behavior of, 198, 255n19; types of, 198–99
genetics, 8–9, 83, 214n15
Gibbon, John, 119–20
Gilpin, William, 80
Globe Consolidated Mine, 195
Godfrey, Edward, 73–75, 77, 78, 82, 86, 87, 88–89, 126
gold mining, 114–16, 118, 197, 199
gold rushes, 48–49, 52–53, 55–56, 147
Grand Central mine, 162, 245n46
Grand Presentation Society Ball, 186–87, 251n43
Grannon, Bessie (Dietrich), 189, 191, 252n51
Grannon, Joseph, 189–91, 252n51
Grant, Ulysses, 95–96, 119, 238n128
Great Britain, 16–17, 22, 33, 34–35, 37
Great Western (steamer), 37, 219n43
Great Western Railway, 219n43
Greeley, Horace, 54, 225n46
greenhorns, 20–21, 39
Grinnell, George, 115
grizzly bears, 117–18
Gros Ventres Indians, 216n6
Grounds, "Billy," 161

Hämäläinen, Pekka, 241n13
Hamilton, Alexander, 75
Hamilton, Louis, 74–76, 77, 78–79, 80–81, 82–83, 84–85, 87–88, 122
Hamilton, Philip, 75

hangings, 37, 55, 158–59, 219n41, 225n51, 244n34
Hay, L. E., 213n2
Helldorado (Breakenridge), 170, 243n27
Helldorado Days, 170
hermaphrodites, 44–45, 220n5, 229n96, 257n8
Heroes, Philosophers, and Courtiers of the Time of Louis XIV, 230n106
heterosexual (word), 11
heterosexuality, 139, 201–2, 230n98
Hicks, Milton, 162
Hihn, Frederick, 61–63
Hincke, Charles, 213n2
Hodges, María Luisa Cota, 61, 62
Holliday, John "Doc," 169, 245n43
Holmes, George, 25–26
homosexual (word), 11
homosexuals and homosexuality: acknowledgment of, 207; surroundings affecting, 7, 198, 202–3, 210–11, 211–12, 214n11; terms for, 4, 7, 8, 11, 12, 254n12; understandings of, 8–11, 194, 197, 202–3, 214nn11–13, 214nn15–16, 256n30. *See also* gay men; lesbians
horses: in accidents, 64–65; changes brought by, 15; companionship of, 131; herding of, 257n9; injuries from, 221n12; of livery stables, 46–48, 221n11, 221n14; military use of, 94–95; runaway, 58, 66, 226–27nn63–64; stolen, 162–64, 246n47, 252n55
Horsley, Joseph "Sugarfoot Joe," 66
hostlers, 44, 46–47, 221n12
Hudson's Bay Company, 22, 23
Hume-Bennett logging, 200
Hunt, Samuel, 155–57, 243nn29–30, 244n31

Hunt, "Zwing," 161, 245n41
hunting, 15–17, 29, 31, 41
Huntley, Florence (Chance), 136
Huntley, Stanley, 132–36, 238n137, 240n161
Hutching's California Magazine, 55
Hyde, Anne, 217n14, 217n16

Illingworth, William, 112, 118
Indians, 79–81, 98–101, 225n53. *See also specific tribes*
Indian Wars, 5, 124
insanity, perceived, 180, 183–84, 252n55
Irish Americans, 92, 94, 125, 224n43
Isherwood, Christopher, 30, 218n30
Issel, William, 253n2
The Ivy Leaf, 187

jackhammer men, 256n34
James, C. L., 215n22
Jay Cook & Company, 101
Jefferson, Thomas, 22
Jewell, Marshall, 132, 137
Johnson, Susan Lee, 214n12
Jonas G. Clark & Company, 222n24
J. S. and E. A. Abbott, 223n28
Juan, María Louisa Cota. *See* Hodges, María Luisa Cota
Juan, Ricardo Fourcade, 62

Kansas City Journal, 189
Kansas City MO, 189, 252n59
Kansas Pacific Railway, 84, 85, 149, 154–55, 232n28
Kellogg, Mark, 120
King Lear (Shakespeare), 185
Kinsey, Alfred: findings of, 7, 196, 198, 202–3, 210, 214n11, 255n19; objectivity of, 256n30; scale developed by, 11, 202; *Sexual Behavior in the Human Male*, 256n30
Kiowa Indians, 86
Kirker, James, 218n29
Klawitter, Emma, 107, 122, 123
Krafft-Ebing, Richard von, 9, 215n17

Lakota Sioux Indians, 99, 100, 115, 119–20, 121, 149, 241n13
Larned, Charles, 97, 98, 99, 105, 235n71
Larpenteur, Charles, 25–26
Las Animas Leader, 154
Las Mariposas (ranch and mine complex), 55–56
Laundress. *See* Noonan, Mrs.
laundresses: anecdotes about, 108–9; and Catholicism, 125; as employees of military, 73, 83–84, 98, 107; living quarters of, 102; reputation of, 89, 107; social position of, 110, 111; work of, 91
Leadville & Aspen Mail & Express, 179, 249n19
LeBarr, John, 158
lesbians, 181, 207, 215n22, 257n2
letters, 32, 34, 53, 107, 132, 181–82, 183, 186, 236n94, 255n14
Lewis, Meriwether, 22
Lewis and Clark Expedition, 22
Lewis Downing & Sons, 50, 223n28
Lincoln, Abraham, 75
Linville, Hiram, 157–58
livery stables, 47, 221n11
L. L. Robinson (locomotive), 224n41
loggers, 196–99, 200, 203–4, 255n14, 255n22
logging camps, 196, 198, 200, 255n17

log houses, 147, 241n9
Logsdon, Guy, 215n23
Los Angeles Herald, 247n62
Lounsberry, Clement, 132
Ludlow, William, 117–18
lumber camps, 196, 198, 200, 255n17

MacDonald, Craig, 222n22; *Cockeyed Charley Parkhurst*, 229n89
Madame La Secher (fictional character), 135–36
mail, 51, 179, 188
Malcolm (correspondent), 233n58
manifest destiny, 5, 55, 60, 77, 80, 146
Manitou Springs CO, 150
Mariposa CA, and area, 55–56, 225n54
Mariposa stage, 54–55
marriage, 8, 13, 18, 23–25, 106–7, 151, 217n14, 217n16
Marrillo, Carlos, 231n12. *See also* Noonan, Mrs.
Marsh, Othniel, 115
Mather, Charles, 187, 251n45
Mathey, E. G., 87
Mayflower Bar, 207, 211, 257n2
McCloskey, Mr., 244n34
McKay, William, 115–16
McLane, Louis, 75
McLaughlin, Charles, 56, 60–61, 226n57
McLaury, Frank, 163, 246n47
McLoughlin, John, 25, 217n14, 217n16
McMasters, Sherman, 162–63, 246n47
Medicine Lodge Treaty, 81–82
mediums, 135–36
Merald, G. W., 159, 244n37
Merrell, Lewis, 96
Methodist church, 241n11
Méti people, 25, 30–31, 217n14, 217n16
migration, early, 213n4

Miles, Nelson, 124
military balls, 109–11, 178, 237n104, 250n23, 251n43
Miller, Alfred, 27, 29, 31–32, 34; *An Attack by Crows on the Whites on the Big Horn River East of the Rocky Mountains*, 35, 218n40
Miller, C. C., 126–27, 239n145
Mills, Frederick, 203, 204
Miner (steamer), 97–98
Miner, William, 8, 214n14
miners, 55–56, 115–16, 196–97
mining: coal, 228n74; dangers of, 205, 256n35, 257n38; decline of, 192, 227n66; equipment used in, 256n36; growth of, 159–60; and stagecoach routes, 53–54; workers in, 199–206. *See also* gold mining; gold rushes
mining camps, 196, 197, 199–202, 205
Mission San Juan Bautista, 59–60
Missouri River, 22, 97, 130–31, 136, 189
Monk, Henry, 54, 64, 69, 225n46, 230n103
Moore, Bartholomew, 44, 49–52, 69–70, 222n24, 223–24nn36–37
Moore, Daniel, 222n24
Moore, Mrs., 222n24
morality concerns, 173–74, 178, 193–94, 210, 249n21, 253n2
Morning News, 250n27
Moss, Charles, 67, 227n72
Moss family, 67
Mount of the Holy Cross (Moran), 251n43
Moving Behind (Indian man), 88
Munguia, Frank, 169
murders, 158, 220n5, 225n53. *See also* shootings: deaths resulting from
Murphy, Lawrence, 213n2
Murray, Charles, 218n27

Murthly (estate), 17, 32, 33–35, 40–41, 218n36

Nahl, Charles, 224n43
Nash, James, 93, 233n58
Nash, Jennie, 93. *See also* Noonan, Mrs.
Nebraska, 12–13
New Orleans LA, 96
New York Times, 5, 223n36
Nez Perce Indians, 123–24
Noonan, John: acquaintances of, 237n118; belongings of, after death, 131–32; character of, 105; Custer family's relationship with, 96, 103, 105–6, 112, 117–18; death of, 131; in fiction, 132–35, 139, 240n156; marriage of, 106–7, 119; reactions to marriage of, 127–31, 132, 239n151; as soldier, 93–95, 120–23, 124–25, 240n161; as widower, 126, 127, 132
Noonan, Mrs.: belongings of, after death, 131–32; clothing of, 108–9, 110–11; Custer family's relationship with, 103, 111–14, 122–23, 137–140; death of, 125–27, 129–30, 239n145; in fictional creations, 132–36, 137, 233n55; heritage of, 77; household skills of, 90; as laundress, 73–74, 83–84, 88–90, 91–92; letters of, 107, 132, 236n94; marriages of, 92–93, 106–7, 124, 233n58; in memory, 140–41; as midwife, 89–90, 97, 111–14; names for, 231n12; in new surroundings, 96–97, 98; personal pleasures of, 107–8; privacy requested by, 73–74; as tailor, 90, 103; as teamster, 74–75, 77–78, 82–83; views of, 240n157
Norse Greenlanders, 21, 216n7
Northern Cheyenne Nation, 99

Northern Light (steamer), 51, 52, 223n35, 224n37
Northern Pacific Railroad, 98–100, 101–2, 130, 134, 136, 235n72, 238n134, 240n166
North Star (steamer), 222n24
North Western Stage & Express Company, 127

O'Connell, Charley, 226n62
OK Corral shooting, 161, 170, 245n44, 246n47
Oklahoma, 210–11
Oklahoma City OK, 209, 211
Old Jennie Nash, 93, 139, 233n58. *See also* Noonan, Mrs.
Old Neutriment (Wagner), 233n58
One Eye Jack, 65
Oregon Company, 38, 219n45
Orman, James, 154, 243n22, 243n24
Orman, William, 243n22
Orman brothers, 153, 154–55
Osage Indians, 39
otters, 21, 22
outlaws, 161, 162, 164, 166–67, 245n42, 247n62
Outlook (reporter), 240n157
Out West, 242n17, 242n20
Overland Mail, 54
Overland Stage, 230n103

Pacific Northwest area, 21–22
paintings, 35–36, 218n40, 241n173, 251n43
Parker, Carleton, 196, 254n13
Parker Vein (steamship company), 224n37
Parkhurst, Charley, 43–46, 220n7; acquaintances of, 48–50, 51–52;

Parkhurst, Charley, (continued)
  birthplace of, 220n8; burial of, 229n95; death of, 67; female anatomy of revealed, 43, 67; health of, 66–67, 229n93; lawsuit against, 62–63; as legend, 227n71; regions lived in, 52, 221n17, 222n24, 224n38; sea voyages of, 51–52, 223n36; speculation about, 67–71, 229n96; stories about, 53, 64–66, 226n63, 228n82; work of, 44, 46–51, 54–56, 58–59, 61, 63, 226n62
partnerships, terms for, 246n56
Patience (opera), 9–10
Pawnee Indians, 39
Philip of Orleans, 232n23
Phoenix AZ, 158–59
Pickering logging company, 254n10
Pinkerton National Detective Agency, 8
Pioche, François, 224n41
Plaza House (hotel), 59
pleurisy, 125
pneumonia, 125, 151, 242n18
poliomyelitis, 229n93
portraits, 1–2, 35–36, 41
postmasters and postmistresses, 175, 178, 179, 181, 187
Pratt, Henry, 37, 219n41
prison terms, 12–13, 216n26
prostitutes and prostitution, 194, 229n87, 233n58, 249n21
Protestants, 224n43
Providence Directory, 44
Providence Journal, 44, 45, 46, 68, 221n17
psychiatrists and psychiatry, 14, 211
Pueblo & Salt Lake Railroad, 243n26

Rabbit Creek robbery, 65
rabies, 26

railroads: changes brought by, 149–50, 210; construction of, 85, 98–100; crews of, 153–54; of logging industry, 195, 254n10; personal disruption by, 192; shootings at depots of, 162, 245n43; weather affecting, 237n106. *See also specific railroads*
ranching, 156–57, 163, 175–76, 207–9, 210
R. B. Forbes, 222n22
Reconstruction, 95
The Red Book of Grandtully, 41
rendezvous, in fur trade, 19–20, 22–24, 26–27, 28–29, 217n18
Reno, Marcus, 121, 129, 239n152
Report of the Exploring Expedition to the Rocky Mountains (Frémont), 219n44
Reynolds, Charlie, 118
rheumatism, 67
rifles, 54, 118, 225n45
rights-of-way, 144, 154–55, 243n27
Roaring Fork River and Valley, 173, 174–76, 182–83, 249n22
robberies, 65, 65–66, 168–69, 214n14, 228n86, 233n58, 247n61
Robinson, Lester, 224n41
Rocky Mountain Fur Company, 22
Rocky Mountain Sun, 174, 176, 182
Rolle, Andrew, 219n44
Rolph, James, 253n2
Romero, Jesus, 244n33
Rosa, Joseph, 245n44
Ross, Horatio, 115–16
Rusk, Howard, 256n30
rustlers, 161–65, 168, 170–71
Rutledge, Keith, 257n1

Sacramento Bee, 194
Sacramento Daily Record-Union, 68

Sacramento Daily Union, 65, 70
Sacramento Valley Railroad, 224n41
The Saga of Billy the Kid (Burns), 170
Sand Creek massacre (1864), 148–49, 241n13
San Francisco and San Jose Railroad, 56, 60–61
San Francisco CA, 53, 193–94, 224n39, 253n2
San Francisco Call, 67
San Joaquin Valley, 55
San Juan CA, 59–61
San Quentin State Prison, 13, 216n28
Santa Cruz area, 59, 60–62
Santa Cruz Sentinel, 222n24
Santa Fe NM, 76
Santa Fe Trail, 76, 82
scalps and scalping, 149, 242n16
Schafer Logging Company, 254n10, 255n17
schools, 178, 243n30, 249nn16–17
séances, 133–35
Seattle WA, 193
Selman, Christopher, 245n42
Seventh Cavalry: duties of, 81, 86; formation of, 78–79; and Indians, 100–101, 119, 124; location of, 82, 93, 96–98; members of, 104, 107, 129, 233n58; on mining expedition, 116; pride in, 94–95; and railroad, 85, 98–100; uniforms of, 104. See also Battle of the Little Bighorn (1876)
Sexual Behavior in the Human Male (Kinsey), 256n30
sexual variation: acceptance of, 14, 67–68, 70–71, 145, 210; rejection of, 12–13, 127–32, 180, 183, 187, 189–91, 210–11
Seymour, Silas, 143–45, 241n1

Shaved Head (Indian man), 124
Shaw, Charles, 192
Shaw, Charles, Jr., 253n64
Shaw, Ora (Chatfield). See Chatfield, Ora
Shehi, Emma, 249n22
Shepard, Jesse, 213n2
Sheridan, Philip, 81, 84, 86–87, 88, 114–15, 118, 123
Sheridan House, 102, 124
shootings: deaths resulting from, 55, 65–66, 161–62, 165, 170, 225n51, 244n33, 245nn43–44, 246n47; injuries resulting from, 56, 167–68, 225n51, 226n57
Sierra Nevada (steamer), 51, 223n33
Silas, 33, 218n35
Sillem, Adolf, 28–29, 218n27
Sioux Indians, 119. See also Lakota Sioux Indians
Sitting Bull (Indian man), 100, 121
Sixth Infantry Regiment, 76
Smith, John, 37, 219n41
Snelling, Marx & Company, 222n24
Snelling, William, 55, 225n51
Snellinghausen, John, 249n22
sociologists and sociology, 195–96
sodomy, 8, 12–13, 215n23, 216n28
soldiers, 89–90, 91–92, 104–5, 106–7, 110
Soquel Augmentation Rancho, 61–62
Southern Pacific Railroad, 63, 162, 168–69, 245n43, 247n62
Spanish, and fur trade, 21
spiritualism, 136
stagecoaching: accidents in, 58–59, 64–65, 226n61, 226n63, 227n64; design of, 57–58, 225n45; drivers for, 49–50, 61, 64, 69, 225n46, 226n62, 230n103; and gold rush, 48–49; management in, 222n20, 226n56; manufacturers in, 223n28; as news

stagecoaching: (continued)
  carriers, 127; railroad replacing, 177; requirements for, 50–51; and robberies, 65–66, 228n86; routes of, 53–55, 55–57, 60–61
Stallard, Patricia, 239n151
stamp mills, in mining, 160
Stanley, David, 99, 101, 235n74
steamers, 53, 82, 98, 100, 102, 130–31, 135, 151. *See also specific steamers*
Stevens, Frank, 49
Stewart, Christine, 18
Stewart, George, 17
Stewart, John, 17, 18–19, 32, 33
Stewart, William, 17–19; on acquaintances, 218n35; *Altowan*, 40–41; with caravan, 20–21, 23; class consciousness of, 18, 36–37; companions of, 25–26, 27–32, 33, 35–37, 218n27, 218n40; contacts of, 19; *Edward Warren*, 40–41; excursion of, 37–40; family of, 216n3; as hunter, 15–16, 24; influences on, 217n12; inheritance of, 32–35, 40–41, 218n36; marriage of, 18; as novelist, 16, 18, 28, 40–41; representations of, in art, 35–36; self-discovery by, 19, 24–25, 26–27, 41–42
Stewart, William George, 18, 40, 216n3
Stilwell, Frank, 168, 245n43, 246n47
St. Louis Daily Globe-Democrat, 230n106
St. Mary's Parish, 239n140
Stonewall Uprising (1969), 14
St. Paul-Pioneer Press, 236n94
Stroesser, Otto, 229n95
Strong, Lisa, 218n40
Stuart, Granville, 208
Sturgis, Samuel, 123, 130
Sublette, William, 32–33, 38, 218n35

Sugarfoot (imaginary bandit), 64, 65, 66, 229n89
suicides, 131, 132–33, 169, 229n87, 240n156, 247n61, 254n6
Sully, Alfred, 86
Swedish logger, 199
Sweet, George, 124, 136, 238n137, 240n166

tailoring, 90, 103
tax collection, from rustlers, 164–65
Teamster. *See* Noonan, Mrs.
teamsters, 58, 74–75, 77–78, 82–83, 140–41, 147, 153
telegraph, 147–48, 174, 192
Telegraph Line of Coaches, 49
Tennant, William, 221n11
Ten Nights in a Bar Room, 187, 251n44
Teren (schooner), 52, 224n37
Terry, Alfred, 120, 121, 123, 238n128
Terry, George, 150–51, 152–53, 242nn17–18
Texans, Confederate, 148
Texas, 207–8, 209
tins, symbolism of, 138
Tombstone AZ, 159–65, 169–70
Tombstone Epitaph, 161, 162
Tonner, Waldemar, 213n2
tourism, 150
transgender (word), 11
transgender people, 2–4, 46, 71, 88–89, 140, 232n23
transitioning, in sexual identity, 83, 141, 232n23
trappers and trapping, 20, 23–24
treaties, 80, 81–82, 115, 119
Truman, Benjamin, 228n82
tuberculosis, 155, 157, 244n31
Turner, Frederick, 213n7

Tweed, Charles, 157, 243n30
Two-Spirit people, 4, 83, 141
Tyler, Oliver, 191–92, 252n62

uniforms. *See* clothing, military
Union Pacific Railroad, 85, 94, 143–45, 149–50, 232n28
United States Gazette, 70
United States Hotel, 242n18
U.S. Peace Commission, 81
Utley, Robert, 239n152

Vallejo, Mariano, 62
Vanderbilt, Cornelius "Commodore," 150–51
Vanderbilt, Cornelius, Jr., 150–53, 166, 242n17, 242nn19–20
Vanderbilt, Ellen, 242n18
Vérendrye, François, 115
Vérendrye, Louis-Joseph, 115
vigilance committees, 53, 158–59, 224n43

Wagner, Glendolin, 240n156; *Old Neutriment*, 233n58
Wallace, Jim, 167–68, 246n59
Webb, J. Watson, 19
Weekly Republican, 244n34
Weightman, Richard, 40
West: as challenging environment, 19; and civilization, 2–3, 5–7, 14, 41–42, 145; East influencing, 193; enterprise in, 254n8; and expansionism, 76, 79–80; extent of, 4–5; and frontier, 5–6; and industrial development, 194–95, 205–6; in personal narrative, 155–57; in popular culture, 169–70; representation abroad of, 34, 35; sense of freedom in, 151; sexual variation in, 2–4, 207–8, 210, 211–12
Weston, J. F., 94, 95, 235n62
Wheeler, Harriet, 248n11
Wheeler, Jerome, 248n11
Wheeler/Stallard house, 248n11
White, Frederick, 165, 246n53
White, John, 183, 186, 190–91, 250n34, 252n55
White, Richard, 224n43, 253n2
White, Sarah (Holtz), 250n34
Whites, 95–96
Whitman, Walt, 28, 140
Wilde, Oscar, 9–10, 160
Wilkenson, John W., 127, 130
Wiseman, Nicholas, 218n40
Wiswell, Oliver, 65, 66, 229n88
With Custer's Cavalry (Fougera), 233n55
Woirol, Gregory R., 254n13
wolf attack, 25–26
Wolverton, W. D., 126–27, 239n145
women: and civilizing force, 178; clothing of, 90–91, 108–9; Hispanic, 92; Indian, 23–24; as laundresses, 83–84, 92, 110; lives of, 107–8; "masculine," 70–71; with military, 73–74, 89, 107, 111; as prostitutes, 229n87; single, 179
Woodhull, Victoria, 8, 214n13
Wounded to the Rear—One More Shot (plaster cast), 106
Wright, Captain, 46, 221n9
Wyatt Earp, Frontier Marshal (Lake), 170

Yates, Annie, 111, 112–14, 137–38, 238n134
Yates, Elizabeth (Bessie), 112, 237n106
Yates, George (father), 109, 112
Yates, George (son), 237n106
Yates, Milnor, 237n106